Progress in IS

More information about this series at http://www.springer.com/series/10440

Christoph Schmidt

Agile Software Development Teams

The Impact of Agile Development on Team Performance

Springer

Christoph Schmidt
München, Germany

This book is based on a doctoral thesis successfully defended at the Business School of the University of Mannheim.

ISSN 2196-8705   ISSN 2196-8713   (electronic)
Progress in IS
ISBN 978-3-319-26055-6   ISBN 978-3-319-26057-0   (eBook)
DOI 10.1007/978-3-319-26057-0

Library of Congress Control Number: 2015958810

Springer Cham Heidelberg New York Dordrecht London
© Springer International Publishing Switzerland 2016

Printed on acid-free paper

Springer International Publishing AG Switzerland is part of Springer Science+Business Media (www.springer.com)

Acknowledgments

Conducting research and writing my dissertation have been an endeavor. This project would not have been possible without numerous mentors, colleagues, friends, and my family who have supported, encouraged, and helped me in many ways. I would like to express my great appreciation and thanks for their contribution and support. This dissertation is the product of a fruitful cooperation between the research group of Prof. Dr. Armin Heinzl at the Institute of Enterprise Systems, University of Mannheim, Germany, and SAP SE, Walldorf, Germany.

First and foremost, I would like to thank my academic supervisor Prof. Dr. Armin Heinzl. He has been a mentor and role model giving me the extraordinary opportunity and research environment for this thesis. I thoroughly thank him for the trust and confidence allowing me to develop my research ideas while guiding and supporting me whenever needed. Moreover, he encouraged me to present my work at international conferences and to develop my work during two research stays abroad. At the same time, I deeply appreciated the continuous support from Dr. Thomas Kude, who has become a close friend to me over the time of my research. Developing, discussing, and challenging my research ideas have always been fruitful, encouraging, insightful, and a lot of fun in our research team with Kai Spohrer. Finally, I would like to thank Prof. Dr. Torsten Biemann for his commitment and for serving as a reviewer for my thesis.

The dissertation project would not have been possible without the great support I received from various colleagues at SAP SE. Through countless discussions, workshops, and experience reports, I had the unique opportunity to learn about agile software engineering from the experts in the field. My special thanks go to Dr. Juergen Heymann. He has always been a supportive and encouraging mentor stimulating me to combine scientific rigor with the usefulness of my research results. Dr. Tobias Hildebrand, Jürgen Staader, Martin Fassunge, Dr. Joachim Schnitter, and Michael Römer introduced me to the software development process at SAP SE. Their support enabled me to make this collaborative research project a successful reality. Moreover, I would like to thank my former colleagues at SAP SE Herbert Illgner, Dr. Kilian-Kehr, Dr. Knut Manske, Günter Pecht-Seibert, and Dr. Dirk Völz for their support. Finally, the empirical study would not have been possible without the support of the around 40 SAP managers who trusted and supported me to conduct the survey. I am well aware of the fact that many of the 500+ study participants have taken the time to fill out the questionnaire on top of their challenging daily work. It is impossible to list them all. On behalf of many, I would like to mention Peter Neumeyer, Alan Southall, and Parmar Yoginder.

I am also very grateful to have had the outstanding opportunity to collaborate with Prof. Dr. John Tripp and Prof. Dr. Dorothy Leidner from the University of Waco, TX, USA, as well as Prof. Dr. Sunil Mithas from the University of Maryland, MD, USA. All three have invited me to a research stay at their university, an unforgettable experience, both from a scientific and a personal point of view. Discussing my research topic with these incredible personalities helped me not only to conceptualize, analyze, and finish my dissertation but also to grow personally.

While working on my dissertation, I worked in a great team of fellow Ph.D. students who have become dear friends to me. The continuous exchange of ideas during various research and teaching projects was always great fun and a unique learning experience. My very special thanks go to Saskia Bick, Jens Förderer, Dr. Erik Hemmer, Dr. Lars Klimpke, Tommi Kramer, Dr. Miroslav Lazic, Tillmann Neben, Dr. Marko Nöhren, Alexander Scheerer, Dr. Sven Scheibmayr, Dr. Kai Spohrer, and Dr. Sebastian Stuckenberg, as well as Behnaz Gholami, Philipp Hess, Dr. Markus Schief, and Sarah Träutlein at SAP SE. In addition, I thank my student assistants Celina Friemel and Fabienne Schneider for their great support in transcribing over 600 questionnaires. Without their support, the thesis could not have been finished. I also would like to thank the chair's assistants Luise Bühler and Ingrid Distelrath as well as the student assistants Olga Oster, Lea Offenberg, Alexandra Lang, and Stefan Eckhardt.

Finally, I would like to thank my family for bearing with me throughout this time. My deepest gratitude goes to my brother Johannes for the enriching discussions, among others, about the essence of research from a natural and social scientist's point of view, his impressive patience and accuracy while proofreading my thesis, and his personal support through challenging times. Last but not least, I thank my parents for their unconditional support in all aspects of my life.

Contents

List of Figures

List of Tables

Chapter 1
Introduction

1.1 Problem Statement

The last decade has seen a tremendous increase in business and consumer software products and services. From cars to smart phone apps to complex business applications, today software is present in almost all areas of life. Gartner Inc.[1] estimates the worldwide revenue of the software industry at \$407.3 billion in 2013 with an annual growth rate of 4.8 %.[2] Software not only expands into growth markets, but also reaches more and more into established markets. Google, Amazon, Airbnb, or Uber are just a few examples of software service providers which have taken market shares from traditional consumer market incumbents. Market experts even claim that software is "upending entire industries, and will do so at an increasingly larger and more rapid rate."[3]

This trend is driven by technological opportunities and economic potential. From a technical perspective, Moore's law has proven to be correct for more than half a century (Moore 1965). Year by year, more and more powerful—and at the same time smaller—computer chips are available, opening up new fields of application for software. For instance, the widespread availability of mobile devices provides the technical basis for software applications at the finger tip. Hence, the general public is using more and more software products on a daily basis. At the same time, an increasing number of computer systems are permanently connected to the global computer network. Computing power is therefore no scarce resource anymore and intensive calculations can be outsourced to powerful computer centers. Mobile applications can access centralized data and conveniently

---

[1]Gartner Inc. is a global information technology research and advisory company.

[2]http://www.gartner.com/newsroom/id/2696317.

[3]http://bits.blogs.nytimes.com/2013/01/10/ben-horowitz-on-the-impact-of-software-everywhere/.

© Springer International Publishing Switzerland 2016
C. Schmidt, *Agile Software Development Teams*, Progress in IS,
DOI 10.1007/978-3-319-26057-0_1

provide useful information whenever and wherever needed. These technological capabilities provide software developers with a degree of freedom to innovate not seen before leading to a constant stream of new software products and services.

Taking an economic perspective, the software industry today leverages unprecedented economies of scale compared to traditional industries providing physical goods. One reason is that virtualization of computer servers and cloud computing leads to decreasing hardware costs. As a consequence, software companies scale their offerings at minimal marginal costs. Many software companies provide their software products globally resulting in exceptional market opportunities.

The combined economical and technological potential attracts many companies. Thus, competition amongst software providers is tough and innovation cycles are short. Only companies with the capabilities to quickly adapt to changing market conditions to exploit emerging technologies stay in the market. Not all companies have developed the required adaptability. The market capitalization of BlackBerry Limited, a Canadian provider of telecommunication devices, for instance, dropped from about $35 billion in 2010 to about $5 billion within 3 years only as emerging technologies were not adopted. In other words, being *agile* is essential to thrive in the information technology industry.

Software development processes are a key success factor. Traditionally, many companies have started their software development projects by detailing software specifications upfront and accurately planning the course of the project in advance. Project managers and software developers subsequently implemented these plans. The software was only released once fully implemented at the end of the software development project (Boehm 2006). The software was mainly tested after the implementation phase during a dedicated testing phase. Consequently, problems mostly occurred only late in the development process. Many projects ran over time or budget. Moreover, it was difficult to flexibly react to changing project conditions. Many projects even failed entirely (Standish 2014).

Since the beginnings of the 2000s, many companies adapted their rigid development processes and transformed to agile development companies.[4] *Agile software development* has fundamentally influenced how companies develop software and developers' daily work routines (Dybå and Dingsøyr 2008; Highsmith 2000). It is an iterative development approach emphasizing close customer collaboration to receive fast customer feedback (Cockburn 2001; Highsmith 2000). Agile software development projects foresee frequent deliveries of incremental software functionality to their customer, instead of a one-time release of the finalized software package at the project end. This development approach forces developers to regularly integrate newly developed software and continuously invest time into quality assurance in order to guarantee that quality requirements are met at all times throughout the development process. Even many software development companies have shifted to an agile software development approach (VersionOne 2012) - or have at least

---

[4]For example, see Microsoft: http://arstechnica.com/information-technology/2014/08/how-microsoft-dragged-its-development-practices-into-the-21st-century.

adopted key ideas of this development paradigm, there is still a lack of theoretical understanding how and why the agile development approach works (Dingsøyr et al. 2012; Dybå and Dingsøyr 2008).

Agile systems development was not derived from managerial principles or academic efforts. Instead, it "evolved from the personal experiences and collective wisdom of consultants" (Dingsøyr et al. 2012) . Over the last 10 years, however, scholars have started to conduct first theory-based studies to evaluate and better understand the development paradigm (Abrahamsson et al. 2002; Dybå and Dingsøyr 2008; Erickson et al. 2005; Maruping et al. 2009a). Nevertheless, a satisfying understanding in what circumstances agile development should be used and reasons for its effectiveness are still missing. This is reflected in the repeated calls for more theory-based investigations and more rigorous industrial studies on agile software development (Abrahamsson et al. 2009; Dingsøyr et al. 2012; Dybå and Dingsøyr 2008).

The agile approach follows the general trend in new product development with teams as the core building block of the development organization (Kozlowski and Bell 2003). Collaborative development work in teams promises greater adaptability, productivity, and creativeness as compared to individuals (Gladstein 1984). Moreover, it provides better solutions to organizational problems (Sundstrom et al. 2000). Nevertheless, there are only few theory-based studies drawing on the extensive knowledge of team effectiveness research to better understand the effectiveness of agile software development teams. Only recently, Dingsøyr et al. (2012) called for "better theories and models of software team effectiveness" in agile software development teams. This study intends to address this theoretical and practical research gap.

1.2 Research Objectives

The objective of this study is to provide a theoretical explanation for the influence of agile software development on the performance of software development teams. The study sets out to answer three separate research questions (RQ1 to RQ3, see Fig. 1.1).

Theory building denotes the rationally justified postulation and empirical testing of causal relationships between theoretical constructs (Bhattacherjee 2012). These

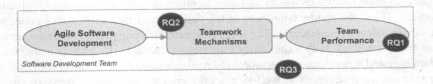

Fig. 1.1 Research objectives

constructs need not only to be clearly defined, but accurate measurement instruments are required to test the postulated theoretical relationships with empirical studies. For this study, *agile software development*, *team performance*, and yet to be introduced *teamwork mechanisms* are the central constructs (see Fig. 1.1). While previous researchers have already suggested different conceptualizations of agile software development on a team level, the team performance concept is still not clearly defined for software development teams. Moreover, no standardized instrument for performance assessment exists. The missing conceptual clarity leads to the first challenge of this study and directs to the first research question:

RQ1: What is the performance of a software development team?

The main proposition of this study is that the repeatedly suggested performance effect of agile software development is based on a mediated effect through various hidden teamwork mechanisms. The study deducts these teamwork mechanisms from team effectiveness literature and combines them with insights described in previous work on agile software development. This approach helps the author raise the second research question:

RQ2: What are the latent teamwork mechanisms affected by agile software development in software development teams?

At the core of the study is a theoretical model explaining the performance effect of agile software development through affective, behavioral, and cognitive teamwork mechanisms in software development teams. The model will be derived from the conceptual and theoretical foundations found while answering RQ1 and RQ2. The proposed research model is an answer to the third research question:

RQ3: How does agile software development influence the performance of software development teams?

The study findings are expected to be of interest for the academic community as well as for decision makers in industry: *First*, this study is amongst the first to elucidate effects of the agile development approach on the performance of software development teams. By taking a teamwork perspective, it provides a new perspective for understanding the complex, hidden mechanisms causing this performance effect. The results contribute to the still nascent, theory-based literature stream on agile software development teams (Abrahamsson et al. 2002; Dingsøyr et al. 2012; Dybå and Dingsøyr 2008). Moreover, the study is one of the rare large-scale, industrial studies on software development. *Second*, the results are an empirical contribution to team effectiveness literature. The study provides an empirical test of central aspects of team adaptation theory and team confidence in the software development domain. *Third*, the results contribute to the definition of the performance concept in software development teams. The study integrates existing performance concepts and combines them with exploratory interview findings of 15 project managers. The suggested measurement instrument is a methodological contribution which may be relevant for researchers as well as practitioners who are interested in assessing or comparing the performance of agile software development teams. *Finally*, a better understanding of the underlying teamwork mechanisms is expected to help decision makers to better understand the impact of agile development on their teams. Hence, the study results will help practitioners decide when to best use the agile development approach.

1.3 Overview of the Research Methodology

This study takes a positivist, epistemological perspective assuming that a social reality exists independent of human consciousness and cognition (Orlikowski and Baroudi 1991). Hence, the study is based on three main assumptions: (1) unilateral causal relationships between latent teamwork mechanisms in software development teams, (2) deduction of these causal relationships from universal laws or principles, and (3) testing of causal relationships with empirical data based on falsification logic (Popper 1935).

The objective of the thesis is to provide a theoretical explanation for the impact of agile software development's influence on the performance of software development teams. Hence, the level of analysis is the software development team. A theoretical research model is derived from teamwork theories combined with knowledge about agile software development and finally tested with empirical data from professional software development teams. The overall structure of the thesis is illustrated in Fig. 1.2.

The research design comprises three stages. In a first step, the latent variables in the research model are defined. A structured review of the literature showed no agreement amongst scholars about a definition of the performance concept of software development teams. To specify the abstract performance concept in the given research context, the author conducted interviews with 15 project leaders. The interviews were analyzed following a grounded theory approach (Strauss 1987). In parallel, existing software development studies were reviewed to analyze scholastic definitions and measurements of the performance concept for software development

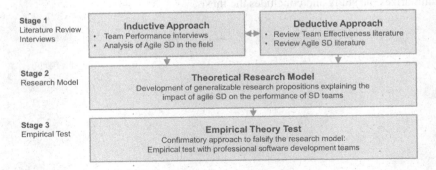

Fig. 1.2 Research organization

teams. Finally, the interview and literature findings were combined. In addition, various teamwork mechanisms relevant for answering the three research questions were derived from previous teamwork studies. Hence, the *first research stage* is both, deductive and inductive in nature (see Fig. 1.2).

The main contribution of this study, however, is deductive theory building and testing. In the *second research stage*, a theoretical research model is derived from teamwork reference models and theories. It proposes a positive impact of agile software development on the performance of software development teams. The study concludes with an empirical test of the research model in the *third research stage*. Hence, the core of the study follows a confirmatory research design.

1.4   Study Organization

The study is divided into seven chapters. Following this introductory chapter, Chap. 2 introduces the agile software development paradigm and outlines the conceptual framework provided by researchers and experienced consultants. Chapter 3 then lays the theoretical and conceptual foundation of the study. It first introduces key concepts of team effectiveness research and team adaptation theory. The chapter further derives the research model which provides a theoretical explanation answering the research questions RQ2 and RQ3. Chapter 4 describes the research context, outlines the overall study design, and specifies the latent variables in the research model including the operationalization and measurement models. Finally, the chapter introduces the statistical methods applied for data analysis and proposition testing. In Chap. 5, the study sample is described in detail. The chapter further introduces a new measurement instrument to assess the performance of software development teams. All research propositions are tested independently and finally integrated into a coherent team performance prediction model. Chapter 6 discusses the study results and explains the theoretical and practical contributions of the study in the context of previous studies. Moreover, limitations of the study are described and promising avenues for future research are discussed. Finally, Chap. 7 summarizes the study and concludes the thesis.

Chapter 2
Agile Software Development

Software is nowadays omnipresent in many consumer and business products. From cars to complex business software over simple smart phone apps, many people regularly use software-based products or services at home or at work. With more than two billion people using broadband internet today, new markets emerge for software companies challenging established market incumbents with software-based services and products. Software brings life to various types of computer systems which have steadily become cheaper, more powerful, more compact, and more energy efficient over the last decades.[1] Consequently, these systems can be integrated into various traditional products to provide diversifying functionality (MacCormack et al. 2001). Andreessen (2011) summarized the trend succinctly: "Software is eating the world".

From a technical point of view, *software* is a "set of programs, procedures, and routines which are associated with the operation of a computer system".[2] Since the first days of programmable machines, both the computer systems and development processes have evolved dramatically. The first software programs were written by electrical engineers and mathematicians in laboratories for military applications in the 1940s. Software development was a very experimental work, with no supporting tools or experience existing. The developed software provided customized functionality for specific purposes. As the hardware and the development process was very expensive, only few applications justified the high expenditure.

Today, the *software industry* is a global industry with an estimated revenue of more than \$400 billion per year.[3] More than half of the revenue is generated by the top ten software vendors, such as Microsoft, Oracle, IBM, or SAP. But

---

[1]Computing power doubled every 2 years (Moore's Law), while energy efficiency double every 1.8 years (Koomey's law) (Koomey et al. 2011; Moore 1965).

[2]http://www.merriam-webster.com/dictionary/software.

[3]http://www.gartner.com/newsroom/id/2696317.

© Springer International Publishing Switzerland 2016
C. Schmidt, *Agile Software Development Teams*, Progress in IS,
DOI 10.1007/978-3-319-26057-0_2

there are more and more small companies providing complementary software products as entry barriers to the software market are ever decreasing (Kude et al. 2012). Small start-up companies can develop and offer software products to large markets at limited costs due to the ubiquitous availability of computers, standardized programming languages, interfaces, as well as reusable software packages with free development tools and supportive development communities. Even amateurs contribute to large-scale software development projects as everybody can develop code for open source communities and participate in the development process (Setia et al. 2012).

The *software engineering* discipline offers solutions to the practical problems of developing software (Sommerville 2004). Today, software engineering is an independent profession and an engineering discipline embedded in computer science and traditional engineering disciplines. It deals with all activities required to economically solve real world problems with reliable software programs. It helps developers with "the application of a systematic, disciplined, quantifiable approach to the development, operation and maintenance of software" (IEEE 1990) and encompasses the application of various theories, methods, processes and tools for the development and maintenance of software within financial and organizational constraints of software development projects.

This chapter first discusses the complex nature of software development projects, to then describe different software development approaches suggested by the software engineering discipline. Three different generations of software development processes are briefly introduced and discussed. *Agile software development* has gained much popularity over the last 10 years motivating this study. The chapter concludes with a brief overview of the practitioner and research literature on agile software development.

2.1   Software Development

Software development is a complex process and many software development projects end in delayed projects results, failure to meet the original project goals, or are even entire project cancellations (Standish 2014). This high failure rate is surprising given the history of more than 60 years of software development projects and numerous best-practices books, studies about project failures, and countless development tools, methods, and processes.

There is a long list of failed project failures. In 2004, for example, one of Britain's biggest retailer, Sainsbury, had to cancel a $525 million IT project intended to automate the supply chain of the company. In the end, the failed system caused the company to hire an additional 3000 people to manually record all its stock items.[4]

---

[4]http://www.computerweekly.com/news/2240058411/Sainsburys-writes-off-260m-as-supply-chain-IT-trouble-hits-profit.

In 2013, the United States government started the website healthcare.org intended to process thousands of users simultaneously. The IT project had been outsourced to several contractors for more than $300 million (Brill 2014). When launched, the information system was not able to adequately process the incoming requests. As a consequence, the project meant a tremendous disaster for the government as it was at the center of a media debate for several weeks.

Project failure is common in numerous industries. However, these are just two examples of a long list of failed software development projects (Charette 2005) and it is particular to software development projects that much money can be spent for no result. The periodical reports of the Standish Group Inc., which examined more than 50,000 IT projects, shows that about a third of IT development projects are canceled before completion. Moreover, about half of the projects will cost almost twice as initially projected. Royce et al. (2009) concluded, there is hardly another field in engineering where such a poor success rate is considered normal, much less tolerated. The economic damage, however, is significant (Standish 2014) which is why analyzing these project failures is not purely an academic exercise. Instead, there is a strong incentive for organizations to understand the reasons for failure and determinants of success.

Despite a history of IT project failures, research on success factors of software development projects remains limited. Sambamurthy and Kirsch (2000) concluded in their literature review article that "deficiencies exist in the knowledge about the effective management of complex systems development processes". Until today, there are no final answers on the successful management of software development projects.

2.1.1 Software Development Complexity

There are several sources of complexity which may explain the high failure rates of software development projects. Reasons include the fundamental characteristics of software, the contexts in which software is used, the complexity of the software development tasks, and the general nature of software development projects. The following sections elaborate on these aspects.

Software Complexity

Software is an intangible good which consist of small functional, closely interlinked modules or components. As these components grow in numbers, it becomes increasingly difficult to keep track and see how they work together, even for the most talented programmers. Most software components can have different possible inputs, outputs, states or dependencies. It is therefore nearly impossible to test all combinations. As testing software comes at a cost, it is often impossible to consider all interactions of a program, even for small programs. Moreover, software inconsistencies may be detrimental as changing one part of the program might have consequences for the functionality of the entire software program. For these reasons, it can be extremely difficult to find errors, measure the quality of a software program, or to properly assess its full functional spectrum. This makes software development so difficult.

The technological progress has provided software developers with almost unlimited computational power, memory, and storage capacity, and a global connectivity of devices. Therefore, software is hardly constrained by physical laws, but only limited to human creativity (Lee 1999). On the one hand, this gives developers a considerable freedom of design. On the other hand, it may add to the complexity of today's software programs.

In addition, the size of the software packages has constantly grown during the last decades. Existing software libraries and standardized software packages from third party providers are integrated into new product development (Spinellis and Giannikas 2012) as software functionality can be reused. This leads to an increasing size of the developed software packages quickly exceeding the cognitive capabilities of developers. For instance, the first operating systems of personal computers, still one of the largest software applications, included between 4–5 million lines of code in the beginning of the 1990s. The latest operating systems are implemented with about 50 million lines of code (Maraia 2006). A modern car is estimated to run with about 100 million lines of code (Charette 2009).

The reuse of software functionality adds to the complexity, as the usage of existing software functionality in unintended environments may cause unpredicted side effects. Brooks (1995) even stated "software entities are more complex for their size than any other human construct" as software is invisible, unvisualizable, and subject to continuous change.

Software Development Task Complexity

Literature has identified three dimensions of task characteristics that constitute task complexity (Wood 1986): *component, coordinative, and dynamic complexity* (Campbell 1988). All three have been found to be inherent in software development tasks.

Software development includes various subtasks such as programming, testing, project management, documentation, requirements specification, installation of development tools, and communication with colleagues or other project stakeholders (Begel and Simon 2010). To succeed, developers need to combine organizational, technical, as well as social skills. Before writing the first line of code, analysis of the software requirements is one of the most critical activities (Hickey and Davis 2004). It requires a solid understanding of the application problem domain and technical expertise. For most projects, this knowledge is dispersed amongst different stakeholders. Mostly, requirements are neither clearly documented nor concisely specified by the users who often only know what they expect upon seeing the final product. Even if requirements can be fully specified, software development remains a non-deterministic activity with no single identifiable path on how to implement a program (Sommerville 2004).

Component complexity is high when a task requires several acts and various information cues to be accomplished. Every software development task involves several sub-tasks to be composed. Moreover, as software is highly modularized, software developers need to consider different components and their interdependence. Both aspects lead to high task complexity. Second, software development has a high *coordinative complexity*. Coordinative complexity is low if a linear function of task inputs leads to the task product. In software development, there are many ways to implement requirements. The inputs of software development tasks are intangible ideas that need to be interpreted. Mostly, there is no single correct way but several options to write a software program. Finally, *dynamic complexity* is caused by changes of the task environments. Software development tasks are often subject to change, e.g. the used technology may change during the development process. Oftentimes, the software requirements change as they are either not clearly defined, misunderstood, or need to be redefined. Overall, software development is a highly complex task with component, coordinative, and dynamic complexity. All three are a central sources of complexity in software development projects.

Software Development Project Complexity

Software development projects are described as inherently complex as they must deal with both technological and organizational factors, often outside the control of the project team. Organizational complexity increases with the number of specialized units as well as the number of relationships between them (Baccarini 1996). Moreover, uncertain environments due to unpredictable markets, changing customer requirements, pressure to shorter time-to-market cycles, and rapidly changing information technologies (Baskerville et al. 2001) can add to it. Many software systems are very large and thus beyond the ability of a single software developer to build, leading to the division of labor amongst different contributors. Many projects include actors from diverse geographic, organizational, and social backgrounds (Dibbern et al. 2004) which increases organizational complexity in software development projects (Kraut and Streeter 1995).

Besides organizational complexity, software development projects mostly face technological complexity (Schmidt et al. 2001). Technological complexity refers to the number of and relationship between inputs, outputs, tasks, and technologies. The previously discussed characteristics of software contribute to technological complexity of a software development project.

Rapid evolution of technology and new product opportunities lead to change and uncertainty as an inherent characteristic of software development projects (Madsen 2007). Uncertainty is broadly defined as the absence of complete information about an organizational phenomenon being studied (Argote 1982). It leads to an inability to accurately predict the project progress (Dönmez and Grote 2013). For software development projects, two fundamental types of uncertainty have been discussed:

requirements and technological uncertainty (Nidumolu 1995). Mellis et al. (2010) find that customers often have difficulties formulating specifications when following a sequential development process as many users and software developers do not have a clear understanding about all software details at the beginning of a project. Consequently, the team has to learn over time what to develop (Lyytinen and Rose 2006). Technological uncertainty is the second critical driver of software development complexity. As technology evolves over time and new technologies are being used, development teams often lack the necessary skills to work with new technology. However, the learning process is often unpredictable as developers have to learn while developing software (MacCormack and Verganti 2003).

Both, technological and requirements uncertainty are major influencing factors of software development projects complexity. To manage this complexity, software development teams either try to minimize project uncertainties by controlling impediments or to flexibly cope with them (Dönmez and Grote 2013). As the sources of uncertainty are often outside of control of the team, flexibility and the ability to adapt to new situations is an important determinant of successful software development teams. The software engineering discipline has proposed different *software development processes* to cope with uncertainty and project complexity. These processes specify general frameworks about structure and organization of software development projects.

2.1.2   *Software Development Processes*

Software development processes define "a set of activities that lead to the production of a software product" (Sommerville 2004, p. 64). As the development of different software systems may require different processes, the software engineering discipline has developed very different processes during the last decades. Nevertheless, there are several tasks that every development projects must include such as *definition tasks* for requirements specification, *implementation tasks* for software design, coding, and testing, and *evolution tasks* for modification, adaptations, and corrections. The different software development processes vary in terms of how strictly and in which sequences these tasks are addressed. Overall, three generations of software engineering development processes can be distinguished: craftsmanship, early software engineering, and modern software engineering.

Craftsmanship

Software development in the 1950s can be best described as *ad hoc* development with no standardized processes, technologies, or development methods. Products were customized for a particular purpose and deployed on mainframe computers. This led to various quality and maintenance issues (Austin and Devin 2009). Software development organizations used simple customized tools, processes, and technologies to program machines with primitive languages. Later, the approach was an unformalized "code-and-fix" approach (Boehm 2006). While the first programmers mostly had an engineering background, more and more people from other disciplines started to develop software.

In the 1970s, the development process was formalized leading to the popular sequential "Waterfall" software development process (Royce 1970). It was a systematic engineering approach that adheres to specific process steps moving software through a series of representations from requirements to finished software (Boehm 2006). This approach assumes software development problems to be fully specifiable and optimal solutions to be predictable and planable in advance. Extensive plans were devised, processes were strictly followed in order to make development an efficient and predictable activity. The waterfall model was later interpreted and implemented as a sequential process with project-gates between clearly defined project phases. Design did not start before definition of a clear set of requirements and coding was not started before completion of the software design. The main idea was to shift from craft to industrial software production imitating manufacturing processes. Therefore, more and more components were built for reuse and process steps were standardized.

Early Software Engineering

In the 1980s, reuse of software functionality increased, new development tools were introduced, and new high-level object-oriented programming languages were developed improving developer productivity. In addition, software organizations used standardized processes to increase productivity. The industry had matured and was transforming into an engineering discipline.

In the 1990s, object-oriented methods were strengthened using design patterns. Modeling languages were introduced and quickly spread with the expansion of the Internet and the emergence of the World Wide Web. Organizations used more and more commercialized software such as operating systems, database systems, or graphical user interfaces and programmed most of the functionality in higher-level programming languages.

Modern Software Engineering

The importance of software as a discriminator of traditional products as well as internet-based software products required faster time-to-market times in the 2000s. In addition, the importance of user-interactive products made fast user feedback important which rendered the formal processes as too rigid. As a consequence, iterative development processes obtained more attention (MacCormack et al. 2001). Today, most of the software is built using standard tools and existing software functionality from commercial products or open source libraries. Typically, only

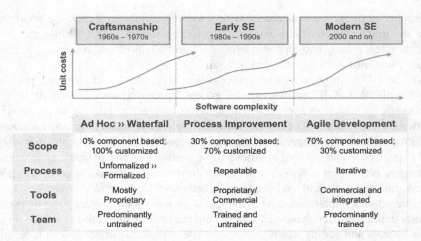

Fig. 2.1 Trends in software engineering (based on Royce et al. 2009)

about 30 % of the components need to be custom built (Royce et al. 2009) allowing more flexible processes.

Figure 2.1 illustrates the three generations of software engineering. The diagram on top of the figure schematically depicts the ability of each particular generation to handle software complexity in terms of cost per unit (Royce et al. 2009). As the complexity of software development projects has constantly risen over time, new approaches were introduced which better suited the given project contexts.

The software industry evolved from a "code-and-fix" paradigm to a professional industry. Many of these changes were incremental. But the late 1990s saw the emergence of a number of agile methods which meant a shift in software development processes and how many software development projects are organized today (Boehm 2006). This study is motivated by the agile software development paradigm. The underlying principles, agile methods, and agile practices are introduced in the following section.

2.2 Agile Software Development

The beginning of the 2000s saw a constant stream of change in the software industry. New technologies emerged and quickly adopted as a consequence of the exchange of ideas among developers through the global connectivity provided by the World Wide Web. The technological potential led to heavy investment into the IT industry. The software industry saw numerous mergers and acquisitions of existing as well as the rise of many new start-up companies. As a consequence, many software development projects faced tremendous organizational changes. In addition, more and more software applications were now developed for the consumer market requiring user-friendly interfaces. For that, user feedback had to be quickly integrated into the development process leading to unpredictable and changing requirements. Overall, rapid change was becoming increasingly inherent to the software industry (MacCormack et al. 2001). Hence, speed-to-market and the ability to change to new requirements or react to customer feedback was essential to succeed in an environment of uncertainty (Baskerville et al. 2003). These challenges could only be met with shorter product life-cycles. As a consequence, the so-called lightweight methods evolved in the 1990s (Larman and Basili 2003) and represented an opposite pole to the heavy-weight plan-driven development processes which were soon considered as too rigid to successfully develop software in such volatile project conditions (Highsmith and Cockburn 2001)

2.2.1 Agile Values and Principles

In 2001, a group of 17 advocates of lightweight software engineering methods gathered to discuss their common grounds to coin the term "agile methods" in the so-called Agile Manifesto.[5] It proposes a set of four core values for agile software development organizations. These agile values were derived from previous light-weight methods introduced by these agilists in the 1990s and early 2000s.[6] The four values constitute the essence of agile software development:

> **Individuals and interactions** over processes and tools[7]
> **Working software** over comprehensive documentation
> **Customer collaboration** over contract negotiation
> **Responding to change** over following a plan

Instead of formalizing the development process with detailed specification of software requirements, agile software development meant a distinct move towards continuous, informal, and close customer collaboration (Highsmith 2000). Unnecessary documentation was avoided as much as possible emphasizing a "lean" mentality adopted from lean manufacturing (Poppendieck and Poppendieck 2007). Agile developers would rather spend their time progressing the final software product instead of working on detailed project plans or extensive documentation of their software. Furthermore, people changed their perception seeing uncertainty

---

[5]See http://agilemanifesto.org/.

[6]Light-weight development methods proceeding agile software development: Adaptive Software Development (Highsmith 2000), Feature Driven Development (Palmer and Felsing 2002), Dynamic Systems Development Methods (Stapleton 1999), Scrum (Schwaber and Beedle 2002), Extreme Programming (XP) (Beck 2000), Lean Development (Poppendieck and Poppendieck 2007).

[7]Fowler (2002) explained that both sides of these statements are valued, but agile software engineering prefers the first over the second.

as an inherent part of software development as opposed to an unforeseeable contingency to be controlled through detailed upfront planning and compliance with strict processes (Dingsøyr et al. 2012).

2.2.2   Agile Methods and Practices

In the late 1990s and early 2000s, various software engineering methods were introduced. These methods are based on the idea of an incremental, iterative, and evolutionary software development process. As they encompass on the four aforementioned core values of agile software engineering, these methods were later called agile methods. Amongst them, *Scrum* and *Extreme Programming* are not only the most influential, but also the most popular today (Maruping et al. 2009a; VersionOne 2012).[8] In the following, both are briefly introduced as they are at the core of this study.

Scrum

Schwaber and Sutherland (2011) define Scrum as a "framework within which people can address complex adaptive problems, while [...] delivering products". Scrum is very popular amongst professional software development teams (VersionOne 2012). It is often referred to as a software development method, but strictly speaking, it is a project management framework. Scrum specifies (1) certain *roles* in the development team, establishes an (2) iterative work mode which centers around development *Sprints*, and defines different (3) *artifacts* that the developers use to coordinate their work. While first being published by Sutherland (1995) and later illustrated by Schwaber and Beedle (2002), the core concepts of Scrum are based on the ideas of Takeuchi and Nonaka (1986). All key elements of Scrum are illustrated in Fig. 2.2.

1. The project framework defines the *Scrum team* as a group of about ten people. There are two specific roles in the Scrum team: the Scrum Master and the Product Owner. The *Scrum Master (SM)* takes the role of a facilitator responsible to maintain the Scrum processes and eliminate impediments that might hinder the team from working efficiently. The *Product Owner (PO)* represent the customer within the team and voices customer requirements. Product owners define the team's development targets in the coming Sprint and bear the responsibility to generate value for the customer. In their daily work, POs define customer

---

[8]Other agile methods are, for instance, Adaptive Software Development (Highsmith 2000), Feature Driven Development (Palmer and Felsing 2002), Crystal Clear (Cockburn 2005), or Kanban (Anderson 2004).

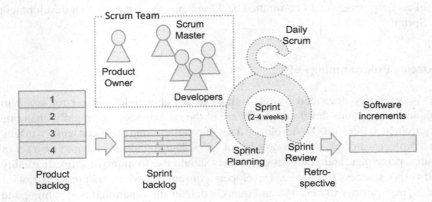

Fig. 2.2 Scrum development framework

requirements, define a list of prioritized development tasks for the team, and review work increments after each Sprint.

All other team members belong to the *development team* and do the actual software development work. They analyze requirements and design, develop, and validate the software. Scrum development teams are cross-functional, i.e. all team members are expected to have the necessary skill set to accomplish all of these software development tasks. Consequently, there are no additional roles in the development team such as user interface developers, testers, or other specialists.

2. Scrum teams pursue an iterative work mode and split the development project into short development cycles, so-called development *Sprints*. These Sprints have a specific length of 1–4 weeks, after which the team delivers new software features to the customer. This approach contrasts the traditional project with sequential phases for planning, development, validation, integration, and software release activities.

   Every Sprint starts with a *Sprint planning* meeting during which the team decides on the features to be implemented. Subsequently, the team members specify sub-tasks and assign them to individual developers. All team members meet daily for about 15 min to synchronize their work and bring transparency to the work progress within the team. All developers inform the team about their accomplishments, describe the current work, and raise issues to be addressed by the team. Every Sprint ends with a *Sprint review* meeting during which the team presents its progress to the product owner or directly to the customer. In addition, the Scrum Master organizes a *Retrospective* meeting for the team to discuss possible improvement to teamwork processes in the future.

3. The team organizes its development tasks using a *product backlog*. The backlog contains a list of prioritized tasks defined by the product owner. The development team breaks this backlog into *sprint backlog items* and tracks its progress during each Sprint in a so-called *burndown chart*. This chart shows the ratio

of accomplished versus committed backlog items for that particular development Sprint.

Extreme Programming (XP)

XP is originally described by the authors as a lightweight method for small to medium-sized teams developing software in the face of vague or rapidly-changing requirements. Beck (2000) developed a set of programming practices while working on a project with Chrysler Group LLC in 1995. The key ideas are based on a set of values, principles, and practices developers should use to improve software quality and responsiveness to change. Developers constantly review system scenarios of the highest priority to business and quickly deliver the functionality (Fruhling and Vreede 2006). Amongst them, frequent releases of new software functionality to the customer and a constant focus on software quality is key. The general idea behind Extreme Programming is to take beneficial ideas and concepts of software engineering to "extreme" levels.

Extreme Programming received significant attention because of its emphasis on communication, simplicity, and testing, its sustainable developer-oriented practices, as well as its interesting name (Larman and Basili 2003). Extreme programmers advocate a strong focus on software code rather than plans or documentation. Furthermore, software quality is the main focus and the quality of the software should be permanently checked with automated tests. Unit tests check whether a particular piece of software works as intended, acceptance tests verify the satisfaction of user requirements, and integration tests validate coherent functionality of different modules of a software. Furthermore, extreme programmers keep the design simple and avoid overmanning features.

Extreme Programming proposes a set of software development practices. These include:

- **Pair programming**, two developers share a single workstation and collaboratively develop software side-by-side. One is actively writing code, the other observes, supports, and challenges the chosen approach in order to find better work results.
- **Code review**, the finalized software code is reviewed by at least one colleague prior to task finalization to obtain feedback and ensure high quality.
- **Test-driven development**, an iterative development practice where developers first write a test case for the wanted software functionality to verify if the software program includes the desired functionality. Only then, developers write software code to pass that test case.
- **Refactoring**, is a development practice including the restructuring of existing software code to improve its internal software quality, i.e. its readability or its structuredness, without changing its functionality. The objective is to increase the long-term maintainability and the extensibility of the software.

- **Continuous integration**, a software development practice where every developer working on a particular code base continuously integrates newly developed or changed software code to prevent integration problems. Mostly, integration tools are used that support the integration process.
- **Coding standards**, a set of rules or conventions of the developers in software development team or community. They include a common programming style which improve readability and the maintainability of a software code.
- **Collective code ownership**, a convention according to which everybody in a team or community owns the code, i.e. everybody is allowed to change any piece of code in a software. Simultaneously, every team member is responsible to ensure its quality.
- **Automated testing**, the use of special software to test the functionality of a software. Test cases check for expected outcomes of the tested software delivered given a set of inputs. These tests are executed for continuous feedback on the software functionality and different abstraction levels, for instance, unit, integration, or user interface tests.

2.3   Literature Review on Agile Software Development

Agile software development has been gaining popularity since the publication of the Agile Manifesto in 2001. Large software providers, such as Microsoft (Begel and Nagappan 2007), SAP (Schmidt et al. 2014; Schnitter and Mackert 2011), Adobe (Green 2011), and many others (VersionOne 2012) have adopted agile methods during the last years. As a consequence, agile software development can today be seen as a mainstream development methodology (West et al. 2010) with an increasing interest among professional software developers in rigorous validations of the effectiveness of the development approach.

During the last decade, researchers have been paying more and more attention to the phenomenon and studied diverse aspects of the agile software development paradigm. Most of these studies were either conducted by researchers in the software engineering (SE) or in the information systems development (ISD) community (Dingsøyr et al. 2012). Trends and findings of both research streams are described and discussed in the following paragraphs.

2.3.1   Information Systems Research

In contrast to the SE literature, there are no review articles about publications on agile software development in the Information Systems (IS) discipline. Therefore, a structured literature search was conducted to provide a comprehensive overview of existing publications. The results help to cluster main areas of interest and to analyze the research results. Beginning with the key words found in the software

Table 2.1 Number of articles found in the reviewed IS research outlets

Journals		Conferences	
European Journal of IS	10	American Conference on IS	14
Information Systems Journal	8	European Conference on IS	16
Information Systems Research	7	International Conference on IS	8
Journal of the Association for IS	1	Pacific Asia Conference on IS	3
Journal of Information Technology	1		
Journal of Management IS	3		
Journal of Strategic IS	0		
MIS Quarterly	2		
	Σ32		Σ40

engineering literature (see Table 2.5 on page 31), a list of search terms was defined:

A {agile, agility}
B {software, information system, information systems, IS}
C {engineering, development}
D {team, teams, method, methods, methodology, methodologies, project}

These search terms were combined as follows: {A1 OR A2} AND {B1 OR B2 ...} AND {C1 OR C2} AND {D1 OR D2 ...} to structurally search the top IS journals[9] and conference proceedings for articles published between 2000[10] and 2014. The resulting list of publications was complemented by articles found through a forward and backward search starting from the list of citations of the most relevant publications in the field. Appendix A.1 presents the full list of 72 papers which could be extracted from these outlets. A brief overview is provided in Table 2.1.

The increasing number of publications over the last years (see Fig. 2.3) shows a great interest in the topic amongst researchers in the international Information Systems community. Moreover, two special issues of the two leading IS journals within the last years (Abrahamsson et al. 2009; Ågerfalk et al. 2009) emphasize its importance (see Table 2.4). Nevertheless, the majority of publications on agile software development can be found in the software engineering outlets.

The extracted publications were analyzed for their research methodology, theoretical foundations, research context, and research focus. The findings are discussed subsequently.

Research Methodology Research on agile information systems development has a clear tendency towards qualitative research methods. About half of the reviewed studies were based on interview-based case studies. The conceptual papers (28 %)

---

[9]IS Basket of Eight: http://aisnet.org/?SeniorScholarBasket.
[10]The Agile Manifesto was published in 2001.

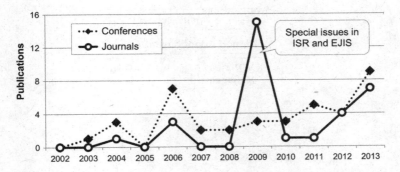

Fig. 2.3 Publications on agile ISD between 2002 and 2013 in the IS research community

are mainly concerned with the definition of agility or discuss the necessity for tools. Only 11 % of these papers report survey results (see e.g. Lee and Xia 2010; Maruping et al. 2009a). Overall, confirmatory research to test the explored results of the qualitative studies are mostly missing. The knowledge of the field is thus primarily derived from single teams working in very different project contexts.

Theoretical Foundations 44 out of 72 paper mention an underlying theory to guide the study. Overall, 29 different theories were found that were applied to understand the agile development approach. This demonstrates the clear response of the research community to the frequent calls for more theory-based studies on agile software development (Dingsøyr et al. 2012; Dybå and Dingsøyr 2008; Ågerfalk et al. 2009). The most frequently applied theoretical lenses were the *Theory of Complex Adaptive Systems* (Ralph and Narros 2013; Vidgen and Wang 2009; Wang and Conboy 2009) (7x), *Theory of Innovation Diffusion* (Mangalaraj et al. 2009; Schlauderer and Overhage 2013) (6x), *Control Theory* (Cram and Brohman 2013; Goh et al. 2013; Harris et al. 2009; Maruping et al. 2009a) (4x), and *Theory of Coordination* (Li and Maedche 2012; Strode et al. 2011)(3x). Furthermore, different theories and models from team effectiveness research have been used such as *Team Adaptation Theory* (Schmidt et al. 2013), *Group Think Theory* (McAvoy and Butler 2009), or *Leadership Theory* (Yang et al. 2009).

Research Contexts Most articles reported results from small, co-located teams, which develop new software products. Other studies researched agile software development aspects in distributed, large-scale, or maintenance project settings.

Research Foci The refined list of publications can be clustered into four main research topics (see Fig. 2.4). First, several articles were concerned with the conceptualization and definition of the software development agility concept. Second, other studies investigated the adoption and adaptation of agile methods in the field. Third, few studies examined the impact and role of standard project management topics, such as funding, leadership, or control of agile software development projects. Finally, different teamwork factors were examined in detail. Authors were interested

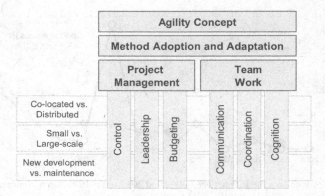

Fig. 2.4 Research foci on agile software development in the IS Community

in the influence of agile software development on specific teamwork factors and, in turn, the influence of these factors on the performance of agile teams. The following paragraphs provide an overview of the most influential publications for each category and summarize the main findings.

Agility Concept

Every good concept needs a strong underlying logic serving as a "theoretical glue" (Whetten 1989). In ISD research, however, it seems that "almost every piece of research adopts a unique interpretation of agility" (Abrahamsson et al. 2009). This conclusion was confirmed by Hummel (2014) who found 17 different definitions of the term after reviewing agile studies in the main outlets of software engineering in information systems research streams.

Among practitioners, the situation is not much different as the following developer quote, found in an internal collaboration forum of SAP SE, illustrates:

> Agility is [in my company] the hyper buzzword these days. Everybody uses it, but nobody tells what is her/his understanding of it. I get goosebumps when I hear it. Some use it as a justification for a chaotic working mode. Some more for agile software engineering. Some see Scrum as part of it. Some not. Who knows. Actually I don't know what people - including [the Chief Technology Officer] - mean when they use that word.

Until 2009, little if any research has focused on the conceptual development of agility in ISD (Conboy 2009). One reason was that agile software development was motivated by the Agile Manifesto, which does not provide a clear definition of the concept. Instead, the four agile core principles are a non-formal definition of agility concept with general guidelines for software developers. In recent years, different perspectives on ISD agility have been provided by researchers without a compromise on definition and conceptualization of software development agility (van Oosterhout et al. 2006).

Table 2.2 Agile software development as a behavior

Abrahamsson et al. (2002)	Agility is defined in respect to the **adoption of agile methods**. Agile development methods are incremental, cooperative, straightforward, and adaptive
Conboy (2009)	Agility is defined in terms of the **adoption of agile methods**. Agility [of a method] is the continuous readiness to rapidly or inherently create change, proactively or reactively embrace change, and learn from change while contributing to perceived customer value
Maruping et al. (2009a)	"We use the term agile software development teams' to refer to teams that are using an **agile methodology**"
Qumer and Henderson-Sellers (2008)	"Agility is a persistent **behavior or ability** of an entity that exhibits flexibility to accommodate expected or unexpected changes rapidly; agility can be evaluated by flexibility, speed, leanness, learning, and responsiveness"
Schmidt et al. (2013)	A team's **behavior** to iteratively and collaboratively accomplish its software development tasks including (1) software specification, (2) software design and implementation, (3) software validation, and (4) software release

The term agility was first used in the field of manufacturing research (Meredith and Francis 2000) and supply chain research. Within the IS discipline, it was first adopted by Overby et al. (2006) to describe the "sensing and responding capabilities" of a firm. Three years later, agility was adopted in the ISD context (Conboy 2009). Subsequently, several authors have provided their perspectives on software development agility since its initial introduction to the software development domain by the group of experienced practitioners in the Agile Manifesto. Researchers generally agree about the multi-dimensionality of the concept including a sensing and a responding dimension (Sarker and Sarker 2009). However, the meaning of agility itself in software development is yet to be fully understood (Börjesson and Mathiassen 2005). Three distinct conceptualizations of agility can be distinguished: Agility as a behavior, agility as a capability, and agility as an attitude.

Agility as a Behavior Several authors conceptualized the agility of a software development team by a team's adoption intensity of agile development methods or development practices (see Table 2.2). Different approaches exist distinguishing agile and non-agile methods. Abrahamsson et al. (2002) suggested to describe incremental (small software releases), cooperative (close communication with the customer), straightforward (the methods are easy to learn and to modify), and adaptive (able to make last moment changes) software development methods as agile. Another, often-cited definition was developed by Conboy (2009), based on a thorough investigation of the agility concept in other research disciplines. Following his perspective, agility comprises two concepts, i.e. flexibility and leanness. Agility does not only incorporate the flexibility to change, but also the team's ability to quickly respond to change. In addition, leanness is the contribution to perceived customer value through economy, quality, and simplicity. Taking this perspective, software development teams are agile teams when adopting software development methods which lead to flexibility and leanness of the software development process.

Schmidt et al. (2013) proposed another perspective. They suggested to conceptualize agility of an software development team by its organization of central development task, such as specification, design, implementation, and software validation. Iterativeness and collaborativeness were suggested as the central behavioral markers of agile teams. Agile teams iterate the aforementioned tasks frequently while involving several team members in the process. In addition, agile teams plan, design, implement, and validate the software in small steps involving the entire team in all steps.

At a higher level of abstraction, Zheng et al. (2011) conceptualize agility as a "collective behavior, instantiated in improvisational behaviour of individuals and groups in their social interactions". They further specify agility as "social actors [...] when engaging with uncertainty and complexity".

Agility as a Capability The second perspective conceptualizes agility as a team capability (see Table 2.3). Agile teams are considered to possess the capability to effectively and efficiently react to change in the project context (Henderson-Sellers and Serour 2005) or, in a narrower sense, to react to changing customer requirements (Lee and Xia 2010). Other authors have specified particular team capabilities such as responsiveness, speed, competency, flexibility, and sustainability (Sharifi and Zhang 1999) or nimbleness, suppleness, quickness, dexterity, liveliness, or alertness

Table 2.3 Agile software development as a capability

Lee and Xia (2010)	"Software development agility is a team's **capability** to efficiently and effectively respond to and incorporate user requirement changes during the project lifecycle"
Sarker and Sarker (2009)	"Agility in a distributed ISD setting is the **capability** of a distributed team to speedily accomplish ISD tasks and to adapt and reconfigure itself to changing conditions in a rapid manner"
Erickson et al. (2005)	"Agility is associated with such related concepts as nimbleness, suppleness, quickness, dexterity, liveliness, or alertness"
Henderson-Sellers and Serour (2005)	"Agility refers to **readiness** for action or change; it has two dimensions: (1) the ability to adapt to various changes and (2) the ability to fine-tune and re-engineer software development processes when needed"
Lyytinen and Rose (2006)	"Agility is defined as the **ability** to sense and respond swiftly to technical changes and new business opportunities; it is enacted by exploration-based learning and exploitation-based learning"
Vidgen and Wang (2009)	"Agile teams can be recognized by their **ability** to work with customers to coevolve business value, work sustainably with rhythm, be collectively mindful, create team learning, adapt and improve the development process, and to create product innovations"
Dingsør and Dybå (2012)	Team **aspects of agility**: "capability, talent, skill, and expertise to foster flexible anticipatory and reactive practices in response to changes in the state environment"

(Erickson et al. 2005) which can be assigned to agile teams. Lyytinen and Rose (2006) describe agility as an organizational capability to learn, explore, and exploit knowledge.

Sarker and Sarker (2009) combine a behavioral and ability perspective in their definition of agility for distributed ISD teams. On the one hand, they consider the capability of a distributed team to "speedily accomplish ISD tasks and to adapt and reconfigure itself to changing conditions in a rapid manner" as a key characteristic of agile teams. On the other hand, they define distinct behaviors of agile teams such as the right resources, the adoption of agile methods, and forging and maintaining of linkages across communicative and cultural barriers among distributed team members.

Agility as an Attitude Moreover, agility can be conceptualized in regards to the attitude of the members of software development teams. Change can either be perceived as a threat or an opportunity. Following this perspective, agile teams "embrace change as an opportunity and harness it for the organization's competitive advantage" (Sharifi and Zhang 1999). Accordingly, agile teams expect and leverage change in the project context rather than assuming predictability. This perspective was not found in ISD literature, but in the manufacturing research stream only. Future research, however, might take this approach to study agile software development teams.

Given this conceptual diversity, Abrahamsson et al. (2009) concluded a need for every organization to appropriately define the agility concept specific to a given context. The same holds true for future research. A single interpretation may not be sufficient to advance research in the field. Nevertheless, a "solid platform on which to build a cohesive body of knowledge" is necessary for future cumulative research (Abrahamsson et al. 2009). This study follows the behavioral perspective and conceptualizes software development teams as agile when using agile development practices (see Sect. 4.3).

Agile Method Adoption and Adaptation

Several studies analyzed the adoption and adaptation of agile development methods and practices. Most studies assume that software development is restricted to small, co-located teams developing non-critical software. Few studies, however, investigate the reasons for developers' deployment of agile methods in other contexts or their combination with the traditional, plan-driven development approach.

Method Adoption Mangalaraj et al. (2009) provide insights into individual, team, technological, task, and environmental factors that determine the acceptance of Extreme Programming practices. They identify individuals' attitude and knowledge about the practices as essential determinants. In addition, development tools as well as the characteristics of the development task can support the adoption intensity. Finally, environmental factors such as time or budget constraints may influence how intensively the development practices are used. McAvoy and Butler (2009) provide a decision support tool based on a "critical adoption factors matrix" to assess the suitability of agile methods in software development projects. The tool is based on insights from workshops with practitioners. Overhage and Schlauderer (2012) examine the long-term acceptance of Scrum, providing a list of acceptance factors evaluated in a single case study. Wang et al. (2012) conducted an exploratory study about the use of agile development practices. They take an 'innovation assimilation perspective' and describe four teams using agile methods during the acceptance, routinization, and infusion phases. Berger and Beynon-Davies (2009) investigate the usage of agile methods in large-scale software development teams. They assume the agile software development approach as primarily adopted by small development teams for short-term projects. In their case study, the authors demonstrate that agile software development can also be applied in the context of hierarchical decision-making, long-term projects, and high complexity. Austin and Devin (2009) provide a basic contingency framework based on the benefit/cost economics to discuss when to use an agile or plan-driven development approach. While most studies focus on new product development, Edberg et al. (2012) explore how information technology professionals define and select a methodology to maintain existing software using grounded theory. They provide a factor model to describe the decision process of software development teams between different components of standard methodologies. Lastly, Balijepally et al. (2009) focus on pair programming. In an experiment, they investigate reasons why and under which circumstances developers use pair programming. They find pair programmers to perform better than the second best programmer independent of the task complexity. Two developers, however, cannot exceed the performance of the best member working individually. In addition, the programmers show higher levels of confidence and satisfaction compared to the second best programmer, but not to the best programmer.

Method Adaptation Other studies examine the adaptation of agile methods to specific work contexts or their combination with the traditional, plan-driven software development approach. Cao et al. (2009) develop a framework for adapting agile development methods proposing a need for Extreme Programming practices to be adapted to different contexts. Based on adaptive structuration theory, the authors explain specific adaptations to address challenges of agile development teams. In a case study, Fitzgerald et al. (2006) exemplify this with Scrum and Extreme Programming at Intel. They propose these methods may complement each others' incompleteness. Port and Bui (2009) run a simulation to better understand the benefits of combining the plan-driven and agile software development approaches for requirements prioritization. Mixed strategies, so they conclude, are likely to yield better results than pure agile or plan-based approaches. Karlsson and Ågerfalk (2009) discuss a formal and methodological approach to tailoring agile software development methods while emphasizing agile values and principles. Finally, Tanner and Wallace (2012) discuss how ISD teams adapt agile methods in distributed work contexts.

Agile Project Management

Different authors investigated project management factors in agile software development teams. These include control, leadership, and budgeting of agile teams.

Project Control Several authors apply control theory to study agile software development projects. Maruping et al. (2009a) examined the project conditions when agile methods are most helpful. Based on a survey with 110 software development teams, the authors find a beneficial use of agile methods in situation of frequent requirement changes and in control mode allowing teams to autonomously decide about the development activities. Goh et al. (2013) conducted a multiple case study. The publication includes a framework proposing project uncertainty and project urgency to be best addressed by an agile team using an interplay of team capabilities and trust-mediated organizational control mechanisms. Harris et al. (2009) studied when to provide teams with the flexibility to modify their directions and team external control of flexibility. The results demonstrate a need for flexibility in situations of uncertain starting conditions and the benefits of combining the traditional control mode with a newly proposed control mode to effectively manage such situations. Emergent outcome control was found to be specific to agile teams and different to behavioral and outcome control. It includes (1) scope boundaries constraining the solution space without specifying the solution and (2) ongoing feedback which is only provided when correction is needed. The studied agile methods were found to implement this control mode. Persson et al. (2012) studied the implementation of project control in a distributed software development team. Formal control practices were found to be enacted through communication media while clan control was predominantly exerted in informal roles and relationships. Cram and Brohman (2013) studied the influence of different development approaches on the control mode of software development projects. They provide a typology of ISD control modes differentiating between preventive and detective or corrective control practices, on the one hand, as well as product and process control objectives, on the other hand. The authors propose that agile projects tend to primarily utilize detective and corrective practices and combine them with process control mechanisms. A similar model was provided by Gregory et al. (2013).

Project Leadership Yang et al. (2009) compare leadership in agile and traditional software development teams to find managers of agile teams in higher need of a transformational leadership style to achieve success. Transformational leaders develop their followers focusing on motivation, morale, and job performance. Transactional leaders, on the other hand, provide rewards for accomplishments and make sure followers comply with defined standards.

Project Budgeting Cao et al. (2013) emphasize that a "just enough planning" mentality in agile project may aggravate funding decisions of project managers. The authors present a framework to explain how organizations' adaptation to the funding approach to accommodate the characteristics of agile projects. According to their results, funding decisions should be based on continuous feedback from project team members and negotiations based on changing customer values. These decision may be implemented through contracts with fixed prices or negotiated scope or pay-as-you go models. Keaveney and Conboy (2006) propose a cost estimate model for agile projects. Essential for the success is expert knowledge and analogy to past projects. Moreover, the authors find fixed price budgets in agile projects to be beneficial for developers and customers.

Agile Teamwork

Most information systems are too large to be developed by a single person. Hence, several developers collaborate in a single or multiple software development teams. During the last 60 years, team effectiveness research has provided extensive knowledge about work teams. The research resulted in many different teamwork models and theories about work team effectiveness (Cohen and Bailey 1997). In recent years, several researchers have built on this knowledge by opening the black-box of agile software development teams and examining the effect on different teamwork aspects. The most popular topics are communication, coordination, and cognition in agile teams. Most of these studies were published in conference outlets indicating opportunities to further development of theses studies. To date, several studies are still at a research-in-progress stage or first steps to an evolving research field.

Team Communication   Rosenkranz et al. (2013) assume the ability to communicate and to reach a shared understanding between the software customer or users and developers at the heard of requirements development. The authors propose the quality of language as a suitable means for "the emergence of coherent and meaningful requirements". The authors provide research propositions and suggest to analyze language use and communication in requirements development in future studies. Hummel and Rosenkranz (2013) propose "social agile practices" to positively influence the communication behavior of an ISD team which, in turn, may lead to higher mutual understanding and better relationship in the team leading to project success. The authors develop a set of research proposition and provided a measurement model for empirical tests, left for future research.

Team Coordination   Xu and Cao (2006) investigate coordination mechanisms in agile software development teams. They distinguish between vertical and horizontal coordination mechanisms, both proposed to determine the performance of agile teams. Vertical coordination involves formal coordination by supervisors while horizontal coordination involves peer-to-peer coordination between team members. Strode et al. (2011) define the concept of "coordination effectiveness" in agile development teams as the "state of coordination wherein the entire agile software development team has a comprehensive understanding of the project goal, the project priorities, what is going on and when, what they as individuals need to do and when, who is doing what, and how each individuals work fits in with other team members work". Li and Maedche (2012) build on this idea and study coordination effectiveness in distributed agile development projects.

Team Cognition Different studies focused on knowledge distribution and knowledge sharing in software development teams. Maruping et al. (2009b) conducted a survey study with more than 500 developers working in 56 teams and found that the two agile practices collective ownership and coding standards moderate the relationship between expertise coordination and software project technical quality. Moreover, collective ownership thereby attenuates the relationship and coding standards strengthen the relationship. The underlying theoretical propositions of the study were derive from transactive memory systems literature. Other studies found "collective mindfulness" to be important in agile ISD teams. According to McAvoy et al. (2013), mindfulness promotes a focus on "continuous attention to detail" and "vigilance to minimize errors and respond effectively to unexpected events". As a consequence, the new perspective allows to study agility in terms of "being agile" rather than "doing agile". Finally, Spohrer et al. (2013) study the influence of pair programming and peer code review on the creation of knowledge in software development teams.

2.3.2 Software Engineering Research

The interest of the software engineering research community in agile software development is primarily evident from the growing number of scientific publications since 2001. Figure 2.5 illustrates the number of publications either published in conference proceedings or scientific journals (Dingsøyr et al. 2012). The most popular conference outlets are the International Conference on Agile Software Development ("XP"), the International Conference of Product Focused Software Development and Process Improvement ("PROFES"), and the International Confer-

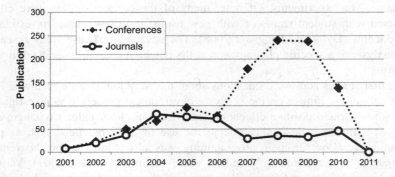

Fig. 2.5 Publications on agile software development between 2001 and 2010 in the SE research community (source Dingsøyr et al. 2012)

Table 2.4 Special issues on agile software development in IS and SE outlets

Outlet	Introductory article	Field
IEEE Computer	Williams and Cockburn (2003)	SE
Journal of Database Management	Siau (2005)	SE
Software Practices and Experience	Greer and Hamon (2011)	SE
Journal of Information and Software Technology	Dybå (2011)	SE
Journal of Systems and Software	Dingsøyr et al. (2012)	SE
Information Systems Research	Ågerfalk et al. (2009)	IS
European Journal of IS	Abrahamsson et al. (2009)	IS

SE - software engineering outlets, *IS* - information systems outlets

ence on Software Engineering ("ICSE"). The major scientific journals publishing on agile software development include IEEE Software, Journal of Systems and Software, Information and Systems Technology, and Empirical Software Engineering. In addition, several special issues addressed the topic indicating a keen interest in the field of software engineering (see Table 2.4).

The findings of these articles were comprehensively summarized by various review articles during the last decade. Table 2.5 on page 31 provides an overview of these review articles and briefly summarizes their conclusions.

Authors from several countries and diverse background have contributed scientific studies for a better understanding of agile software development (Chuang et al. 2014). Moreover, several special issues in leading SE journals have addressed the topic and there are periodical conferences on the topic, e.g. International Conference on Agile Software Development. While the first studies were mainly best-practice reports or success stories (Abrahamsson et al. 2002), more and more studies are published with scientific rigor and relevance (Sfetsos and Stamelos 2010). Nonetheless, "most [of the studies] are inspired by practices emerging in industry" (Dingsøyr et al. 2012).

Chuang et al. (2014) classified about 70 % of the studies as case studies, design simulations, or experiments. Of note, many of theses case studies were either conducted with student teams or with new teams; only few studies investigated mature teams (Dybå and Dingsøyr 2008). The advantage of case study research is an analysis of a specific phenomenon at the potential cost of generalizability of the results.

The first studies addressed questions about the adoption of agile methods. In a second phase, the impact on the software development process was investigated. Some studies found positive effects on team learning, knowledge exchange, and improved software code quality due to the use of agile practices such as pair programming. However, pair programming was also found to be "extremely inefficient", "very exhausting'", and "a waste of time" (Tessem 2003). Various studies found effects on better collaboration in the team, an improved "faith in their own abilities", respect and trust in software development teams (Robinson and Sharp 2005). Some studies investigate the role of personality of software developers

Table 2.5 Publications on agile software development in SE outlets

Review	Period	Scope	Findings/Conclusions
Abrahamsson et al. (2002)	≤ 2002	Experience reports	– Only a limited number of empirically validated studies found – Studies are mainly with anecdotal evidence from "success stories" – Agile methods are "effective and suitable for many situations" – More empirical studies to evaluate effectiveness needed
Cohen et al. (2004)	≤ 2004	Experience reports, research studies	– Insights from workshops, experiments, surveys, and seven case studies – Adoption and first experience with Extreme Programming and Scrum – Agile will not replace the traditional development approach – Both paradigms will find their areas of applications
Erickson et al. (2005)	≤ 2005	Experience report, research studies	– Mainly case studies about Extreme Programming – Most case studies promote the success of Extreme Programming – Need for more structured research in comparison to other approaches – "hard, empirically-based economic evidence is lacking"
Dybå and Dingsøyr (2008)	≤ 2005	Research studies	– Thirty three studies found with acceptable rigor – Four streams: (a) introduction and adoption, (b) human and social factors, (c) customer and developer perception, (d) comparative studies – Focus on human and social factors suggested for future studies – Lack of theoretical and methodological rigor – Need for a research agenda to increase quality and quantity of studies
Sfetsos and Stamelos (2010)	≤ 2009	Research studies	– Forty six empirical studies with "acceptable rigor, credibility, and relevance" – Three streams: studies on (a) test driven development, (b) pair programming, (c) XP practices – Test automation: better software quality as key benefit – Pair programming: better code quality and improved teamwork

(continued)

Table 2.5 (continued)

Review	Period	Scope	Findings/Conclusions
Jalali and Wohlin (2012)	1999–2009	Experience report, research studies	– Studies in distributed settings with globally distributed teams – Reviewed studies are mostly industry experience reports – Most studies focus on a particular Extreme Programming practice – Comprehensive framework to understand agile SE is needed
Dingsøyr et al. (2012)	2001–2010	Research studies	– Research community shows growing interest in agile SE – Limited number of studies with theoretical support – (a) knowledge management, (b) personality theories, or (c) learning theories – However: "general perception that agile research tends to be a-theoretical" – "Urge to embrace a more theory-based approach in the future when inquiring agile development"
Chuang et al. (2014)	2001–2012	Research studies	– Review of the key outlets and contributions to agile ISD literature – About half of the studies are case studies; only 7 % are surveys – Only 2 % pursue theory development – "Research on agile development methods remains at the infancy stage" – Call for more industrial and scholarly research studies
Hummel et al. (2013b)	≤ 2013	Research studies (IS & SE)	– Review about the role of communication in agile IS development – Communication process within agile ISD is still not well understood – Theories of communication, collaboration, cognition, and sense-making for future research

(Young et al. 2005). Other studies investigated developers' perception and found 95 % of the employees using XP would like their company to continue using agile methods (Mannaro et al. 2004). Finally, several studies compare the productivity of the agile versus the traditional software development showing positive to neutral impact (Ilieva et al. 2004; Wellington et al. 2005) while most studies found a positive impact on software quality (Layman et al. 2004; Wellington et al. 2005).

Critical studies on agile software development question the novelty of agile software development, criticize a lack of focus on long-term architecture, claim that it would only fit to small software development teams, and predict that Extreme Programming may lead to inefficient teamwork (Dybå and Dingsøyr 2008; McAvoy and Butler 2009).

Most of the studies in the software engineering outlets are neither concerned with theory development nor do they refer to existing theories from other fields to explain the effectiveness of agile software development. Instead, they are mainly descriptive with a lack of theoretical and conceptual foundation in the research stream (Abrahamsson et al. 2009). Only recently, few articles were published in a special issue of the Journal of Systems and Software exploring the "theoretical underpinnings of agile development" (Dingsøyr et al. 2012). The focus was on coordination, decision making, and social factors in agile software development. In conclusion, four key results can be found in the software engineering literature:

- The software engineering research community shows great interest in the topic
- Studies are mostly case studies
- Studies are mainly descriptive with no or limited theory-based explanations
- Many studies find evidence for a positive impact on software quality and teamwork factors, but there is a lack of integrated or cumulative research

2.4 Discussion of the Literature

In recent years, many software development organizations have shifted their development processes to agile software development (VersionOne 2012). As a consequence, agile software development can be described as mainstream today (West et al. 2010). At the same time, research on agile software development has matured from "practitioners' success-stories" (Abrahamsson et al. 2002) to a covered domain in the software engineering as well as the information systems research community. Both communities have shown particular interest in the topic as the extensive list of publications (see Figs. 2.3 and 2.5) and various special issues on agile software development indicate (see Table 2.4).

In 2008, Dybå and Dingsøyr (2008) reviewed the research body of knowledge on agile software development. They found a number of research studies, but also identified the need for more rigorous studies to advance the evolving field. In the meantime, several researchers have responded to this call resulting in an increasing number of publications on agile software development. Many of these studies are exploratory in nature and draw their insights from single or multiple case studies (see Appendix A.1). In addition, most of them explore small, co-located software development teams or projects while only few studies researched distributed or large-scale development settings. The exploratory character of the field allows researchers to better understand the implementation of agile software development. Against this background, this study aims to provide generalizable research findings to advance the research field.

Agile software development is a phenomenon primarily driven by experienced practitioners and consultants in the software industry (Boehm 2006). Hence, several researchers have first discussed how and why software development organizations use and adapt agile methods (see section "Agile Method Adoption and Adaptation").

Moreover, they evaluated how customers', developers', or students' perception of the agile development approach. Other studies assessed the development approach in terms of productivity, software quality, and job satisfaction (Dybå and Dingsøyr 2008). Many of these studies were primarily descriptive in nature.

Until today, the research community is still far away from fully understanding why, how, or in which project contexts agile software development works. In other words, there is still a long way for researchers to develop a theoretical understanding of agile software development. Such a theoretical perspective could not only explain the success of agile software development, but also guide professionals when and how to use the agile development approach.

A structured search of studies in the IS field revealed that more than 60 % of the publications build on a theoretical model or framework (see Appendix A.1). This shows that more and more studies seek to contribute to theory development in this field of research. This study intends to contribute to this literature stream and advance the theory-based understanding of agile software development.

As with every evolving research field, key concepts need to be discussed to ensure a common understanding in the research community for cumulative research success. The last years have seen valuable contributions to this discussion (see section "Agility Concept"). Various perspectives have been provided and there is agreement of agility being a multifaceted construct (Sarker and Sarker 2009). However, there is no agreement what agility is or how it should be conceptualized. This is one reasons why research on agile software development is still fragmented, as the boundaries and key concepts are not aligned. Another reason may be a lack of a clear definition of the dependent variable of many studies. While some studies are interested in the impact on software quality, delivered scope, in-time or in-budget delivery, other are curious to understand the impact on communication, coordination, or knowledge structures in software development projects or teams.

Overall, researchers have studied very diverse aspects of agile software development. Missing boundaries as well as a missing understanding about the definition of software development agility complicates the integration of the research stream. Therefore, this study intends to clearly define how it conceptualizes the multifaceted concept of agile software development as well as how it defines software development team performance (see Sect. 3.3.1).

In conclusion, agile software development is a software development approach with growing popularity since the early 2000s. Research on agile software development has advanced from best-practice success stories to more rigorous research studies with a predominantly descriptive character. The extant knowledge of teamwork research may provide a promising theoretical lens for this research direction. Due to the relevance for software development organizations, such a model should not only be generalizable but also validated with data from professional software developers. Since research on agile software development is very fragmented, every study needs to clearly define the conceptualization of agility and the dependent variable. Only then, follow-up studies can build on the study's results to advance the field towards an integrated research prospect. Dingsør and Dybå (2012) summarized the field of research in a call for future studies. They demanded (a) a better measurement of teamwork aspects in software development, (b) more rigorous industrial cases, (c) better understanding of dynamic configurations, (d) increased emphasis on team cognition, and (e) a better understanding of multicultural context of software development teams to advance the understanding of agile software development teams. This study seeks to contribute to the reviewed literature streams addresses these research challenges.

The author agrees to these conclusions seeing both an interest among researchers and a need for further research on agile software development. First, the results of the extensive literature review indicate an imbalance of applied research methods skewed towards qualitative research with only a limited number of quantitative studies. Second, theory-guided research on agile software development remains limited and many studies are still based on experience lacking theoretical support. Despite the strong focus on teamwork and collaboration in agile software development teams, only few studies draw on the extensive body of knowledge about the effectiveness of work teams to better understand agile software development. Finally, there is still no agreement among researchers about the definition of agility. As a consequence, study results are not comparable leading to a lack of cumulative studies and knowledge about agile software development. Overall, there is a need for more rigorous, theory-supported studies with insights from professional software developers.

Chapter 3
Theoretical and Conceptual Foundations

This chapter provides the theoretical and conceptual foundations of the study by introducing a theoretical research model with five empirically testable research propositions. The theoretical basis of the study was developed with insights from team effectiveness research and literature on agile software development. The central proposition of this study is that agile software development not only directly influences the performance of a software development team, but that it also triggers affective, behavioral, and cognitive teamwork mechanisms. Insights into these hidden effects within agile teams are expected to advance the theoretical understanding and evaluation of agile software development by integrating previously separated literature streams.

This chapter first introduces the related teamwork concepts. In particular, Sect. 3.1 categorizes Scrum teams as work teams and introduces the selected teamwork theories. Then, team adaptation theory and the impact of a work team's level of confidence on team effectiveness are discussed. A combination of both concepts lays the theoretical basis of the research model. Section 3.2 provides an overview of previous approaches to conceptualize software development team performance, i.e. the dependent variable of the research model. This leads to Sect. 3.3, which develops the research propositions to explain the impact of using agile practices on the performance of software development teams.

3.1 Team Effectiveness Research

Many failures of software development projects relate to a missing recognition of software development as a largely social process (Hirschheim et al. 1996). In many agile software organizations, these social processes are embedded in work team structures characterized by the Scrum framework (VersionOne 2012).

© Springer International Publishing Switzerland 2016
C. Schmidt, *Agile Software Development Teams*, Progress in IS,
DOI 10.1007/978-3-319-26057-0_3

Scrum suggests to develop software in stable, cross-functional teams of about ten developers (Schwaber and Beedle 2002). Regular Scrum team meetings foster the interactive and collaborative work mode in line with the agile development paradigm (see Sect. 2.2.1). Scrum not only directs the social processes but also reinforces team-based structures in software development projects. Hence, a fundamental understanding of the widely studied teamwork mechanisms may provide valuable insights for this study on agile software development.

A work team is defined as "a collection of individuals who are independent in their tasks, who share responsibility for their outcomes, who see themselves and are seen by others as an intact social entity embedded in one or more larger social contexts, and who manage their relationships across organizational boundaries" (Sundstrom et al. 2000). A wide variety of different types of teams have been discussed in the literature. As conclusions for one type of team may not apply to other team contexts or tasks, it is important to categorize software development teams. According to Kozlowski and Ilgen (2006), work teams are "composed of two or more individuals who (a) exist to perform organizationally relevant tasks, (b) share one or more common goals, (c) interact socially, (d) exhibit task interdependencies (i.e., work flow, goals, outcomes), (e) maintain and manage boundaries, and (f) are embedded in an organizational context that sets boundaries, constrains the team, and influences exchanges with other units in the broader entity". Given the characteristics of Scrum teams (see Sect. 2.2) and the aforementioned definition of a work team, this study classifies Scrum teams as work teams and subsequently borrows from work team effectiveness research.

3.1.1 Theory Selection

In the last decades, substantial knowledge about work teams has accumulated with hundreds of primary studies, several meta-analyses, and review articles in the fields of social psychology, organizational psychology, and management research (i.a. Bettenhausen 1991; Ilgen et al. 2005; Kozlowski and Ilgen 2006; Salas et al. 2005; Sundstrom et al. 2000). Scholars have developed several teamwork theories focusing on specific mechanisms in work teams forming the conceptual and theoretical foundation of this study (see i.a. Bettenhausen 1991; Cohen and Bailey 1997; Mathieu et al. 2008). Team effectiveness research distinguishes between three fundamental domains: affective, behavioral, and cognitive mechanisms evolving in and characterizing work teams. This study proposes agile software development to affect all three domains (see Fig. 3.1).

Team Affection Agile software development emphasizes on collaboration among software developers. Besides, many agile methods embrace social aspects in the software development process (see Sect. 2.2.2). This intensified level of interaction

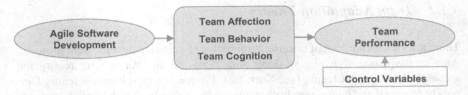

Fig. 3.1 Research framework

among developers may impact team affection. Various scholars have suggested that a team's belief in its own capabilities (team confidence) is a reliable determinant of team performance (Bandura 1977; Gully et al. 2002). First studies have also confirmed the effect in software development teams (Akgün et al. 2007). To the author's best knowledge, however, no previous study has investigated agile software development's influence on the level of confidence of a development team. This study proposes a positive relationship between using agile development practices and the level of confidence of a development team (see Sect. 3.3).

Team Behavior and Team Cognition Agile software development was originally the response of software engineers to rapidly changing project conditions (see Sect. 2.2). At its core, agile development promises to help software development teams work more effectively in highly uncertain environments (Beck 2000; Highsmith 2000) and to increase software development teams' ability to adapt to new situations. The adaptation aspect has not been studied so far despite team effectiveness' theory on team adaption which exactly explains how teams adapt. This gap in the literature has also been identified by Dingsøyr et al. (2012).

Team adaptability theory (Burke et al. 2006b; Rosen et al. 2011) describes the interplay of a team's behavior and its cognitive emergent states. Emergent states are "cognitive, motivational, and affective properties of teams that are typically dynamic in nature and vary as function of team context, inputs, processes, and outcomes" (Marks et al. 2001). For instance, team members may develop a feeling of trust or conflict (affection), a shared belief in their own capabilities (motivational), or a shared understanding (cognitive) when working together over time. Emergent states are considered to act both as team inputs and proximal outcomes of work teams. According to the theory, provision of feedback and help among team members (backup behavior) and a common understanding in the team (shared mental models) are the central markers for adaptive team performance. This study argues a positive influence of agile software development on aspects of team adaptation mediating the overall performance effect of agile software development on team performance (see Sect. 3.3). Team adaptation theory provides the theoretical background for this effect, the following paragraphs will introduce the theory (see Sect. 3.1.2).

3.1.2   Team Adaptation Theory

There are various sources of uncertainty inherent to software development projects. As a consequence, dynamic working conditions are an ever present reality for software development teams (see Sect. 2.2). Frequently, development teams face poorly specified and consequently changing tasks, technological disruption, or team instability (Kude et al. 2014). Contingency plans, waiting until conditions clear up, or having enough resources to handle unpredictable events are possible approaches to handle project uncertainty (Klein and Pierce 2001). In many situations, however, the only option is to adapt to the new situation which is why this study assumes a software development team's ability to adapt to be a key determinant of its success. To better understand the adaptation of work teams, the study relates to team adaption theory (Burke et al. 2006b; Rosen et al. 2011).

   Team adaptability is defined as the "ability to adjust strategies based on information gathered from the environment through the use of backup behavior and reallocation of intra-team resources. Altering a course of action or team repertoire in response to changing conditions" (Salas et al. 2005). A related, but different concept is team adaptation. *Team adaptation* refers to a team behavior, i.e. a "change in team performance, in response to a salient cue, that leads to functional outcomes for the entire team" (Burke et al. 2006b). Team adaptation theory postulates team adaptation to be the result of *adaptive team performance* (Burke et al. 2006b). Team adaptation is manifested in the innovation of new or modification of existing structures, capacities, and/or behavioral or cognitive goal-directed actions. *Adaptive team performance*, in turn, is the result of a team's ability to iterate through *adaptive cycles*. These cycles are described as a sequence of four team processes and their interplay with a team's cognitive emergent states (see Fig. 3.2). Teams with a better adaptive team performance, i.e. teams better iterating the adaptive cycle, are expected to possess a superior ability to adapt to new situations.

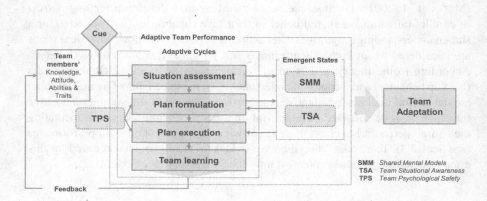

Fig. 3.2 Team adaptation model (simplified, based on Burke et al. 2006b)

Adaptive Cycles

The theory takes a procedural perspective assuming that *adaptive team performance* is not a consequence or a result of action, but an action itself. This collective action evolves over time while a team progresses through recursive adaptive cycles. The characteristics of these cycles, both, influence and are influenced by a team's cognitive and behavioral structure. According to the theory, adaptive teams successfully manage to

1. assess a new situation and build a coherent understanding of a new situation,
2. adjust their plans accordingly,
3. coordinate their work to fit the new situation,
4. and learn by evaluating the effectiveness of their performance.

During the first phase of the adaptive cycle (*situation assessment*), the environment is scanned by the team members for potential cues. A cue is any kind of non-routine event, whether previously known or unknown, with the potential to disturb or affect the current process (Louis and Sutton 1991). After the cue has been recognized and identified as a source of disruption for the ongoing process, the respective team member recognizing the cue ascribes a certain meaning to the raw data based on previous experience. Following the interpretation of the situation, it is communicated to the rest of the team (Burke et al. 2006b; Rosen et al. 2011). During the second phase, the *plan formulation* phase, the team works on a plan to address the identified cue in order to meet the original goal. This includes mission analysis, creation of a contingency plan (Marks et al. 2001), differentiation of team member roles, and conflict management. The third phase of the adaptive cycle, called *plan execution*, is the actual adaptive performance phase. During this phase, several processes on the individual and the team level happen dynamically, recursively, and simultaneously. The central process during the plan execution phase is coordination. To successfully coordinate, mutual monitoring, back-up behavior, and systems monitoring are key processes (Marks et al. 2001; Salas et al. 2005). The last phase of the adaptive cycle is *team learning*. During this retrospective phase, the team recapitulates prior actions to build a common understanding of a situation. Finally, the team formulates lessons learned for similar situations in the future.

Plan Execution

The plan execution phase is at the core of the adaptive cycle. Team adaptation theory describes various processes that a team conducts simultaneously for the success of this step. Typically, it involves coordination behavior (mutual monitoring, backup behavior, communication) and leadership (Burke et al. 2006b).

- *Mutual monitoring* has been defined as team members' ability to "keep track of fellow team members' work while carrying out their own ... to ensure that everything is running as expected and ... to ensure that they are following procedures correctly" (McIntyre and Salas 1995). According to Salas et al. (2005), mutual monitoring affects team performance by identifying errors subsequently mitigated through backup behavior.

- *Team backup behavior* is defined as the "discretionary provision of resources and task-related effort to another ... [when] there is recognition by potential backup providers that there is a work-load distribution problem in their team " (Porter et al. 2003). Marks et al. (2001) identify three means of providing backup: (a) providing feedback and coaching to improve performance, (b) assisting teammates in performing a task, and (c) completing a task when overload is detected. Backup behavior is particularly important for tasks that are difficult to assess in terms of quality and progress as individuals may not be aware of their own deficiencies (Salas et al. 2005). To effectively engage in backup behavior, team members have to be able to detect a need for help (monitoring capability), but to effectively judge the trade-off between helping other team members and accomplishing their personal tasks. Consequently, a common understanding of tasks and team member responsibilities (shared mental models) fare essential to effectively provide assistance or performance feedback in respect of team objectives. Only if team members understand their colleagues' task, they are capable of (a) assess if the provision of feedback helps the overall team performance and (b) to provide feedback/help to their fellow team members (Dickinson and McIntyre 1997). Hence, shared mental models and mutual monitoring are necessary for teams to provide internal team backup.
- *Communication* is the "process by which information is clearly and accurately exchanged between two or more team members in the prescribed manner with proper terminology; the ability to clarify or acknowledge the receipt of information" (Cannon-Bowers et al. 1993). It is essential during the adaptive cycles for updating the shared mental models and effective monitoring behavior. Moreover, backup can be provided through feedback and communication is hence a facilitating mechanism.
- The *leader* of a team is essential for team effectiveness in his or her role as coordinator, point of contact to other teams or management, and as guide for a team's vision (Burke et al. 2006a). According to team adaptation theory, team leaders can significantly influence the coordination of work within the team in the face of change. Hence, leaders are facilitators of team adaptation.

Emergent Cognitive States

According to team adaptation theory, adaptive teams develop emergent cognitive states while iterating the adaptive cycle. These emergent states serve as both, proximal outcomes of the process steps as well as inputs for the adaptive cycle. The theory postulates three central cognitive states: shared mental models, team situational awareness, and psychological safety.

- *Shared Mental Models* (SMM). Mental models are "dynamic, simplified, cognitive representations of reality that team members use to describe, explain, and predict events" (Burke et al. 2006b). Team member can develop similar mental models, so-called shared mental models.

- *Team Situational Awareness* (TSA), a "shared understanding of the current situation at a given point in time" (Salas et al. 1995).
- *Team Psychological Safety* (TPS), the degree to which team members have a shared belief of safety in the team with respect to interpersonal risk taking. It describes a team climate of interpersonal trust and mutual respect and enables team members to take appropriate actions to accomplish work (Edmondson 1999).

Team adaptation theory assumes teams to develop a shared perspective during the situational awareness phase. Shared mental models help team members to interpret information similarly and develop situational awareness at team level. Team psychological safety is assumed as a key determinant of a team's readiness to react to environmental changes while developing a plan. Hence, TPS is considered as an input for team adaptation by team adaptability theory. Moreover, teams are expected to update their shared cognition during the plan formulation phase. Hence, producing a new plan as part of the adaptive cycles is expected to influence the shared mental models of teams. Furthermore, the theory predicts shared mental models themselves to influence the quality of plan execution of a team. Thereby, shared mental models play a central role for adaptive team performance.

Markers of Adaptive Teams

Team adaptation theory integrates several perspectives from organizational, behavioral, and cognitive sciences; it is a multidisciplinary, multilevel, and multiphasic model (Rosen et al. 2011). For these reasons, the model is quite complex. To reduce complexity when studying the theory or parts of it, Rosen et al. (2011) suggested to reduce the number of constructs and only consider the relevant *behavioral or cognitive markers* of team adaptation. There are two main aspects which are at the core of team adaption on which the study will be focusing (Salas et al. 2005): **team backup behavior** and **shared mental models**, two central mechanisms of adaptive team performance.

3.1.3   Team Confidence

Previous literature proposed team confidence as an important determinant of team performance (Gully et al. 2002; Stajkovic et al. 2009). A large number of empirical studies have confirmed this positive relationship (Gully et al. 2002; Jung and Sosik 2003; Stajkovic et al. 2009). Originally, Bandura (1977) had introduced the confidence concept of *self-efficacy* as the cognitive component in social-cognitive theory on the individual level. Self-efficacy refers to "people's judgments of their

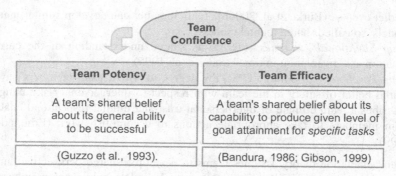

Fig. 3.3 Team confidence, team potency, and team efficacy

capabilities to organize and execute courses of action required to attain designated types of performances" (Bandura 1986). Bandura explains that self-efficacy influences the way how people control and direct their own actions. Individuals with a higher self-efficacy exert more efforts to attain goals, set more challenging goals, are more persistent in face of difficulties.

Later, Bandura (1986) suggested to extend the concept to the team level. He proposed the same antecedents and consequences on both the individual and an the team level. Various authors build their work on Bandura's argumentation arguing that a team's effectiveness is not only determined by the qualities of the individual team members (individual level input), but also by team members' perception of these qualities (collective emergent state).

Team Confidence Concepts

There are two basic ways to conceptualize a team's level of confidence: team potency and team efficacy (Kozlowski and Ilgen 2006). Both presume a shared collective belief by the team members (see Fig. 3.3). Team potency is a generalized confidence construct, while team efficacy is task-specific.

- *Team potency* refers to a team's shared belief about its ability to be successful (Guzzo et al. 1993; Jung and Sosik 2003).
- *Team-efficacy* refers to a team's belief of its collective capability to organize and execute courses of action required to produce given level of goal attainment for specific tasks (Bandura 1986; Gibson 1999).

Antecedents

There are different factors influencing the confidence of a team (Bandura 1977): (1) *Past performance accomplishments* are an important influencing factor of a team's belief in its capabilities, (2) *vicarious experiences* can positively influence the

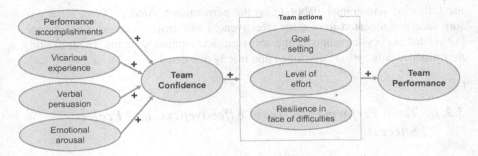

Fig. 3.4 Antecedents and consequences of team confidence

level of confidence. They can either be realized directly through one's own success or indirectly through the success of someone similar, (3) *verbal persuasion* may determine team confidence, and (4) *physiological and emotional arousal* can affect the level of confidence.

Consequences

Team confidence was theorized to influence team effectiveness because teams are expected to change their actions as they become more confident about their own capabilities (Gully et al. 2002). More confident teams are expected to *set higher goals*, *exert more effort* into achieving these goals, and *show greater persistence* in the face of obstacles, challenges, or setbacks. In other words, teams with a 'we can do it' attitude perform better as their confident affection influences what a team does and in which way it chooses to do its tasks (see Fig. 3.4).

Kozlowski and Ilgen (2006) reviewed the literature on team effectiveness research and concluded that "it is likely that contextual factors such as team task and culture, may affect the link between team confidence and team effectiveness". For instance, Gibson (1999) showed team efficacy to not be related to group effectiveness when technological uncertainty is high, work is independent, and collectivism is low. With the opposite situation, the relationship was found to be positive. In their meta-analysis of 67 empirical studies, Gully et al. (2002) found a stronger impact of confidence on team performance when the interdependence of a team's task was higher ($\rho = 0.45$) and less impactful when interdependence was lower ($\rho = 0.34$).

3.2 Software Development Team Performance

The focus of this study is the influence of agile software development on the performance of software development teams. While the conceptual foundations of agile software development were already discussed in section "Agility Concept", the following paragraphs elaborate on the performance concept. First, team performance is delineated from team effectiveness and project success, i.e. separate, but related success concepts in the software development domain. Then, existing performance concepts are described and briefly discussed.

3.2.1   Team Performance, Team Effectiveness, and Project Success

Project Success

A software development project widely considered successful when satisfying the traditional project management objectives, such as delivery on time, within budget, meeting quality expectations (Jugdev and Müller 2005). These success indicators might, as disputed by other, suffice to fully describe software development projects and their inherent communication, coordination, learning, or negotiating challenges (Sarker et al. 2009). To resolve this dispute, project success can be conceptualized in a broader sense comprising of a *product perspective*, e.g. meeting cost and on schedule delivery, and a *process perspective*, e.g. user and project stakeholder satisfaction how the software is delivered (see Fig. 3.5 and Procaccino et al. 2005).

ISD Team Effectiveness

This study considers software development teams as an integral part of a software development project. Therefore, team effectiveness is conceptualized as an important aspect of project success (see link (a) in Fig. 3.5) in a multifaceted construct with three particular dimensions: *behavioral outcomes* (e.g., absenteeism,

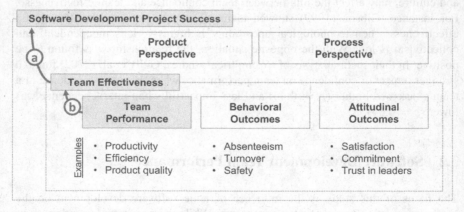

Fig. 3.5 Team performance, team effectiveness, and project success

turnover, or safety), *attitudinal outcomes* (e.g., satisfaction, commitment, or trust in management) and *team performance* (e.g., productivity, efficiency, product quality) (Cohen and Bailey 1997; Ilgen et al. 2005; Sundstrom et al. 2000). Among them, "performance is the most widely studied criterion variable in the organizational behavior and human resource management literature" (Bommer et al. 1995). However, there is no agreement how *team performance* is defined (Ilgen et al. 2005; Sundstrom et al. 2000).

Team Performance

In line with previous team effectiveness models (i.a. Cohen and Bailey 1997), this study considers team performance as a sub-dimension of team effectiveness (see link (b) in Fig. 3.5).

3.2.2   Review of Existing Team Performance Concepts

A structured review of the literature showed no agreement among scholars on the definition of the performance of a software development team or on appropriate measurement (Münzing 2012)[1]. Some authors study performance dimensions relevant for individual team members or stakeholders, others are interested in outcomes at the team or the project level. Overall, all scholars have conceptualized team effectiveness as a multidimensional construct. The dimensions are either *task outcomes,* i.e. team assessments based on a team's work outcomes as well as the required team effort, or *team outcomes,* i.e. effects on team members' attitude and behavior. Figure 3.6 provides an overview of all performance dimensions found in the analyzed publications. The numbers at the bottom of the figure indicate the number of publications considering a particular performance dimension as part of the dependent performance variable in the study.

Most studies examine software development projects of the traditional "plan and document" paradigm, i.e. the studied projects have a dedicated planning phase before the team starts developing software. Consequently, team performance can be assessed relative to a predefined project plan. Most of these studies are interested in the delivered *scope* (Bok and Raman 2000; Stewart and Gosain 2006; Yang and Tang 2004), *quality* (Maruping et al. 2009a; Sawyer and Guinan 1998), and *in-time* or *in-budget* delivery (Espinosa et al. 2007; Faraj and Sproull 2000; Henderson and Lee 1992; Henry and Todd 1999; Huckman et al. 2009; Ryan and O'Connor 2009;

---

[1] Münzing (2012) conducted a structured literature review as part of his Master thesis. The review was initiated and supervised by the author of this study. Overall, 74 publications found in the *Information Systems* and *New Product Development* literature streams were analyzed.

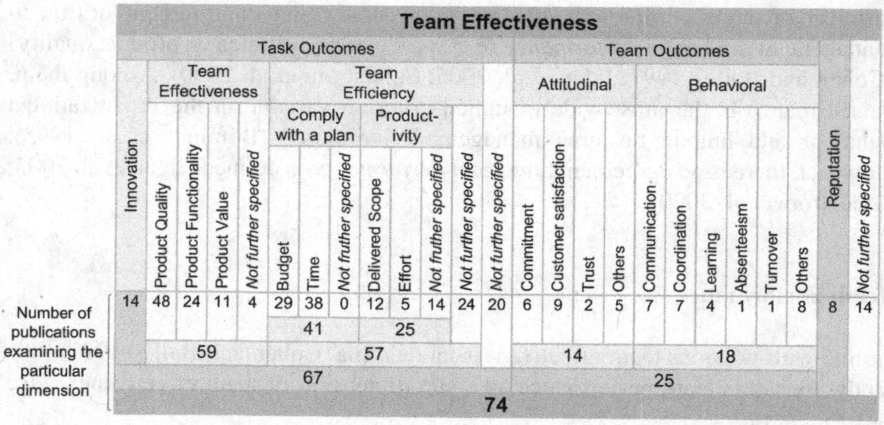

Team Effectiveness

	Task Outcomes												Team Outcomes											
	Team Effectiveness				Comply with a plan			Product-ivity					Attitudinal				Behavioral							
Innovation	Product Quality	Product Functionality	Product Value	Not further specified	Budget	Time	Not fruther specified	Delivered Scope	Effort	Not further specified	Not further specified	Not further specified	Commitment	Customer satisfaction	Trust	Others	Communication	Coordination	Learning	Absenteeism	Turnover	Others	Reputation	Not further specified
14	48	24	11	4	29	38	0	12	5	14	24	20	6	9	2	5	7	7	4	1	1	8	8	14
					41			25																
	59				57								14				18							
	67												25											
	74																							

Fig. 3.6   Team effectiveness dimensions in previous studies

Sawyer 2001). Other studies take a more general perspective and examine *product innovation* (Guinan et al. 1998) or *customer satisfaction.*

Moreover, software development studies vary in terms of *how* they measure team performance. Most authors ask team stakeholders to subjectively rate different performance dimensions in retrospective. Münzing (2012) found 54 out of 74 publications to use ratings on agreement scales from survey data. Other studies quantify team outcomes with direct objective data from firm records, files, or other archival data. For instance, line-of-code, feature-points or number of error messages have been previously used as proxy variables for team performance (i.a. Maruping et al. 2009a). These performance measures, however, can be problematic as the data might be subject to manipulation, may reflect only specific performance aspects, or might not be accurately measured (Henderson and Lee 1992). Furthermore, it might be difficult to compare this data for software development teams working on different product types, e.g. data-based software vs. software applications, or at different points of time in the product life-cycle.

In conclusion, scholars provide a heterogeneous view *what* the performance of a software development team is and *how* to measure it. Table 3.1 on page 49 provides an overview of existing measurement instruments for software development team performance including three popular measurement instruments to demonstrate the conceptual diversity. Due to the lack of reliable measurement instruments for agile software development teams, this study develops a new instrument to assess the performance of software development teams. This instrument was developed based on insight from interviews with project managers and the literature mentioned earlier. Further details are outlined in Chap. 4.

Table 3.1 Performance concepts in software development research

Author	Definition	Adopted by
Henderson and Lee (1992)	**ISD Team Performance** is assessed by non-team stakeholders in terms of *efficiency*, *effectiveness*, and *elapsed time*. For each category, different measurement items were provided and rated by the assessors on a 7-point Likert scale	Faraj and Sproull (2000); Guinan et al. (1998); Kang et al. (2006); Sawyer (2001); Sawyer and Guinan (1998); Zhang et al. (2008)
Nidumolu (1995)	**ISD Project Performance** includes *process performance* (learning during the project, process control, and quality of interactions) and *product performance* (operational efficiency of software, responsiveness of software, and flexibility of software)	Lee and Xia (2010)
Hoegl and Gemuenden (2001)	**ISD Team Performance** includes *effectiveness*, *efficiency*, *work satisfaction*, and *learning* as the central performance dimensions. The technical quality of the software solution, including the satisfaction with the software solution from different perspectives (effectiveness). Another five items were used for measuring the teams' adherence to schedule and budget (efficiency). Team members' work satisfaction and learning were assessed separately	Carmeli et al. (2011); Huang et al. (2008); Huang and Jiang (2010)
Misra et al. (2009)	**Success of (Agile) Software Development (Projects)** reduces delivery schedules, increases return on investment (ROI), increases ability to meet with the current customer requirements, increases flexibility to meet with the changing customer requirements, improves business processes	
Siau et al. (2010)	**ISD Success** refers to the *system usage* of and *perceived satisfaction* with the developed system. System usage includes system success (maintainability, agility, and efficiency) information or data quality (integration, unification, effectiveness, and efficiency), and system usage. User satisfaction can include satisfaction with the system quality, effectiveness, or efficiency	

3.3 Research Model

Literature in social and organizational psychology as well as the organization and management sciences provided numerous models to analyze and explain the effectiveness of work teams. Researchers distinguish between static and dynamic team work models.

Dynamic models focus on teams' evolution or development over time. Consequently, time is as an important model parameter. Various dynamic models assume that teams go through different phases of formation, maturation, and evolution. For instance, Tuckman's classical model describes a team's maturation through a forming, storming, norming, and performing phase (Tuckman 1965). The dynamic teamwork model by Marks et al. (2001) describes various process steps which teams constantly iterate. The model distinguishes transition and action phases which determine how a team works.

This study takes a static perspective to analyze the effectiveness of agile software development teams. *Static team work models* describe mature teams which are assumed to have reached a stable state that can be described, analyzed, and measured. Most static models follow an *Input-Process-Output (IPO)* framework which has strongly influenced how researchers have been discussing team effectiveness and its determinants during the last 50 years of research. The IPO perspective was originally introduced by McGrath (1964), later refined by Gladstein (1984), and further extended by various other authors (see e.g. Cohen and Bailey 1997; Hackman 1987; Ilgen et al. 2005; Kozlowski and Bell 2003; Mathieu et al. 2008; Salas et al. 2005; Sundstrom et al. 2000). It considers input factors at the individual, team, and organizational level to influence various team processes which, in turn, mediate the effect of these inputs on team outcomes.

- *Inputs* are a team's resources such as knowledge, skills, abilities, personalities, demographics or external stimuli such as rewards, group structure or organizational climate.
- *Processes* are inhibitory or enabling team activities and team members' interactions while accomplishing team tasks. Team processes combine the "cognitive, behavioral, and motivation/affective resources" (Kozlowski and Ilgen 2006) of a team to achieve team outcomes.
- *Outcomes* are criteria to assess the effectiveness of a team.

It is important to note that the IPO model is not a theory, but an organizational systems model that helps to structure the research process (Cohen and Bailey 1997). The relationships between the input and output components of this study are explained in the following paragraphs with the help of existing conceptual and theoretical assertions.

The research model of this study builds on an extension of the initial IPO model, the *Input-Mediator-Outcomes (IMO)* model based on Mathieu et al. (2008), see Fig. 3.7. This model distinguishes between *team processes* and *emergent states*

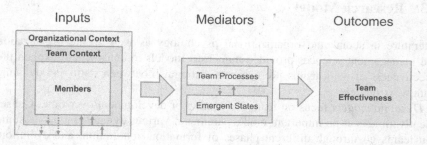

Fig. 3.7 IMO model in team effectiveness research (based on Mathieu et al. 2008)

that teams developed over time. Emergent states are "cognitive, motivational, and affective properties of teams that are typically dynamic in nature and vary as a function of team contexts, inputs, processes, and outcomes" (Marks et al. 2001).

In the subsequent sections, the research constructs are defined and the research propositions are deducted. The chapter concludes with the integration of the proposed propositions into a coherent research model.

3.3.1 Model Constructs

Six latent research constructs form the building blocks of the research model, i.e. the theoretical core of this thesis. These six constructs are briefly introduced in this section. In addition, definitions for all constructs are provided (see Table 3.3 on page 63). Following the Input-Mediators-Outcomes perspective, agile software development is considered as an input factor of software development teams and team performance is modeled as the outcome variable of the research model. The effect of agile software development on the outcome variable is further explained through affective, behavioral, and cognitive team processes and emergent states.

Input

Agile Software Development. As outlined in section "Agility Concept", there are two fundamental concepts of agile software development. Researchers either conceptualize agile software development as a *capability* (e.g. Lee and Xia 2010; Lyytinen and Rose 2006; Sarker and Sarker 2009) or a *behavior* of a software development team (i.e. Abrahamsson et al. 2002; Maruping et al. 2009a). This study takes a behavioral perspective and conceptualizes agile software development in terms of a team's intensity of using agile development practices. More specifically, agile software development is measured in terms of a team's intensity of using pair programming, automated testing, and code review (see Sect. 2.2.2). These three development practices have been suggested to help teams to adapt to unpredictable and changing environments (Beck 2000). Furthermore, software development teams using these development practices instantiate an iterative development approach. The practices focus on high software quality and running software during the entire development process. Thus, the core ideas of agile software development are reflected in the induced team behavior. When using these three development practices, software developers instantiate the agile development approach. Thus, the team can be considered as an agile team.

Outcome

Team Performance. Until today, there is no consensus among scholars about the conceptualization of the performance of an software development team (see discussion in Sect. 3.2). Therefore, the author conducted a pre-study to better understand the assessment of team performance by project managers in the given research context (for details see Sect. 5.2). The results show a multifaceted approach to the topic. The specific dimensions are discussed in Sect. 5.2 and illustrated in Fig. 5.6. Overall, *team performance* refers to the stakeholder perception of the overall success of a software development team as perceived by a team's project leader.

Mediators

Affective, behavioral, and cognitive team processes and emergent states. Shared mental models are a team members' shared and organized understanding and mental representation of knowledge about key elements of the relevant environment and tasks (Klimoski and Mohammed 1994). For this study, they represent the cognitive emergent state of the model. *Backup behavior* refers to the discretionary provision of resources and task-related effort to another member of one's team intended to help achieve the goals upon suspected failure (Porter et al. 2003). Finally, a team confidence level is discussed in terms of *team potency*, i.e. the collective belief of a team that it can be effective (Guzzo et al. 1993). It provides the affective perspective for the research model.

Control Variables

In line with other studies on the effectiveness of work teams, the research model controls for the number of people in a team (*team size*) and the *diversity of experience* of its team members, and the extent of well-established work procedures *not* available to solve the tasks at hand (*technological uncertainty*).

3.3.2 Effects on Team Cognition

Team adaptation theory (Burke et al. 2006b) holds that shared mental models are particularly important for teams working in volatile environments. The theory builds on shared mental model theory and its central tenet that congruency in team members' mental models facilitates efficient teamwork leading to higher team performance (Uitdewilligen et al. 2010). Work teams with more similar mental models have been shown to communicate more effectively, collaborate better, and being more willing to work with team members in the future (Rentsch and Klimoski

2001) compared to teams with underdeveloped shared mental models. Shared mental models allow team members to interpret information in a similar way to anticipate needs and actions in similar ways and thereby 'implicitly' coordinate the joint behavior. This, in turn, results in better communication and coordination within a team (Burke et al. 2006b; Cannon-Bowers et al. 1993; Klimoski and Mohammed 1994).

Mental models are an explanation of someone's thought about how something works in the real world, i.e. a representation of the world or relationship between parts of the world (Klimoski and Mohammed 1994). They are particularly helpful to solve abstract tasks, such as software development tasks. For instance, software engineers develop mental models about the software architecture, their software's data or process models, or the application domain and purpose of a software.

Collaborative software development is not only an abstract, but modularizable task. Software development teams split the overall team task into distinct, but inter-dependent sub-tasks to be solved by individual developers or sub-teams. This work style requires a common understanding among the developers to ensure efficient coordination of the tasks and integration of the final work results. Considering these task characteristics, this study assumes that a high sharedness of team members' mental models is particularly important for high performance software development teams. In the same vein, He et al. (2007) found that a shared understanding of the team task is a critical element for successful development teams as it helps the team to form common explanations and coordinate activities efficiently (Levesque et al. 2001).

Klimoski and Mohammed (1994) suggested *social interactions*, such as frequent communication, information sharing, participation, or negotiation, to be the primary mechanism for shared mental models to develop. Moreover, *spending time together* on task implementation helps team members to appreciate their peers' mental models and strongly influences the development of a shared understanding (Uitdewilligen et al. 2010). Furthermore, *role differentiation* plays a major role in the development of shared mental models (Levesque et al. 2001). For teams with specialists roles, cross-training and adopting other team members' duties can have a positive influence on the development of shared mental models (Levesque et al. 2001; Marks et al. 2002). Finally, *performance monitoring* and *self-correction* was found to be positively related to higher mental model congruency (Rasker et al. 2000; Salas et al. 2005).

Developers working in a pair with a programming partner socially interact over a longer period of time. Both developers discuss how to solve the assigned development task. Beforehand, both partners need to developed a common under-standing about the task to be solved. Then, the two programmers jointly implement the software code, simultaneously monitor each others' behavior, and provide instant feedback. Both aspects have been shown as important antecedent for the development of shared mental models (Rasker et al. 2000). Often, developers with different skills or expertise pair up to solve complex problems. Some teams use pair programming for cross-training between experienced and junior developers. The two developers learn from each other while spending time to jointly solve their task.

Overall, the more intensively a team uses pair programming, the more intense are the social interaction among the individual team members. Due to the intensified social interaction, pair-programming-based team behavior is expected to lead to a higher sharedness of the mental models within a team if the programming partners frequently rotate within the team. Frequent in-depth discussions about the programming tasks are a consequence of intense pair programming sessions leading to a better and more shared mental models, for instance, about the software architecture or the development tasks of the team. Finally, two developers solving a development task might exchange and build on their ideas to, first, better understand the development tasks and, second, come up with better solutions compared to developers working alone. Hence, pair programming may not only lead to more congruent mental models within the team, but also to better mental models.

Pair programming can be viewed as an extreme form of the agile code review development practice. Code review means that the implemented software code is reviewed by a second person in retrospective, i.e. after the implementation task is finalized by one developer and before the code is integrated into the team's common code line. This agile development practices induces the reviewer and the reviewee to interact, to give feedback, and to discuss the proposed solution or opportunities for improvement. Hence, code review and pair programming have comparable social interaction patterns and may therefore both enhance the sharedness and the quality of team members' mental models following the same line of reasoning outlined for pair programming.

Test automation is another central aspect of agile software development. Agile developers write automated tests to continuously check the correctness of newly developed or modified software. For that purpose, agile development teams continuously run all team members' tests in order to receive instant feedback on the software's behavior. In particular, automated test cases check if the software behaves as expected given a certain set of input conditions. When writing automated test cases, software developers make their mental model explicit, i.e. the test cases represent each developer's expectations how the software should behave for specific input conditions. Thus, test-based software development induces developers not only to specify the behavior of the software, but also to explicate their expectations writing executable test cases. Taking a cognitive perspective, the developers define and explicate their mental models about the software's behavior.

Agile development teams share their automated test cases by integrating them into a so-called 'test suite'. Test suites contain all test cases developed by all developers contributing to a software. Test suites can thus be understood as a technical mean to integrate a team's mental models to check for compliance of a team's software with its mental models. Consequently, the shared development and usage of a team's test suite facilitates the sharing and application of all developers' mental models.

The test-automation based work style requires a team to develop quality norms. This common understanding of good software quality evolves through continuous discussion within the team. Hence, the test automation-based software development approach motivates team members to share and discuss their perspectives about acceptable software quality. All three agile development practices are expected to improve the sharedness of team members' mental models. Hence, the following proposition is put forth:

Proposition 1: *The more intensively a team uses agile practices, the more shared are the mental models of the team members.*

3.3.3 Effects on Team Behavior

McIntyre and Salas (1995) have argued that backup behavior is a decisive team behavior of high performance teams. Team backup behavior can take many forms such as helping, carrying out a task, or providing feedback to team members. The intention is to achieve the team goals when potential failure is apparent (Porter et al. 2003). Marks et al. (2001) identify three means of providing backup including (a) providing feedback and coaching to improve performance, (b) assisting team-mates in performing a task, and (c) completing a task when overload has been detected. Backup behavior is different from helping behavior as it results from the realization of the necessity of help to ensure team performance and not individual performance. Thus, team backup behavior can be a way to dynamically adjust a team's work load to perform at a level not possible if the team would work according to plan.

Previous literature suggests *mutual monitoring* and *team orientation* as central antecedents of team backup behavior (Salas et al. 2005). This study suggests that both are more pronounced in software development teams adopting agile development practices. The following paragraphs elaborate on this idea.

Mutual performance monitoring relies on a team's common understanding about its members' weaknesses or lapses (McIntyre and Salas 1995). In software development, small deficiencies, i.e. software bugs, can have a tremendous impact on the functioning of the entire software. Hence, a team's ability to monitor its performance is essential for its performance. During pair programming sessions or when reviewing each others' code, team members build up awareness about the software quality as they scrutinize each others' work results. Hence, the more code is reviewed by a second pair of eyes, the higher the likelihood of catching errors. The increased awareness allows the team to shift priorities, provide feedback, and help each other fix problems. Due to the more collaborative development approach and common awareness of problems, developers can immediately address occurring mistakes and take measures to avoid them in the future. Hence, mutual monitoring induced by the agile development practices is one reasons for more feedback, verbally and behaviorally, within agile software development teams.

When programming with a partner or during intensive code review sessions, developers collaborate intensively. Instead of working by themselves, agile software development practices, such as pair programming and code review, encourage developers to engage with each other when implementing their tasks. The personal interaction is expected to raise team members' orientation and awareness of the team. Team orientation is the preference of an individual to work in a team (Salas et al. 2005). As previous research has shown, it is an important antecedent of team backup behavior (Salas et al. 2005). In combination with the awareness of performance deficiencies, teams using agile practices are expected to provide more backup to each other compared to non-agile teams.

When writing automated tests, developers outsource and automate the monitoring procedure for future quality checks. When executing these automated tests, developers are able to monitor the team's work outcome for potential failure. The gained transparency allows developers not only to be aware of existing issues, but also to provide verbal feedback, help each other, and shift workloads if needed. Hence, agile software development practices support the team in instantiating backup behavior within the team. Many teams work with continuous integration servers that automatically execute test cases after integrating new features into the code base. When a single test fails, the entire team gets noticed. Hence, the team can decide whether the error can be solved by the original developer or if further assistance is needed. As such, running automated test cases provides a convenient way to implement mutual monitoring and feedback on the current status of the software.

Moreover, automated tests themselves can be considered as backup behavior themselves. Previous expectations on the software's behavior are made explicit with an automated test to be used in the future or by other developers in the team. Therefore, automated tests can be considered as a backup behavior or as provided feedback that would otherwise be given, at best, verbally upon manual testing. Also, automated testing implies constant integration of one's own code into the team's shared code-base, thus increasing the team orientation of individual team members.

In conclusion, agile practices are argued to improve the mutual monitoring process and improve team members' orientation towards the team. Both have been theorized to positively influence backup behavior in the team (Salas et al. 2005). Moreover, the agile development practices instantiate verbal and behavioral feedback in the team. The following proposition is added to the research model:

Proposition 2a: *The more intensively a team uses agile practices, the more intensive is the provided backup within the team.*

Backup behavior is a response to a genuine request for assistance and means that a team member only provides assistance to a colleague if help is actually needed (Porter et al. 2003). Consequently, team members first have to assess if providing assistance is beneficial for the team and simultaneously be able to provide verbal or behavioral feedback for a particular team member. To judge if a request is legitimate and whether deviating from an original task distribution within a team is advantageous for the overall team performance, members must have a common understanding about their peers' tasks, team members' skills, and their work progress (Porter et al. 2003).

In software development teams, backup behavior requires developers to have a common understanding of each others' implementation tasks, their colleagues' approach to solve their tasks, as well as a similar understanding of the technology and the architecture of the software. Otherwise, the team is not able to effectively shift work within the team and work, as a collective, more effectively than the original developer on his or her own.

Software development is knowledge work and interim results often do not provide visual cues. Therefore, it is oftentimes difficult to assess the progress and quality of a software feature. While this positive relationship between shared mental models and the provision of backup may also be true for other work teams, the abstract characteristics of the software development tasks emphasizes its significance for software development teams.

Another reason why backup behavior is particularly important for software development teams is that individual developers are often even not aware of their own performance deficiencies. Software engineers develop a product used in very different contexts and at a high level of complexity encapsulated in different software layers (see Sect. 2.1.1). Therefore, it can be very tedious to find one's own mistakes (bug fixing) or finish a task. Team members have to recognize the need for help and effectively judge the trade-off between providing help or accomplishing their own task to effectively engage in backup behavior. To make that decision, team members need a common understanding of other team members' tasks, skills, and engineering capabilities as well as of the software architecture to provide backup (Dickinson and McIntyre 1997). In line with previous assertions in literature (Burke et al. 2006b; Salas et al. 2005), the following proposition is put forth:

Proposition 2b: *The more shared the mental models of the team members, the more intensive is the provided backup within the team.*

The structural contingency perspective ·provides another useful perspective for this study. In organization theory, technology has typically been defined as the processes or tasks involved in transforming inputs into outputs. There is a general perspective that the most appropriate structure (i.e., the structure that maximizes organizational performance) is contingent on the uncertainty confronted by the organization (Fry 1982). Underlying the structural contingency perspective is an information processing viewpoint of the organization. Performance is determined by the match between the uncertainty in a unit's tasks and the ability of the unit's structure to process the information required to cope with uncertainty (Tushman and Nadler 1978). The better the match, the higher the performance. Hence, uncertainty is considered as a critical contingent factor for the performance of organizations and, thus, also for team performance.

For software development teams, technological uncertainty was found as a critical risk factor for project success (Nidumolu 1995). Already in 1981, McFarlan described the organization's experience with technology (hardware, operating systems, databases, application languages) as a key source of uncertainty (McFarlan 1981). Today, technologies develop at ever fasting rates and developers have to learn and adapt to more and more new technologies to keep pace with their competitors.

In addition, previous studies empirically confirmed that technological uncertainty is inherent in the work of software development teams (c.f. Kude et al. 2014; Lee and Xia 2005; Nidumolu 1995) and a central risk factor for software development projects.

Many agile software development consultants claim that agile teams are better equipped to cope with uncertainty compared to non-agile teams (Beck 2000; Schwaber and Beedle 2002). Based on this perspective, this study included project uncertainty into its research focus. While various scholars had already studied the effect of agile software development on team performance in the face of *requirements uncertainty* (see Lee and Xia 2010), this study focuses on *technological uncertainty* which was found as another central uncertainty dimension for software development projects (Nidumolu 1995). Technological uncertainty refers to uncertainty concerning work practices and procedures needed to convert requirements into a software system. It requires software development teams to find new ways, build up new knowledge, and develop new work procedures to solve a task rather than using preexisting work patterns.

During the last years, software development teams increasingly reuse software functionality from existing software packages to improve their development efficiency. Examples include open source software libraries, underlying software platforms, or databases. Despite these positive effects of software reuse, it can lead to external dependencies and unpredictable side-effects for the software development process, for instance, software package updates can lead to a change of the interfaces of these packages. Hence, teams have to react to these changes. Thus, reuse can be a source of technological uncertainty for a software development team. Another source of technological uncertainty can be changing software development tools. For instance, test frameworks, development environments, or programming languages might change during a development project.

When facing technological uncertainty, preexisting work procedures or available knowledge may not be of help for a software development team. Backup provided between team members may provide a helpful mechanism to cope with uncertainty (Marks et al. 2002) as previous research has shown that backup behavior is particularly important for volatile work environments (Porter et al. 2003). In such situations, individual team members most likely face workloads surpassing their capacity. Other team members need to take over to avoid negative impact on the team performance. To compensate, team members shift workloads within the team to adapt to novel situations. However, only when underutilized team members assist their overloaded colleagues, the team can adjust and perform at an otherwise unachievable level. For routine tasks, however, backup can even be detrimental for the performance as misplaced backup behavior might lead to redundant rather than complementary teamwork. In conclusion, the following proposition is formulated:

Proposition 3: *In case of high technological uncertainty, the more backup a team's members provide to each other, the better is the team performance.*

3.3.4 Effects on Team Affection

The level of confidence of a team has been theorized (Bandura 1977) and empirically confirmed as a strong determinant of high performing teams (Gully et al. 2002). As discussed in Sect. 3.1.3, scholars distinguish between a team's general belief in its success (team potency) and a task specific belief, e.g. that the team is good in developing software (team efficacy). Based on many years of experience of various experts in the research context, this study focuses on team potency, i.e. a team's common belief that it can be successful in general (Gully et al. 2002).

There are several teamwork factors which increase a team's confidence level (see Fig. 3.4 on page 45). These include past performance accomplishments, various experiences, verbal persuasion, and emotional arousal (Bandura 1977). For software development teams, Akgün et al. (2007) found that the level of trust and empowerment as well as a team's experience determine the collective belief that the team can be successful (team potency). This study takes a different perspective and posits the use of agile development practices to trigger the aforementioned determinants of team confidence. Therefore, teams using agile development practices are expected to have a higher level of confidence than non-agile teams. The following paragraphs elaborate on that idea.

When programming with a partner, developers are more likely to experience vicarious moments compared to working alone. They directly experience that a similar working behavior can lead to success. Moreover, the close collaboration over a longer period of time may cause emotional arousal when both developers go through challenging and awarding phases during the development process. Finally, both developers constantly provide feedback to each other. When facing problems, both developers might push each other towards accomplishing their task. After successfully finishing their development task, the two developers may be jointly excited over performance accomplishment. Teams with a high level of pair programming frequently change their programming partners. The effect is hence not limited to dyads of developers, but emerges to the team level. Thus, pair programmers may be more prone to believe in the strengths of their team if they have opportunities to learn about the skills and experiences of their team members and share positive interactions (Chen et al. 2002). Not only pair programming, but also code review sessions may create these collaborative opportunities for team members. For instance, when providing or receiving feedback from team members, developers learn about the competencies of others and engage in positive communication (Prussia and Kinicki 1996).

When writing automated software tests to ensure the successful integration of code fragments from different developers, individual team members acquire knowledge about the specifics of the code developed by others. This may strengthen the collective believe in the team's skill set. As the entire team is noticed in case of test case passing or failure the team may gradually develop a higher level of confidence in case of continuous positive feedback. At the same time, developers are aware of their colleagues' success in accomplishing their tasks. While these vicarious experiences and interaction can be particularly effective in fostering team potency, they can also be difficult to achieve in organizational contexts due to time pressure. In the context of software development teams, institutionalizing personal and impersonal quality assurance development practices through using the three agile development practices may ensure enough time for team members to produce high-quality work and subsequently facilitating confidence at, both, the individual and the team level.

Furthermore, previous literature found an important antecedent of a team's confidence in group norms (Lee et al. 2002). They lead to a higher level of confidence because norms imply possibilities for individuals to exert influence on the group and increase confidence in fellow team members to orient their behavior towards accepted standards. In the case of software development, team norms often refer to coding and quality standards. Agile software development practices aim to develop and enforce such standards (Maruping et al. 2009b). For instance, software developer working with a programming partner have to agree on common coding conventions subsequently enforced in pairing situations. Team members' belief in the entire team's adherence to these standards may increase their confidence to successfully accomplish its software development tasks.

Overall, the three agile development practices trigger different influencing team factors proposed to increase a team's level of confidence. While each development practice may influence the overall team level of confidence via different mechanisms, the global effect is expected to be the same, an increased confidence level of the entire team. Hence, the following proposition it put forward:

Proposition 4: *The more intensively a team uses agile practices, the more confident is the team.*

In team effectiveness research, much effort has been dedicated to study the impact of a team's confidence on its effectiveness (Guzzo et al. 1993; Jung and Sosik 2003). Team potency was theorized to have a positive impact on team performance outcomes through its effect on the team members take, the level of effort, as well as resilience of team members upon unsatisfactory task performance. There is a large body of empirical research supporting the positive relationship between team potency and different forms of team performance outcomes (see e.g. the meta analysis by Guzzo et al. 1993). Akgün et al. (2005) found a positive relationship between the level of confidence of a software development team and decreased development costs, increased speed-to-market, as well as increased market success.

In line with this literature stream, the collective belief of a team to be effective is proposed to positively influence the performance of a software development team. Previous literature on team potency suggests a persistence of teams with a high level of confidence in coordinated task-related efforts, even when faced with setbacks and challenges (Bandura 1986). Also, teams with high confidence were found to accept ambitious goals more readily (Whitney 1994). Thus, high-potency software development teams may be more willing to accept and more persistent to reach the goal of delivering high-quality software in a short period of time. Moreover, teams with a high level of confidence are more likely to compare themselves and compete with other teams (Little and Madigan 1997). This may be an incentive for delivering quickly. Hence, team outcomes can be assumed to be more desirable for managers and customers. In addition, software projects are often delivered close to or even after deadlines. Previous studies found team confidence to be particularly beneficial when approaching deadlines, as high-confidence teams cope better with entailing pressure (Little and Madigan 1997). These arguments lead to the following proposition:

Proposition 5: *The more confident a team, the better is the performance.*

3.3.5 Integrated Research Model

All research propositions are summarized in Table 3.2 and illustrated as an integrated research model in Fig. 3.8. In addition, the study controls for two context factors expected to account for variation in the performance of studied software development teams. As suggested in previous research, the diversity of *programming experience* is an important predictor of team performance (Banker et al. 1998). Moreover, *team size* is a typical control variable in team studies as an increasing team size has been argued to create coordination problems, affecting team performance (Table 3.3).

Table 3.2 Research propositions

No.	Proposition
P1	The more intensively a team uses agile practices, the more shared are the mental models of the team members.
P2a	The more intensively a team uses agile practices, the more intensive is the provided backup within the team.
P2b	The more shared the mental models of the team members, the more intensive is the provided backup within the team.
P3	In case of high technological uncertainty, the more backup a team's members provide to each other, the better is the team performance.
P4	The more intensively a team uses agile practices, the more confident is the team.
P5	The more confident a team, the better is the team performance.

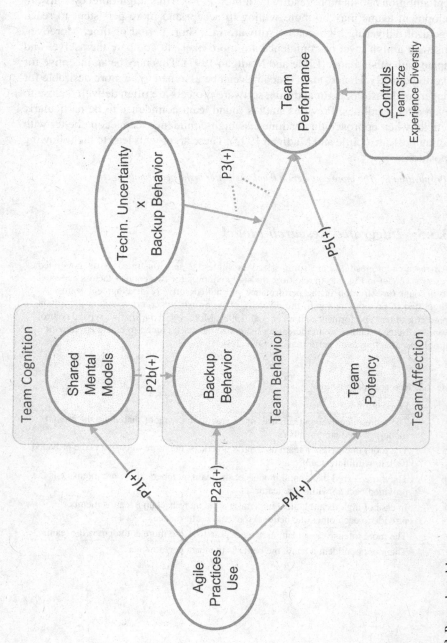

Fig. 3.8 Research model

Table 3.3 Overview of the constructs in the research model

Construct	Definition	Source
Agile Practices Use	Use of Pair Programming (PP), Code Review (CR), and Automated Testing (AT) PP: Pair programming is an agile software development technique in which two programmers work together at one workstation. The driver writes code while the navigator reviews each line of code as it is typed in. The two programmers frequently switch roles. CR: Code review is a quality assurance practice in which new or modified code is reviewed by at least one colleague. AT: Test automation is the automated execution of test cases to compare the actual and predicted functional outcomes of a piece of software or parts of it.	Based on Beck (2000); Maruping et al. (2009a)
Shared Mental Models	Team members' shared, organized understanding and mental representation of knowledge about key elements of the team's relevant environment and tasks. Technically, the degree of similarity among the mental models of members.	Klimoski and Mohammed (1994); Mohammed and Dumville (2001)
Backup Behavior	Discretionary provision of resources and task-related effort to other team members in order to help obtain the goals as defined by his or her role when it is apparent that the team member is failing to reach his or her goals.	McIntyre and Salas (1995); Porter et al. (2003)
Team Potency	Collective belief of the team that it can be effective.	Akgün et al. (2007); Guzzo et al. (1993)
Team Performance	Stakeholders' perception of the overall success of a software development team.	Self-developed
Team Size	Number of team members in a software development team.	–
Experience	Diversity of experience in professional software development within the software development team.	–
Technological Uncertainty	Extent to which well-established work practices and procedures *cannot* be used to convert requirements into a software system.	Based on Nidumolu (1995)

Chapter 4
Research Methodology

The previous chapter introduced the theoretical research model of this study to be tested with data from professional software development teams. This chapter explains the data collection process and methodology for analysis of the study results in the following chapters. Section 4.1 introduces the given research context; Sect. 4.2 describes the survey study design with three role-specific questionnaires for developers and the teams' Scrum Masters, and the respective Product Owners. An overview of the measurement instrument for all latent variables in the research model is given in Sect. 4.3. Finally, two statistical techniques - both used to analyze the collected data and to test the research hypotheses - are introduced and briefly discussed in Sect. 4.4.

4.1 Research Context

The study was conducted at SAP SE, a world leader in enterprise software and software related services with more than 65,000 employees worldwide.[1] The company was founded in 1972 and is today a global organization with locations in more than 130 countries (Leimbach 2008). SAP applications and services enable more than 250,000 customers to efficiently operate and improve their businesses. The company has a global development organization of more than 15,000 software developers. The majority works in development locations in Germany, the US, Canada, Bulgaria, India, and China.

---

[1]http://global.sap.com/corporate-en/our-company/history/index.epx.

© Springer International Publishing Switzerland 2016
C. Schmidt, *Agile Software Development Teams*, Progress in IS,
DOI 10.1007/978-3-319-26057-0_4

Over the last decade, SAP has fundamentally changed its software development methodology. When agile development methods obtained broader public interest around 2004, the first SAP development teams piloted Scrum and started to experiment with Extreme Programming[2] (Schnitter and Mackert 2011). During the following years, around 120 projects - more than 10,000 software developers - shifted to an agile development paradigm (Mackert et al. 2010). The transition of the entire development organization was completed in 2012. In the new organizational setup, Scrum teams are the central unit of business as opposed to the former structure organized around development projects with individual developers and project managers.

4.1.1   Organizational Context

Large-Scale Scrum

Scrum was originally introduced as a development method for small development projects (Schwaber and Beedle 2002). Most of SAP's development projects, however, have several Scrum teams; some projects even comprise of up to several hundred software developers. Therefore, SAP has implemented a popular approach by Larman and Vodde (2009) to scale Scrum for large-scale projects.

SAP's standard Scrum teams have a dedicated *Product Owner* (PO) and about ten developers. In multi-team projects, POs of all project teams meet regularly in a so-called *product team* to discuss the project direction (Mackert et al. 2010). These meetings are headed by an *Area Product Owner* (APO) defining the strategic direction of the whole project. APOs interact with the customer and define a product vision. The product team refines this product vision, defines a project backlog, and coordinates the assignment of tasks to their development teams.

SAP's Scrum teams are very heterogeneous in respect to programming languages (Java, C, and ABAP[3]) or the software type (database software, on-premises and cloud-based business applications, development tools, mobile applications, etc.). This setup provided the required heterogeneity among the study subjects, i.e. the participating software development teams, even though the study was conducted at a single company.

Agile Software Engineering Training

Scrum neither helps developers to develop software nor gives it guidance to the team between the Scrum planning and review meetings. To fill this gap, SAP offered a specific training program to familiarize developers with agile software development

---

[2]Scrum and Extreme Programming were introduced in Sect. 2.2.2.

[3]ABAP is SAP's proprietary programming language.

practices. The training intended to improve developers' programming skills and the teams' ability to reliably deliver high quality software after each Sprint (Al-Fatish et al. 2011; Scheerer et al. 2013). The training was established in 2010 as part of a strategic program focusing on better software quality and more frequent software releases.

During a week's class room training, entire development teams were trained with agile software development practices through hands-on exercises. Afterwards, experts coached the teams in their usual work environment for three weeks. The training also covered development practices relevant for this study: *automated testing, code review, and pair programming* (see Sect. 2.2.2). In addition, it offered an update to the agile *Scrum* framework. The content of the training is not specific to SAP, but taken from standard agile software development books (see Sect. 2.2).

After 2011, the training program was scaled globally (Heymann 2013; Schmidt et al. 2014). Up until 2014, more than 5,000 SAP developers participated in the training and more than 180 development teams were trained in Germany only. Despite the tremendous investment, the company did not pressure developers to use the taught development practices after the training program. Instead, the teams decided themselves about the appropriate adoption intensity.

4.1.2   Participatory Research Setup

The author of this study worked as a research assistant at SAP between 2011 and 2014. During that time, he attended various trainings for software developers and contributed to 'continuous improvement workshops' with participants from different development teams and areas. In addition, he conducted specific exploratory studies at the company. Among them were multi-day observations of four software development teams, interviews with more than 30 developers from different teams, informal talks with coaches for agile software engineering, and interviews with several project managers. Results of these studies are related to this study and have already been documented elsewhere (see e.g. Kude et al. 2014; Scheerer et al. 2013; Schmidt et al. 2013, 2012; Spohrer et al. 2013). This participatory research setup provided valuable insights into SAP's development organization, the software development processes, and the company-specific terminology to conduct this study.

The embedded research work allowed to pre-test a preliminary version of the presented research model at SAP in summer 2012 with more than 900 invited developers. The pre-test results revealed the adoption intensity of the taught agile development practices after the training as well as the perceived impact on developers' work (Schmidt et al. 2014). In particular, the study asked developers' belief to deliver better software, to have a higher frequency of delivering new software features, and their perception about improved or worsened teamwork aspects after participating in the training program.

The pre-test results provided valuable insights in the studied population and helped to improve the questionnaires for the main study. First of all, the findings motivated the re-evaluation and extension of the original research model. Second, the low response rate in the pre-test led to a fundamental change in the research design. While the pre-test was conducted as an online survey, the main study collected data with a paper-based questionnaire filled in by the developers during a 30 min meeting. The change bolstered the response rate up to over 70 % per team compared to about 20 % in the pre-test (see Sect. 5.1). Finally, the pre-test findings led to significant improvements in the measurement instrument of the main study. Details are described in the following section.

4.2   Study Design

The following paragraphs explain the selection of a survey-based study design, describe the three role-specific questionnaires for developers, Scrum Masters, and Area Product Owners, and finally outline the data collection procedure.

4.2.1   Survey Field Study

Social scientists can select from a broad spectrum of research strategies such as experimental, cross-sectional, longitudinal or case study research designs (Bryman and Bell 2011). The research design considerably influences the external[4] and internal validity[5] of the research results, i.e. it influences (1) the generalizability of the results, (2) the control of contextual variables and thus measurement precision, and (3) the realism of the research context.

This study investigates the results of a paradigm shift in software development. During the last 10 years, many companies have changed their development processes and shifted towards an agile software development approach (see Sect. 2.2). Consequently, realism and generalizability of the research results were considered as important factors for the study design decision.

Previous studies mostly focused on in-depths analyses from a limited number of professional software development teams or derived their findings from student experiments (see Sect. 2.3). This research project, however, had the unique opportunity to collect data from a large number of professional software development teams. Leveraging this opportunity, the author conducted a cross-sectional field study with professional software development teams to test the proposed research model.

---

[4]*External validity* refers to the generalizability of the research results across times, settings and individuals (Scandura and Williams 2000).

[5]*Internal validity* refers to the extent to which a concept, conclusion or measurement is well-founded and corresponds accurately to the real world (Scandura and Williams 2000).

Cross-sectional field studies investigate research questions by collecting data from representative subjects in natural settings at a single point of time. The study participants are selected to randomly differ in those variables relevant to the research question. Statistical analysis methods help determine the differences between these subjects and extract underlying patterns between the study participants. The cross-sectional research design does neither controls for independent or contingent variables nor does it involve manipulations of treatments. Instead, it maximizes the realism of the context while mindfully accepting potential drawbacks from lower precision of measurement and control of contextual variables.

The selected research design as well as the applied data analysis techniques strongly influence the quality of cross-sectional field studies. Hence, Edmondson and McManus (2007) emphasize a necessary methodological fit for cross-sectional field studies in management research. In this thesis, the author discusses various research contexts proposing specific research methods. It draws thereby on a large body of knowledge from different research streams and develops clear research hypotheses that can be tested. Furthermore, the study examines the relationship of clearly defined constructs for which quantitative data can be measured. As such, the overall purpose of the study is to extend and test an existing theory in a new research setting. This study follows the advise of Edmondson and McManus (2007) to structurally "obtain data from field sides that measure the extent or amount of salient constructs" and to "apply inferential statistical methods for testing the proposed hypotheses and to ensure methodological fit".

At the core of this dissertation is a large-scale survey with professional software teams from SAP. Survey research primarily uses questionnaires to measure characteristics, behaviors, affections, or other aspects in cross-section field studies (Bhattacherjee 2012; Dillman et al. 2009). The following paragraph specifies the questionnaire that was used for this study.

4.2.2 Questionnaire Design

The survey included three role-specific questionnaires for developers, Scrum Masters, and Area Product Owners. This design parallelized the data collection process and simultaneously reduced the cognitive load for the participants. Moreover, the chosen design implemented a procedural mitigation of common methods bias in the data (Podsakoff et al. 2003) by collecting crucial variables in the research model from different sources in the teams.

The paper-based questionnaires comprised of seven pages for the developer, ten pages for the Scrum Masters, and six pages for the APOs (see Appendices A.5, A.6, and A.7). The cover page of each questionnaire informed the respondents of the purpose of the study and the overall study design. The remaining pages contained

Table 4.1 Overview of the role-specific questionnaires

Developer questionnaire	Scrum master questionnaire	APO questionnaire
Agile practices use	Team context	Software quality
Shared mental models	Extent of scrum	Delivery quality
Backup behavior	Development process	Task characteristics
Teamwork aspects	Teamwork aspects	Team performance
Impact of agile practices		

the measurement scales for the variables in the research model. Although the study was conducted in Germany, all questions were asked in English as not all participants were literate in German. English, however, is the company's business language. Table 4.1 and the following list provide an overview of the questionnaires:

- **Developer Questionnaire** The responding developers indicated in the first part of their questionnaire the adoption intensity of the studied agile development practices. In the second part, they rated the similarity of their mental models with three other colleagues as well as the level of backup amongst each other. Then, the developers were asked for insights into various teamwork aspects. Finally, developers rated the perceived impact of agile software engineering on their work performance. This last section of the questionnaire was not part of the research study, but of interest to the company only (see Appendix A.5).
- **Scrum Master Questionnaire** The Scrum Masters were asked to provide insights into the team setup and its work context, for instance, the team size or the programming language. Then, the questionnaire covered the adoption intensity of the Scrum methodology in the team. Further, it asked for various parameters of the team's software development process such as release frequency or customer involvement. Finally, Scrum Masters provided their perspective on various teamwork aspects (see Appendix A.6).
- **Area Product Owner Questionnaire** Complementary to the team-internal perspective given by the developers and the Scrum Masters, the respective APOs were invited to assess the performance of the participating teams from a team-external perspective. In the first part of the questionnaire, APOs evaluated the software quality delivered by the teams. The second part examined the teams' performance in terms of their ability to reliably deliver new software. The third section of the questionnaire asked APOs to characterize the tasks their teams were assigned to. Finally, APOs provide an overall performance score for their teams (see Appendix A.7).

4.2.3 Data Collection Procedure

The data for this study was collected in four SAP locations in Germany between December 2013 and February 2014. The author approached managers of 120 software development teams for participation in the study. These teams were randomly selected out of the about 180 teams which had already participated in the training program at that point in time. All teams developed enterprise software applications or supporting software technology in SAP's software stack.

After managerial approval, the author approached the respective Scrum Masters and asked for their team's participation in the study, with about 80 teams enrolling in the study. All members of the volunteering teams were invited to a team meeting to fill the respective questionnaire. Even if a team had collectively agreed to participate in the study, each individual team members' participation was still on a voluntary basis. This procedure was in agreement with the company's workers' council as well as SAP's data privacy officer.

The meetings lasted between 30 and 60 minutes and followed a standardized procedure (see Appendix A.3). After explaining the overall purpose of the study, the questionnaires were handed out to all team members. On average, it took about 20 min to complete the questionnaires. During the entire meeting, the interviewer was present in the room to clarify any misunderstandings or upcoming questions. The APOs were approached separately, only after their teams had participated in the study. For some teams, the product owner completed the APO questionnaire instead or in addition to the APOs. All returned questionnaires were independently and redundantly transcribed by two research assistants for quality assurance.

Different incentives were offered to encourage participation and to express gratitude for contribution to the study. All teams received a customized team report that contrasted the team's answers with the answers of all other participating teams (see Appendix A.8). Furthermore, each team got a small gift in form of a USB traffic light (see Appendix A.4). The teams use these devices to display the status of their automated test suites. Second, all teams participated in a lottery and two teams were drawn. These winner teams were invited to a go-cart event. Third, all participants were offered sweets while completing the questionnaires.

This study introduced a new approach to measure shared mental models and team backup behavior. All developers rated their work relationship with three randomly selected colleagues. For that purpose, all developers drew a number plate and positioned it in front of them (see Fig. 4.1). The front side of these number plates identified each developer with a unique number. The back side told the developers the numbers of three colleagues in the room for whom they were asked to answer the respective questions (see Fig. 4.2). A set of different number plates was prepared for every possible team size and designed for the highest possible coverage of bidirectional relations in the team.

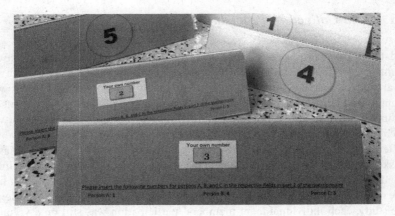

Fig. 4.1 Number plates for developers

4.3   Construct Operationalization

The research model contains various latent variables without the possibility of direct observation. For instance, the sharedness of team members' mental models or the performance of a software development team cannot be directly measured. Therefore, these latent variables are inferred from a set of observable indicators, the so-called measurement scale or measurement model (Homburg and Giering 1996), see Fig. 4.3.

In survey studies, measurement indicators—also referred to as measurement items—are typically devised through questions in questionnaires (Dillman et al. 2009). The respondents were asked to provide their answers on quantifiable agreement, frequency, or bipolar scales. Usually, each latent variable is measured with multiple measurement items for reasons of reliability. The provided answers are aggregated to a single latent variable score for each sample subject (see Fig. 4.3). There are two basic approaches to measure latent variables with indicators: formative or reflective measurement models (Bollen and Lennox 1991; Jarvis et al. 2003).

- *Reflective measurement items* are caused by the latent variable they measure, i.e. variation in the construct causes variation in the measurement indicators. The indicators reflect the latent variable, indicators share a common theme, are highly correlated, and interchangeable (see Latent Variable A in Fig. 4.3).
- *Formative measurement items* cause the latent variable. A single indicator directly influences the latent variable, i.e. variation in a measurement indicator causes variation in the construct. Hence, formative indicators do not correlate and dropping a single indicator may change the conceptual domain of the construct (see Latent Variable B in Fig. 4.3).

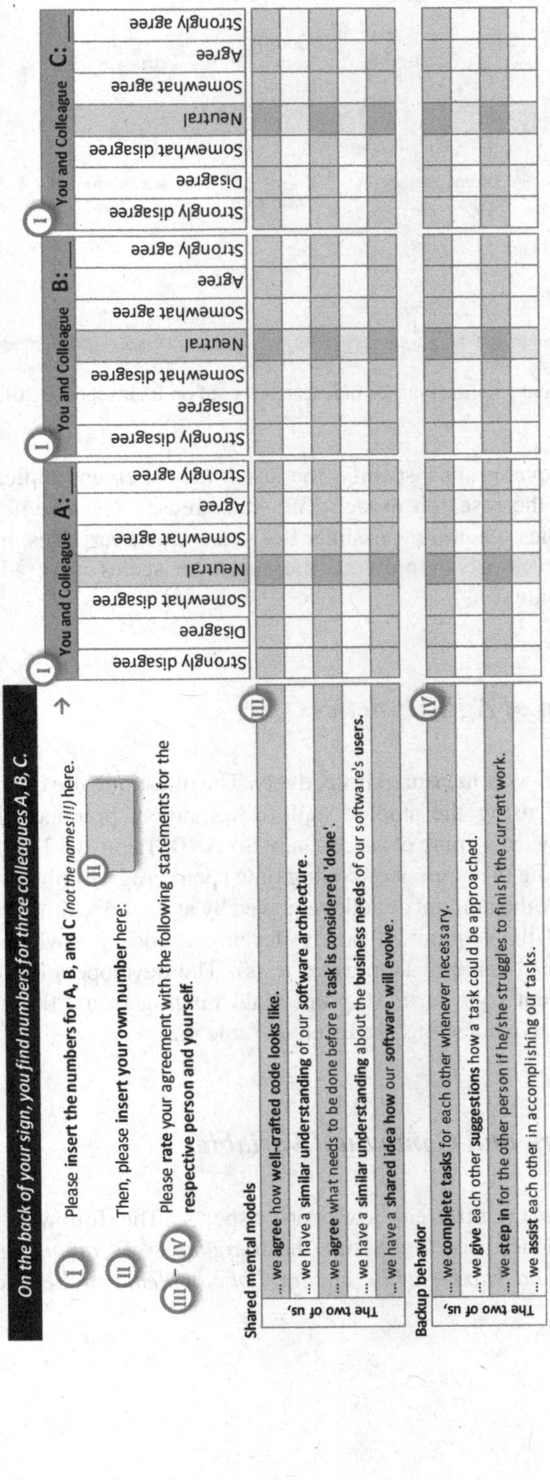

On the back of your sign, you find numbers for three colleagues A, B, C.

(I) Please insert the numbers for **A, B,** and **C** *(not the names!!!)* here.

(II) Then, please insert **your own number** here:

(III) – (IV) Please **rate** your agreement with the following statements for the respective person and yourself.

Shared mental models

The two of us,

... we agree how **well-crafted code** looks like.

... we have a **similar understanding** of our software architecture.

... we agree what needs to be done before a task is considered **'done'**.

... we have a **similar understanding** about the business needs of our software's users.

... we have a **shared idea** how our software will evolve.

Backup behavior

The two of us,

... we **complete tasks** for each other whenever necessary.

... we give each other **suggestions** how a task could be approached.

... we **step in** for the other person if he/she struggles to finish the current work.

... we **assist** each other in accomplishing our tasks.

Response scale for each of You and Colleague A:, You and Colleague B:, and You and Colleague C:: Strongly disagree, Disagree, Somewhat disagree, Neutral, Somewhat agree, Agree, Strongly agree.

Fig. 4.2 Questionnaire design for shared mental models and backup behavior

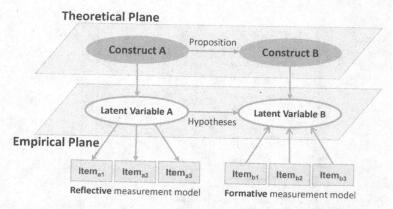

Fig. 4.3 Theoretical and empirical planes in research (based on Bhattacherjee 2012)

The following paragraphs specify the used measurement indicators for all latent variables in the research model. The study reused measurement indicators from previous studies whenever possible. For some latent variables, however, new indicators were developed or previous measurement scales were adapted to the present research context.

4.3.1   Adoption of Agile Practices

Agile practices use was measured reflectively. The questionnaire quantified developers' intensity of using the studied agile development practices. In line with previous studies (e.g. Maruping et al. 2009a,b; So 2010; Tripp 2012), the developers were asked to indicate the amount of coding time spent programming with a partner (pair programming), the amount of code reviewed by at least one other team member (code review), and the amount of newly developed code for which they wrote automated test cases (usage of automated tests). The developers had to rate their personal development style on a 10-point scale ranging from "0–10 %" to "90–100 %". The respective questions are listed in Table 4.2.

4.3.2   Teamwork and Contextual Variables

This study focuses on different teamwork aspects. The following paragraphs describe the approaches used to measure the *sharedness of team members' mental models*, the level of *backup behavior*, and *level of confidence* of the studied teams.

Table 4.2 Questions to assess agile practices use

ID	Indicator
PP1	How much of your code do you develop with a programming partner?
PP3	With how many of your team members do you pair program regularly?
PP2	How much of your coding time do you work with a programming partner?
TEST1	For how much of your new code do you write automated tests before writing the productive code?
TEST2	For how much of your new code do you write automated tests at all?
TEST3	For how many of your new tests do you use test isolation (test double, mocking, etc.)?
TEST4	How much of your new functionality is regularly tested with automated integration tests?
CR1	How much of your new code is reviewed by at least one colleague?
CR2	How much of your modified code is reviewed by at least one colleague?
CR3	How many of your team members regularly review code you have developed?

10-point scale ranging from "0–10 %" to "90–100 %" (coded 0.0–0.9)

Shared Mental Models Measuring shared mental models is challenging in team effectiveness research (DeChurch and Mesmer-Magnus 2010; Wildman et al. 2013) and existing literature offers no consistent measurement approach. Some studies defined the construct in terms of *accuracy* of team member's mental models, others in terms of the level of *sharedness*. The diversity of elicitation techniques include paired similarity ratings, concept maps, card sorting task or rating scales (Mohammed et al. 2010; Uitdewilligen et al. 2010).

Moreover, mental models are context sensitive and hardly comparable for teams working in different environments. Consequently, existing measurement instruments differ considerably. All approaches require not only a profound understanding of teams' specific work contexts but are also very time-consuming. Therefore, primarily qualitative research designs use them to measure shared mental models of a limited number of teams. This study, however, pursues a quantitative study design with a large sample size. Therefore, existing approaches were not applicable and a new measurement instrument had to be developed.

There were three fundamental challenges: (1) diverse background of the studied teams in software products developed, used technology, and work contexts, (2) a large number of professional software development teams, and (3) potentially high costs due to participants sacrificing work time. Therefore, a context-insensitive and time-efficient measurement was needed.

This study measures the *sharedness* of team members' mental models with a reflective measurement model. In line with previous literature, "sharing" is interpreted in the sense of "having in common" rather than "dividing up" (Cannon-Bowers et al. 1993). Hence, developers rate the similarity of their understanding of four specific knowledge domains with three other colleagues. The domains were (a) knowledge about the application domain of the software, (b) the underlying

Table 4.3 Questions to assess shared mental models and backup behavior

ID	Indicator
SMM1	We agree how well-crafted code looks like
SMM2	We have a similar understanding of our software architecture
SMM3	We agree what needs to be done before a task is considered done
SMM4	We have a similar understanding about business needs of our software's users
SMM5	We have a shared idea how our software will evolve
BB1	We complete tasks for each other whenever necessary
BB2	We give each other suggestions how a task could be approached
BB3	We step in for the other person if he/she struggles to finish the current work
BB4	We assist each other in accomplishing our tasks

7-point Likert scale from "strongly disagree" to "strongly agree" (coded 1–7)

technology, (c) the development procedure, and (d) the overall project vision, as specified by He et al. (2007). The questionnaire items were developed accordingly. For instance, each participant evaluated the following statement with respect to three colleagues on a 7-point Likert agreement scale: "*we have a similar understanding of our software architecture*" (see Table 4.3). Subsequently, average values of the provided answers were calculated for each developer and then aggregated to a single score for each team.

Backup Behavior To the author's best knowledge, no previous study has measured backup behavior of software development teams using a questionnaire. Consequently, a new measurement instrument had to be developed. The used questionnaire items address central aspects of the construct. These are providing feedback, giving work suggestions, and finishing other persons' work. The same measurement procedure, as described for shared mental models, was applied. Developers were asked to rate the amount of provided or received feedback, support, and backup to or from three randomly selected members of their team. For that purpose, three statements are provided in the questionnaire for which the developers rated their agreement on a 7-point Likert scale ranging form "strongly disagree" to "strongly agree". The team values are then calculated by averaging these answers. The measurement model is reflective.

Team Potency Measurement instruments for operationalizing team confidence have been widely discussed and applied in team effectiveness research (Gully et al. 2002; Jung and Sosik 2003). This study adopts the reflective 7-item measurement model described by Guzzo et al. (1993). The items assess the team's belief to deliver high quality software and to solve problems upon hard work. The team potency items have the team as reference. Thus, aggregation is not necessary for further analysis on the team level.

Technological Uncertainty This study includes technological uncertainty as a moderating variable in the research model. The measurement instrument was borrowed from Nidumolu (1995), see Table 4.4 and reversed for the statistical

Table 4.4 Questions to assess team potency and technological uncertainty

ID	Indicator
POT1	Our team has confidence in itself
POT2	Our team believes it can become unusually good by producing high-quality work
POT3	Our team expects to be known as a high-performing team
POT4	Our team feels it can solve any problem it encounters
POT5	Our team believes it can be very productive
POT6	Our team can get a lot done when it works hard
POT7	No task is too tough for our team
TUN1^R	Concerning the last six months, the team faced tasks for which there was a clearly known way how to solve them
TUN2^R	Concerning the last six months, the team faced tasks for which the team's preexisting knowledge was of great help to solve them
TUN3^R	Concerning the last six months, the team faced tasks for which the team's preexisting work procedures and practices could be relied upon to solve them

7-point Likert scale from "strongly disagree" to "strongly agree" (coded 1–7)
^{R} - reversed coding

analysis. It comprises of three measurement items adopted with minor adaptations to ensure fit for the given research context. One item of the original instrument had to be deleted based on feedback in the pre-test. As the three technological uncertainty dimensions are disjunct, the measurement model was formative.

4.3.3 Team Performance

As discussed in Sect. 3.2, team performance is a multi-faceted construct and researchers neither agree on conceptualization nor measurement. Nevertheless, two popular approaches have been used repeatedly which were originally introduced by Henderson and Lee (1992) and Hoegl and Gemuenden (2001). Moreover, various instruments exist for non-software development teams. For several reasons, these measurement instruments could not be adopted for this study. First, the non-software specific team performance measurement models were too generic to capture the marginal performance differences of the studied teams. Second, the software development specific measurement instruments were used for software development teams in traditional project contexts with detailed upfront planning. Hence, the teams were evaluated relatively to this plan. SAP teams, however, follow an agile development approach. Therefore, they neither have a fixed project duration nor do they define budgets or feature scope upfront. Consequently, these measurement scales were not applicable in the given research context either. Previous studies used objective data to capture the performance of the studied software development teams. For instance, Maruping et al. (2009a) used objective, quantitative indicators for bug severity and software complexity as objective measures of project quality.

Unfortunately, the research context of this project did not provide access to these or similar performance indicators. Therefore, a new measurement scale had to be developed to assess the performance of the studied teams.

Team Performance In previous studies, stakeholders provide reliable performance ratings in the absence of objective performance indicators (Henderson and Lee 1992; Hoegl and Gemuenden 2001). For the given research context, APOs were the central stakeholders of the studied teams (see Sect. 4.1.1). They were directly affected by the output of the teams, in charge of several teams and can therefore compare the performance of every single team with its peer teams. Hence, APOs were asked to assess the performance of the studied teams.

The author conducted an exploratory interview study to define the relevant performance dimensions in the specific research context. In a first step, existing ISD and software development team studies were reviewed to compare existing team performance concepts. Thereafter, 15 APOs were interviewed for about 1 h between May and June 2013 to elicit the essential team performance dimensions. These APOs were in charge of more than 50 development teams working in diverse software development projects. All interviews were recorded, transcribed, and finally analyzed with the NVivo Software Package.

To analyze the data, grounded theory was used (Strauss 1987), i.e. a qualitative research approach that enables researchers to create structure about what they see solely from the data at hand, and not from prior assumptions or theories. This approach is particularly useful when uncertainty about data to be collected and its importance is high. The process includes three phases. First, the data is scanned for artifacts that are tagged and labeled (open coding). Second, the detected labels are related to one another (axial coding). Finally, the labels are organized into a coherent story which can either build the basis for a theory or a categorization of the labels. The analysis of the interview data revealed three major performance dimensions (see Fig. 4.4):

Fig. 4.4 Extracted team performance dimensions

1. *Software Quality*. The quality of the delivered software was mentioned by all APOs as a distinguishing performance indicator. Following the ISO norm (ISO/IEC 2001), there are internal and external software quality aspects. *Internal software quality* determines the ability of the team to move forward on a project. It includes aspects such as software maintainability, flexibility, reusability, readability, testability, or structuredness of the software code. *External software quality* aspects are functional correctness, software usability, reliability, accuracy, and robustness. External quality determines the fulfillment of stakeholder requirements, i.e. it covers software quality aspects that are relevant to the software user while internal quality is relevant for the software developer who extends, modifies, or maintains the software in the future (Kan 2003).
2. *Delivery Quality*. The interviewed APOs evaluated their teams in terms of *how* they delivered new software. In particular, differences in teams' progress were described, i.e. the velocity of the teams to deliver new software features. As one interviewee concluded "I know how much the team delivers at the end of the Sprint [...] that is my performance assessment". Furthermore, the teams differed in their *predictability*, i.e. how reliably they delivered the software in comparison to what they had forecasted before the Sprint ("I can be sure that high performance teams deliver what they promise"). Finally, the APOs assess how well the teams report occurring issues or challenging, i.e. their level of *transparency*. The interviewees explained that some teams directly report problems while others rather conceal them. One interviewee stated "I certainly expect that teams make it transparent if problems come up".
3. *Innovation Quality*. Finally, APOs appreciate novel ideas by their teams on what to develop ("innovation team") instead of just accomplishing their tasks ("execution team"). As one APO concluded "a high performance team thinks outside the box [...] is innovative, works independently, and is proactive".

Based on these results, a questionnaire was developed with measurement scales for these performance dimensions (see Table 4.5 on page 80). All performance dimensions were conceptualized with reflective measurement models. First, four items for the overall performance of a team were defined (PERF1-PERF4). Second, several items were specified to measure the quality of the software (QEXT1-QEXT7, QINT1-QINT5) and finally items for the progress (PROG1-PROG4), the predictability (PRED1-PRED4), and the transparency (TRANS1-TRANS3) of the teams. Even though the innovativeness of the team was found as an important team outcome, it was not hypothesized to be directly influenced by the use of the studied agile practices. Hence, the study limited the performance perspective to the software and delivery quality performance dimensions.

The quality items were rated on a 10-point frequency scale while the remaining items used a 7-point Likert agreement scale. Table 4.5 summarizes the measurement scales the APOs used to assess the performance of the participating teams. The full instrument can be found in the Appendix A.7.

Table 4.5 Questions to assess team performance

ID	Indicator
PERF1	When asked for a high performance team, other SAP teams would reference this team
PERF2	I consider this team a high performance team
PERF3	Reports on the performance of this team are always favorable
PERF4	Peer teams consider this team a great success
PROG1	This team has a high velocity of delivering new features
PROG2	The progress of the team is always satisfying
PROG3	The team continuously makes excellent progress with new features
PROG4	This team is a high performance team regarding the speed of delivering features
PRED1	I trust the team to deliver at the end of a development cycle what it forecasts before the cycle
PRED2	The team always meets the objectives that are set at the beginning of a development cycle
PRED3	When the team promises to do something, I am sure it does so
PRED4	I am confident that the team delivers forecasted features
TRANS1	The team communicates issues to affected stakeholders whenever necessary
TRANS2	Product stakeholders (PO&APO) are always well-informed about problems
TRANS3	Whenever problems occur, the team informs affected stakeholders
7-point Likert scale from "strongly disagree" to "strongly agree" (coded 1–7)	
QEXT1	When the team presents new features, the team's software does what it is supposed to do
QEXT2	The team's key stakeholder (in a Scrum context: product owner) is satisfied with the software quality the team delivers
QEXT3	When the team presents new features, they could fearlessly be shipped to the customer
QEXT4	The capabilities of the software meet the needs of the team's customers
QEXT5	Overall, the team's software contributes to SAP's reputation as a high quality software company
QEXT6	The team delivers software that fully covers the requested functionality
QEXT7	The software the team delivers meets technical requirements
QINT1	The team complies with done criteria
QINT2	The software code is reusable
QINT3	The software code is maintainable
QINT4	The software code is easily testable
QINT5	The software code is clean

10-point scale from "Never" to "Always" (coded 1–10)

4.3.4   Instrument Validation

The final measurement instrument comprises of measurement scales for all variables in the research model. Three pre-tests were conducted to assess its usability in terms of comprehension, the layout of the questionnaires, as well as the data collection procedure (Fowler 2002, p. 112). Various versions of the instrument were reviewed by several experts at SAP to check its face and content validity (MacKenzie et al. 2011). In particular, feedback from three APOs, two coaches of the agile software engineering training, and various developers from different SAP software development teams helped to improve the quality. Some questions appeared to be redundant, i.e. too similar in the wording, and were therefore removed from the measurement instrument. Other items, that were taken from previous studies, were also removed as they were too difficult to understand by the German non-native English speakers. In addition, faculty and postgraduate students at the University of Mannheim checked the questionnaires for understandability and respondent-friendliness. Both are generally considered as critical factors to achieve a high response rate (Dillman et al. 2009).

The final questionnaires were tested with four graduate student teams and two professional software development teams at SAP. These university teams, six students each, had participated in the author's class on software engineering methods. For a period of three months, they had been working as a small software development team when the validation test of the measurement instrument took place. The main purpose of the class was to learn and apply the agile software development methodology based on a hands-on software development project. Therefore, all students were able to comprehend the questionnaire despite its context-specific language.

Finally, the author validated the newly developed measurement scales using a card-sorting exercise with more than 150 undergraduate and graduate students. The answers were used to check content and discriminant validity of the measurement scales based on the results of an exploratory factor analysis (MacKenzie et al. 2011; Moore and Benbasat 1991).

4.4 Analysis Methods

There are several statistical techniques to analyze survey data. This study uses multivariate *regression analysis* (Wooldridge 2013) to test the proposed research hypotheses and *component-based structural equation modeling* (Chan 1998) to develop a performance prediction model for software development teams. Both techniques are introduced in this part. Furthermore, advantages and disadvantages of both analysis techniques are briefly discussed.

4.4.1 Regression Analysis

Regression analysis is the most widely used analysis technique for empirical analysis in economics and social sciences (Wooldridge 2013). In its basic form, simple regression can be used to study the relationship between two scalar variables. The most common form is linear regression based on a linear relationship between the explanatory independent variable x and the dependent variable y. The relationship is modeled as $y = \beta_0 + \beta_1 x + u$ with β_i as the model parameters and u as the error term in the relationship. Multiple regression models accommodate multiple explanatory variables and coefficients $\beta_i x_i$ that may help to explain higher variance in the dependent variable to build better models predicting this variable.

The ordinary-least square (OLS) is the most common approach to estimate the regression model parameters based on a population sample. The approach minimizes the squares of the residuals, the differences between the actually observed and the fitted, predicted model value. The OLS approach takes several assumptions: (1) a linear relationship between the dependent and the independent variable, (2) independence of the error terms, i.e. the expectation value of the error terms is zero, (3) constant variance of the error terms (homoscedasticity), and (4) normality of the error term distribution (Wooldridge 2013).

Dependent and independent variables are random variables that are estimated based on data from a population sample. The overall object of the linear regression method is to reject the path-specific null hypotheses of no-effect and to explain variance (R^2) of the dependent variable (Gefen et al. 2000). Hence, the regression results include confidence intervals for the estimated model parameters. The linear regression approach can be used for exploratory and confirmatory research purposes.

The sample was collected from several sources in the team (developers, Scrum Masters, and Product Owners). Consequently, non-responsiveness of individual persons lead to structural missing values for several teams (see Fig. 5.1). The OLS analysis approach allows to test the postulated hypotheses independently. Thus, the maximal number of data points could be used for testing the research hypotheses as partially filled out questionnaires could still be used for the analysis. While the structural equation modeling approach incorporates other advantages it lacks the ability to consider data sets with missing data.

4.4.2 Structural Equation Modeling

Structural equation modeling (SEM) comprises of a group of multivariate statistical analyses primarily used to estimate and test relationships between latent variables in theoretical models (Gefen et al. 2000). Furthermore, they are deployed in exploratory research designs, prediction models, or in theory building. SEM analysis combines ideas from *econometric modeling* for prediction models and *psychometric modeling* for measuring latent variables. They are widely used in the IS research (Ringle et al. 2012) and adjacent social sciences (Reinartz et al. 2009; Shah and Goldstein 2006; Williams et al. 2004). The popularity is based on a number of advantages: *First*, SEM offers a great flexibility to estimate latent variables with observable indicators "obtained through self-reports, interviews, observations or other empirical means" (Petter et al. 2007, p. 625). *Second*, SEM techniques can

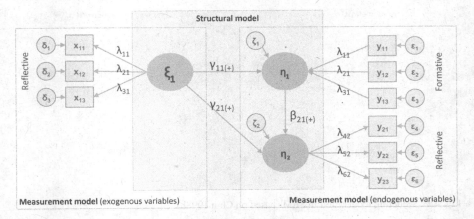

Fig. 4.5 Exemplary SEM model (based on Chin 1998b)

estimate complex models with multiple dependent variables or interaction effects. *Third*, SEM incorporates measurement errors for model testing, thus improving the overall model validity. *Fourth*, scholars can compare different parameter model estimation results based on standardized fit statistics. *Finally*, the simultaneous estimation of the measurement and the structural model produces better results compared to linear regression analysis (Chin et al. 2003).

SEM models consist of two major components (see Fig. 4.5):

- The *structural model* specifies the hypothesized relationships (γ_{ij}) between the latent variables. Exogenous variables (ξ_i) are hypothesized to cause the endogenous variables (η_i) in the model. The structural model mirrors the theoretical research framework.

- The *measurement model* defines how the above mentioned latent variables are measured, i.e. how the collected empirical data manifest the latent variables of the structural model. In social sciences, most studied variables are not directly observable. Therefore, subjective measures have to be combined to operationalize the latent variables of interest (Homburg and Giering 1996). SEM analysis hereby takes measurement errors, that all empirical data contains to some extent, into account. The path model adds error terms δ_i and ϵ_i for every observed indicator. Moreover, the latent variables are measured as a combination of several indicators x_i or y_i to build the measurement model of a latent variable. In the reflective mode, each indicator represents the latent variable, i.e. the different items are expected to be redundant to each other. Higher numbers in the latent variable are reflected in higher numbers of all variable indicators. In the formative mode, the indicators are independent of each other and capture a specific aspect of the latent variable they represent. Only upon combination, they form the entirety of the latent variable.

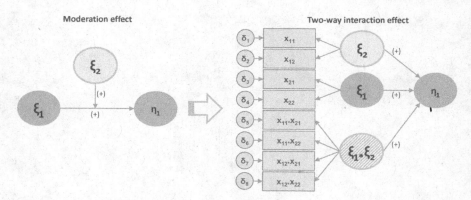

Fig. 4.6 Modeling moderation in SEM (based on Chin 1998b)

SEM analysis can estimate complex research models with *moderation* or *mediation* effects of *multidimensional* or *second-order constructs* (Gefen et al. 2011). This study entails moderation effects. Moderating variables affect the strength or direction of the influence of an independent variable on a dependent variable. In other words, the slope of the relationship between the dependent and the independent variable is affected by a third variable, called the moderator. In case of continuous variables, moderation is generally modeled as a two-way interaction as illustrated in Fig. 4.6. The moderator (ξ_2) directly influences the dependent variable (η_1) as does the independent variable (ξ_1). The product term of both variables ($\xi_1 * \xi_2$) is an additional predictor available for testing the dependent variable. The product term is operationalized with the product terms of all indicators of the independent and the moderator variable. Moderation can be illustrated by plotting the effect slope between two variables at different levels of the moderating variable. Aiken and West (1992) recommend to graphically illustrate the slope at the mean as well as at the mean plus and minus one standard deviation level of the moderator.

The structural and measurement models can be formalized as a system of linear equations. The endogenous variables η_i can be explained as linear combinations of the exogenous variables ξ_i plus the error terms ϵ_i. This equation system can be written in matrix notation as $\eta = \Gamma\xi + B\eta + \zeta$. B and Γ contain the regression parameters while ζ holds the error terms. The measurement model for the exogenous $x = \Lambda_x\xi + \delta$ and for the endogenous variables $y = \Lambda_y\eta + \varepsilon$ complement the formalized SEM and allow to estimate the model parameters with the empirical data x and y.

There are two fundamental approaches to solve this system of linear equations to estimate the model parameters. They differ in their objective of the analysis, the statistical assumption, the estimation algorithm, and the corresponding fit statistics:

Component-Based SEM[6] (Chin 1998b; Wold 1982) has the overall objective to explain variance of the dependent variables. It seeks to show R^2 values as well as the significance levels of rejecting the null hypotheses of no-effect between the model variables (Gefen et al. 2000). Hence, the approach is best applied to predictive applications and theory building. Technically, the algorithm first runs a principle component analysis to estimate the loadings Λ_x and Λ_y for the endogenous and the exogenous variable based on the given empirical data. The calculated component scores are the estimated values for the latent variables in the structural model. Based on these scores, the coefficients Γ of the structural model are then estimated in an iterative way using path analysis regression. The PLS-approach seeks to simultaneously minimize the variance of the error terms in the dependent variables (Chin 1998b) to best reproduce the empirical data with the estimated model. The estimation approach follows the principle of ordinary least-square regression analysis. Hence, there are no assumptions about the distribution of the used empirical data or restrictions to the sample size (Weiber and Mühlhaus 2012). SmartPLS[7] or PLS-Graph[8] are popular software packages that implement this algorithm.

Covariance-Based SEM (CBSEM) test for insignificance of the null hypotheses, i.e. the algorithm tests whether the provided theoretical model is plausible when constrained by the empirical data (Gefen et al. 2000). The overall objective of CBSEM is hence theory testing. The approach estimates the parameters of the structural and the measurement models to fit the covariance matrix implied by the theoretical model and specified by SEM as closely as possible to the empirical covariance matrix observed in the data sample. The estimated parameters describe the accuracy of the proposed model in regards to the fit of the data compared to a best-fitting covariance structure. The confirmatory factor analysis is the key idea of this estimation approach. The latent variables are interpreted as factors driving the indicators in the measurement model. After calculating the empirical correlation matrix of all indicators, the algorithm estimates the parameters to minimize the differences between the empirical and the theoretical correlation matrix. The factor loading between the measurement indicators are then estimated to best reproduce the empirical correlation matrix. CBSEM assumes the empirical data to be normally distributed and requires large sample sizes of at least 100 data points (Hair et al. 1995). The algorithm is implemented in different software packages, such as AMOS,[9] LISREL,[10] or Stata.[11]

---

[6]The approach is also known as partial-least square (PLS) or variance-based approach.

[7]http://www.smartpls.de.

[8]http://www.plsgraph.de.

[9]http://www-01.ibm.com/software/analytics/spss/products/statistics/amos.

[10]http://www.ssicentral.com/lisrel.

[11]http://www.stata.com/stata12/structural-equation-modeling/.

4.4.3   Selecting an Appropriate Analysis Technique

Multiple regression analysis is the most popular and flexible statistical multivariate analysis method in social sciences (Wooldridge 2013). The first generation regression techniques find their application for prediction models with a single dependent variable. SEM analysis allows researchers to systematically and comprehensively answer a set of interrelated research question (Gefen et al. 2000) consisting of complex research models with multiple dependent variables. The second generation analysis techniques simultaneously estimate the measurement and the structural model. This approach improves the overall assessment and validity power of the model (Bollen 1989).

PLS and CBSEM are different regarding their analysis objectives, their limitation to model complexity, and the required sample size in the empirical data:

- *Objective of the two SEM methods.* PLS focuses on maximizing the explained variance for all endogenous variables in the model. It is therefore better suited for early stage research during theory development and for less developed measures for the model variables. The focus is on prediction. CBSEM seeks to reproduce the empirical covariance matrix by adjusting the parameters in the SEM. It focuses on confirming theoretical relationships, i.e. theory testing. The approach relies on well-established measurement models.
- *Model complexity.* PLS can deal with an almost unlimited number of reflective *and* formative measurement models as it first calculates the latent variable scores. CBSEM, in contrast, is limited to formative constructs and limited in the complexity of the models feasible to estimate due to increasing effort of calculating the covariance matrices.
- *Sample size.* PLS runs a series of OLS regressions with component scores and was shown to produce good results for small sample sizes (Reinartz et al. 2009). For CBSEM with maximum likelihood estimation, a sufficient sample size of at least 100 data points is required (Hair et al. 1995).

This study aims at explaining the effect of agile software development practices on the performance of software development teams. The research on agile software development is still limited. Due to limited research in this field, there is no consensual theory published. Consequently, to answer the research question of this study, the study aims at new theory development. The resulting hypotheses provided in the research model can be tested with the gathered survey data. These research hypotheses were first tested independently using multiple regression. Thereafter, all hypotheses were integrated into a single model and estimated as a single predictive performance model. Due to the limited size as well as the missing normality in the data, PLS was used for the second analysis step.

Chapter 5
Empirical Validation

This chapter describes the analysis of the collected survey data and testing of the five hypotheses in the research model. Section 5.1 outlines the study sample providing an overview of studied population. In Sect. 5.2, the newly developed team performance measurement instrument and the gathered performance data is discussed. Testing of the research propositions are described in Sect. 5.3 and the final integration into a performance prediction model is summarized in Sect. 5.4.

5.1 Sample Overview

5.1.1 Survey Response

In total, 491 developers working in 81 software development teams participated in the study (see Fig. 5.1). Overall, the response rate is 68 % out of the invited 120 teams. This sample covers 45 % of the German development teams which had already participated in the training program at the point of time when the study was conducted.[1] On average, 7.1 team members (developers plus Scrum Master) participated in the voluntary survey. The average team size in the sample was 9.0 (see Fig. 5.2 for details) concluding to an average response rate of 79 % per team. In general, the response rate is very high compared to other survey studies (Dillman et al. 2009).

Seventy nine Scrum Masters completed their questionnaires. Furthermore, 36 team product owners and 50 Area Product Owners (APO) of 81 teams participated. For 17 teams, only the product owner responded. For 32 teams, there are answers from both, the APO and the PO. For 18 teams, the performance was only assessed by the teams' APO (see Fig. 5.1). This adds up to a final sample of 67 teams for

---

[1]The company does not allow to disclose the overall number of teams working in Germany.

© Springer International Publishing Switzerland 2016
C. Schmidt, *Agile Software Development Teams*, Progress in IS,
DOI 10.1007/978-3-319-26057-0_5

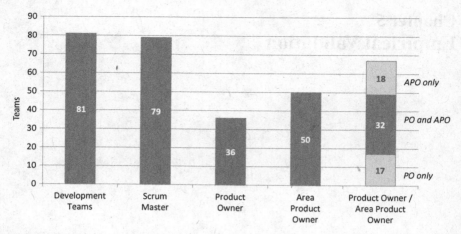

Fig. 5.1 Sample overview

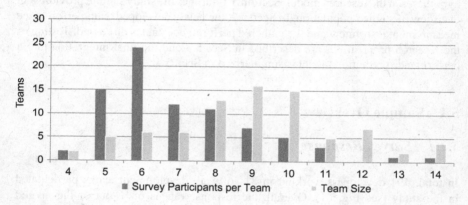

Fig. 5.2 Response rate per team

which all three perspectives are available, i.e. returned questionnaires from at least four developers, the Scrum Master, and the PO or the APO.

All participating teams followed the Scrum development framework, are located in Germany, and develop standard enterprise software. The products range from customer relationship management, over banking, and logistics application software to database technologies. The following paragraphs provide an in-depth analysis of the study sample.

5.1.2 Sample Characteristics

Individual Characteristics

The first part of the questionnaire asked the developers about their personal experience in professional software development and their affiliation with the team.

By and large, the participating software developers are very experienced and loyal to their teams. The average developer acquired more than 10 years of working experience, one third even more than 15 years. The studied teams were very stable, the majority of the developers had worked for more than 2 years in the same development team (see Fig. 5.3).

The study's pre-test revealed developers periodically working on tasks not related to software development. Therefore, the questionnaire specifically asked each developer for the time attributed to software development tasks, i.e. understanding requirements, coding, testing, integration, or bug fixing activities that are directly related to software development. On average, every developer works about 70 % of their work time on tasks related to software development (see Fig. 5.4). Only 12 % of the respondents indicate to work less than 50 % of their time on software development tasks.

Team Characteristics

All 81 participating teams are located in Germany disseminated over four different SAP locations. The average team size was nine, with a maximum of 14 team

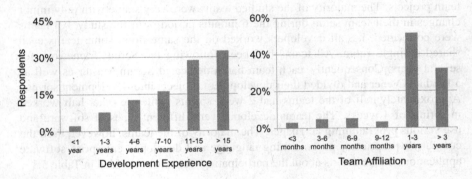

Fig. 5.3 Developer experience and team affiliation

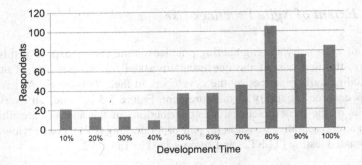

Fig. 5.4 Developers' time dedicated to software development tasks

Table 5.1 Data sample: team characteristics

Team size		Project size	
<7 Team members	15 %	<4 Teams	58 %
7–9 Team members	44 %	4–6 Teams	27 %
10–12 Team members	35 %	7–9 Teams	10 %
>12 Team members	6 %	>9 Teams	5 %
Team setup		Location	
		Walldorf	74 %
Same room	16 %	Rot	5 %
Same floor	84 %	St. Ingbert	9 %
		Markdorf	12 %
Programming language[a]		Software type[a]	
Proprietary language	78 %	Software platform	23 %
Java	29 %	Software application	76 %
Java Script	43 %	Mobile Apps	19 %
C / C++ / C#	5 %	Others	9 %

[a]Multiple selection possible

members. On average, the teams collaborated with three other teams in multi-team projects. The majority of the studied teams were very stable with only minor changes in their team setup during the 6 months period prior the study. All teams were co-located, i.e. all developers worked on the same floor, some teams even shared a single room. All teams had been following the Scrum framework for several years. Consequently, each team had a dedicated Scrum Master as well as a Product Owner and divided their development projects into development sprints. Approximately half of the teams had 2 week sprints while the other half worked in sprints of 4 weeks. The teams developed very different types of software and use various programming languages. The majority of the teams, however, used the company's proprietary programming language and developed enterprise software applications. More details about the participating teams are provided in Table 5.1.

5.1.3   Extent of Agile Practices Use

The use of agile software engineering practices is the central aspect of this study. Therefore, the first part of the questionnaire asked for the intensity of adoption of the studied agile practices by the developers in their daily work. At least three questions ensured reliability of measurement. Figure 5.5 provides an overview of the results of the three practices. The distributions of the answers are illustrated based on a representative question for pair programming (PP1), code review (CR1), and automated testing (TEST2) and summarized in Table 5.2.

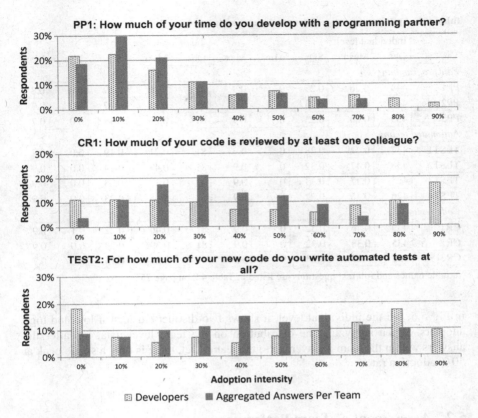

Fig. 5.5 Agile practices use

Pair Programming On average, the respondents used pair programming for about a quarter of their development time. The adoption intensity, however, varied strongly between the individual developers as well as amongst the studied teams. High adopters use the development practice for more than half of their time while the low adopter almost never program with a partner.

Code Review Code review is used more intensively than pair programming. The developers get about half of their code reviewed by at least one colleague. Similarly to pair programming, there is a wide spread between low and high adopters. Some respondents have almost all of their code reviewed, while low adopters' is only rarely reviewed.

Automated Testing On average, developers write automated tests for about 45 % of their code. The data sample further shows high variance in respect to using automated tests. Low adopters only write tests for about 20 % of their code whereas high adopters write tests for almost 80 % of their code. Even within the teams, there is high variance how intensively the practice is used. The distribution is illustrated

Table 5.2 Agile practices use: descriptive statistics

Var.	Individual level					Team level				
	Obs	Mean	SD	Min	Max	Obs	Mean	SD	Min	Max
Pair programming										
PP1	444	0.26	0.25	0	0.9	81	0.26	0.19	0.0	0.8
PP2	442	0.25	0.23	0	0.9	81	0.25	0.17	0.0	0.7
PP3	435	0.26	0.23	0	0.9	81	0.26	0.17	0.0	0.7
Automated testing										
TEST1	437	0.22	0.28	0	0.9	81	0.21	0.19	0.0	0.8
TEST2	438	0.47	0.32	0	0.9	81	0.47	0.24	0.0	0.9
TEST3	423	0.37	0.33	0	0.9	81	0.37	0.23	0.0	0.9
TEST4	426	0.46	0.32	0	0.9	81	0.45	0.23	0.0	0.9
Code review										
CR1	439	0.46	0.32	0	0.9	81	0.46	0.22	0.1	0.9
CR2	435	0.38	0.32	0	0.9	81	0.39	0.23	0.0	0.9
CR3	432	0.24	0.23	0	0.9	81	0.24	0.15	0.0	0.7

Variable names and full text questions are listed in Table 4.2 on page 75

in Fig. 5.5. On the individual level, it shows two distinct clusters of low and high adopters. When analyzing the distribution on the team level data, i.e. after the answers within the team are average to the team level, there is only a single peak at 50 % adoption rater.

5.2 Assessment of Team Performance

Measuring the performance of software development teams remains a challenge due to a lack of standardized measurement instruments. Moreover, existing measurement instruments had proven to be inapplicable to the given research context for various reasons (see discussion in Sect. 4.3.3). Therefore, a new performance assessment instrument was developed and deployed to evaluate the performance of the participating teams in the survey. The instrument comprises of various performance aspects previously extracted from interview findings with 15 Area Product Owners at SAP (see Sect. 4.3.3).

The newly developed instrument distinguishes between outcome and process oriented performance components (see Fig. 5.6). On the one hand, internal and external *software quality* was evaluated by the participating product owners (outcome-oriented perspective). On the other hand, the teams' *velocity* to deliver new software features, their *transparency* of communicating arising problems, and the quality of the team to correctly *predict* the scope of newly developed software features after each sprint were estimated (process-oriented perspective). Complementary, the product owners provided an *overall team performance* score for each team (see

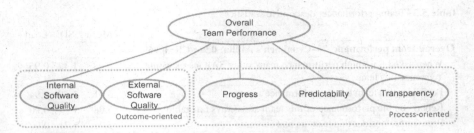

Fig. 5.6 Team performance dimensions

Appendix A.7). The final survey data set includes complete performance evaluations for 67 teams.

First of all, the interdependence of the extracted performance dimensions and the overall team performance score was analyzed. For that purpose, the prediction quality of each performance dimension of the overall team performance score was evaluated. The data was used to test a performance model with the team performance score as the dependent variable and the performance sub-dimensions as independent variables (see Fig. 5.6).

There are various statistical analysis techniques to test such a model and to further provide the strength and confidence levels of each antecedent. This study uses component-based partial least square (PLS),[2] initially introduced for prediction models in exploratory research contexts (Chin 1998a; Fornell 1989). The PLS algorithm evaluates the ratio of variance explained in the dependent variable and finds if the studied performance dimensions can be used as reliable predictors for the overall performance score. Moreover, PLS can estimate the importance of each performance dimension for the performance model.

Measurement Model Validation

First, the measurement quality of the team performance model was examined. For that purpose, convergent validity, individual item reliability, composite reliability, and discriminant validity were analyzed. Exploratory factor analysis showed no discrimination of internal and external quality measures. Consequently, all quality items were henceforth used as measures for a single quality dimension in the analysis. In addition, the factor analysis revealed the necessity to remove some quality-related measurement items to comply with the specifications of standard psychometric measurement requirements. Table 5.3 shows the final list of measurement items, the descriptive statistics, as well as the loading for each measurement item. The initially deployed measurement instrument can be found in the Appendix A.7.

---

[2]Details on this analysis technique are described in Sect. 4.4.2.

Table 5.3 Team performance: descriptive statistics

	Mean	SD	Load
Overall team performance[a]—Cronbach's Alpha: 0.96; CR: 0.96			
When asked for a high performance team, other SAP teams would reference this team	4.98	1.42	0.95
I consider this team a high performance team	5.11	1.59	0.94
Reports on the performance of this team are always favorable	5.08	1.27	0.90
Peer teams consider this team a great success	5.05	1.21	0.90
Software quality[a]—Cronbach's Alpha: 0.94; CR: 0.94			
When the team presents new features, the team's software does what it is supposed to do	8.19	1.20	0.87
The team's key stakeholder is satisfied with the software quality the team delivers	8.22	1.45	0.76
The capabilities of the software meet the needs of the team's customers (SAP internal or external)	7.72	1.52	0.78
When the team presents new features, they could fearlessly be shipped to the customer	7.70	2.26	0.87
Overall, the team's software contributes to SAP's reputation as a high quality software company	8.34	1.50	0.89
The team delivers software that fully covers the requested functionality	7.62	1.60	0.87
The software the team delivers meets technical requirements	8.40	1.23	0.80
The software code is reusable	7.60	1.76	0.72
The software code is maintainable	8.23	1.48	0.73
Transparency[b]—Cronbach's Alpha: 0.86; CR: 0.92			
The team communicates issues to affected stakeholders whenever necessary	6.09	1.03	0.93
Product stakeholders (PO&APO) are always well-informed about problems	6.06	1.01	0.90
Whenever problems occur, the team informs affected stakeholders outside the team	5.70	1.24	0.93
Predictability[b]—Cronbach's Alpha: 0.93; CR: 0.95			
I trust the team to deliver at the end of a development cycle what it forecasts before the cycle	5.43	1.32	0.88
The team always meets the objectives that are set at the beginning of a development cycle	5.21	1.37	0.90
When the team promises to do something, I am sure it does so	5.63	1.24	0.93
I am confident that the team delivers forecasted features	5.52	1.28	0.93
Progress[b]—Cronbach's Alpha: 0.95; CR: 0.96			
This team has a high velocity of delivering new features	4.97	1.67	0.95
The progress of the team is always satisfying	5.01	1.38	0.87
The team continuously makes excellent progress with new features	4.74	1.38	0.92
This team is a high performance team regarding the speed of delivering features	4.94	1.74	0.88

[a]10-point scale from "Never" to "Always" (coded 0.0 to 0.9)
[b]7-point scale from "Strongly disagree" to "Strongly agree" (coded 1 to 7)

The factor loadings of these measures were above the recommended threshold of 0.7 (Chin 1998a). The average variance extracted (AVE) of each latent variable is greater than 0.5 indicating satisfying convergent validity. Discriminant validity is also given as the square root of the AVE of each construct exceeds the constructs correlation with all other constructs (see Table 5.3). Finally, composite reliability (CR) (Fornell and Larcker 1981) and Cronbach's alpha (α) scores show satisfying values (see Table 5.4).

Analyses and Results

PLS and bootstrapping with 1000 re-samples was used to estimate the performance model. The estimation results including the standardized coefficients, significance levels, and the amount of variance explained (R^2) are presented in Fig. 5.7. Based on the significance coefficients, three dimensions are found that help to predict the overall team performance score. Overall, they account for 76 % of the variance of all performance measures.

The velocity of a team to deliver new features is the strongest predictor ($\beta = 0.55$, $p < 0.01$) but the quality of the software ($\beta = 0.19$, $p < 0.05$) and the team transparency ($\beta = 0.27$, $p < 0.01$) also significantly contribute to the quality of the team performance prediction model. The predictability measures show no significant effect on the dependent variable (see Fig. 5.7).

Table 5.4 Team performance: correlations and average variance extracted

	(1)	(2)	(3)	(4)	(5)
(1) Overall team performance	0.86				
(2) Predictability	0.63	0.82			
(3) Progress	0.81	0.58	0.86		
(4) Software quality	0.72	0.69	0.66	0.66	
(5) Transparency	0.65	0.66	0.49	0.61	0.79

Average variance extracted (AVE) on the diagonal of the matrix

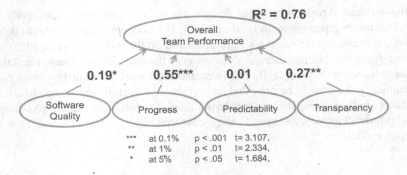

Fig. 5.7 Team performance assessment

Discussion of the Results

In general, the participating product owners assess their teams rather in terms of their delivery quality than how good the quality of their software is. Software quality constitutes an important factor, but a team's ability to deliver new features and to reliably report upcoming problems was considered to be more important for the participating product owners' evaluation of the team performance. In line with previous literature (Ilgen et al. 2005; Mathieu et al. 2008), the data supports the understanding that team performance is no one-dimensional concept.

Conclusion

This study set out to better understand the influence of agile software development practices on the performance of software development teams. Instead of focusing on particular performance aspects, such as the software quality or diverse process outcomes, an abstract perspective is taken. This is reflected in the conceptualization of team performance. Hence, the first four items in Table 5.3 are used in all subsequent models to measure team performance of a software development team. Nevertheless, these findings improve the understanding of APOs' perception of their teams' performance.

5.3 Hypotheses: Test and Evaluation

This section first discusses the measurement models for the latent variables in the research model. Then, the research hypotheses are tested using regression analysis.

5.3.1 Measurement Model

As the software development team defines the level of analysis of this study, all model variables represent team level concepts. For conceptual and methodological reasons, however, some variables were measured on the individual or dyadic work relationship level. For instance, all developers of the participating teams rated their personal intensity of using agile practices and their work relationships with three colleagues in the team. The provided answers were therefore aggregated to a team level score before testing the research hypotheses. The following paragraphs discuss these multilevel aspects and specify the measurement scores for all variables in the research model.

Data Aggregation

Phenomena on team level often emerge from lower-level data manifested among individuals, within team member dyads, or in subgroups of a team. Measuring higher level phenomena on a lower level provides increased measurement accuracy compared to assessing higher level indicators only. For instance, aggregating the ratings from team members' perception of their level of trust within the team is expected to be a more reliable rating than the perception of a single informant only. Multi-level research provides the theoretical and methodological foundation to discuss these conceptual and methodological aspects (Klein and Kozlowski 2000; Mathieu and Chen 2011; Morgeson and Hofmann 1999).

Scholars argued that higher level phenomena are either independent from lower level characteristics, only emerge in case of homogeneity within lower level units, or occur only in case of lower level heterogeneity (Klein and Kozlowski 2000). For instance, the behavior, affection, or cognition of a team can either be reflected or caused by its individual team members. Therefore, multilevel phenomena need to be carefully conceptualized and measured with appropriate measurement model to ensure alignment between the theoretical argument (theoretical plane) and the measured empirical data (empirical plane). Moreover, choosing the corresponding statistical techniques for data aggregation is essential to accurately interpret higher level phenomena from lower level data.

Latent variables in multilevel studies are often rated by several respondents answering several measurement questions. This results in three dimensions in a multilevel research data set as illustrated in Fig. 5.8. The empirical data set

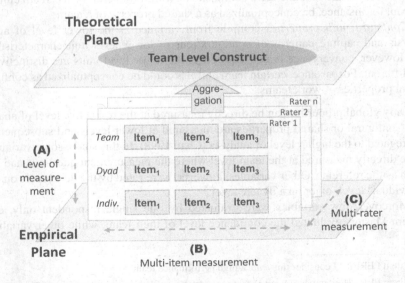

Fig. 5.8 Aggregation of multi-level research data

describes a multidimensional data vector. The vector can be further transformed into the appropriate dimensionality defined by the theoretical level of analysis. The theoretical level of analysis, in turn, is defined by the research question, i.e. the level to which generalizations are made (Rousseau 1985).

- The *level of measurement* (A) is the level at which data are collected to assess a construct. Team level constructs may be measured at the team level, the dyadic, or the individual level.
- Multi-item measurement ensures reliability of the latent construct by measuring several items, so-called *multi-item measurement* (B).
- Multi-rater measurement describes data collection using single or multiple raters, so-called *multi-rater measurement* (C).

Klein and Kozlowski (2000) distinguish between *global, shared,* and *configural* constructs when classifying multilevel concepts:

- *Global unit properties* originate at the highest level of analysis as single-level phenomena. They are mostly descriptive, easy to observe characteristics of a team as a whole without relevance for internal variance. Examples are the size or age of a team.

In contrast, shared and configural unit properties originate at lower levels but manifest at higher-levels. They emerge from individual level behavior, experience, values, cognition or team member characteristics (Klein and Kozlowski 2000).

- *Shared units properties* are similar across lower level units and represent composition forms of emergence. They describe common characteristics within members of the unit and are a composite of within-unit consensus. Team culture can, for instance, be conceptualized as a shared property of a team.
- *Configural unit properties* compile from variance at the lower level of analysis and capture patterns of configurations of lower level unit characteristics. However, convergence is not required as the lower level units are distinctively different. For instance, certain team abilities could be conceptualized as configural properties of work teams.

Only global properties can be directly measured at the respective level of analysis. Configural or shared properties are measured at lower levels and subsequently aggregated to the higher level of analysis (Chan 1998). In this study, some variables were directly measured at the team level where the measurement questions had the team as the referent.[3] Other variables, however, were rated by the developers on the individual[4] level, other on a dyadic level.[5]

Moreover, few variables were evaluated by one single respondent only, e.g. Scrum Masters evaluated the confidence level of their team, while other variables

---

[3] See item PERF2: "I consider this *team* a high performance team".

[4] See item PP1: "How much of *your* code do you develop with a programming partner?"

[5] See item SMM1: "The two of us, *we* agree how well-crafted code looks like."

Table 5.5 Measurement level, raters, items, and aggregation method

Construct	Unit-level type	(A) Level of measurement	(B) Items	(C) Rater	Aggregation
Agile practices use	Configural	Individual	8	Devs	Mean[a]
Team potency	Configural	Team	5	SM	Mean[a]
Tech. uncertainty	Global	Team	3	SM	Sum
Shared mental models	Configural	Dyad	5	Devs	Mean[a]
Backup behavior	Configural	Dyad	4	Devs	Mean[a]
Team performance	Global	Team	4	APO	Mean[a]

Devs - Developers, *SM* - Scrum Master, *APO* - Area Product Owner
[a] Arithmetic mean

were quantified with the combined perceptions of several developers. Table 5.5 provides an overview of all variables illustrating the level of measurement, the number of items used to measure each latent variables, and the number of raters. The measurement models for each variable are further discussed in the following paragraphs.

Measurement Scores

Extent of Agile Practices Use The use of agile practices was conceptualized as a configural property of the team. The initial studies at SAP had demonstrated that each and every developer in a team can independently decide how he or she implements the development task. Consequently, the studied agile development practices are flexibly and variably used and the use of agile development teams was considered as a composite of each developer's behavior. Therefore, each developer's intensity of using the studied practices configured the team behavior.

Chan (1998) distinguishes different compositional models in multi-level research. In *additive models*, the higher level unit is an aggregation of the lower level units regardless of the variance among these units. The average is a typical operational combination process of the lower level scores to the higher level variable, but there is no requirement for homogeneity at the lower level of analysis. As the use of agile practices was conceptualized on the team level, the arithmetic mean was used to aggregate the answers from the responding developers to the team level.

An exploratory factor analysis showed that the respective items (pair programming, code review, and testing) loaded on a single factor after two items were removed (TEST1, TEST3). The answers to the remaining eight items were averaged with equal weights to calculate a team level score labeled *AGILE*. This index represents the team's extent of using agile development practices. The descriptive statistics can be found in Table 5.2 on page 92, the correlation matrix of these variables in Table 5.6.

Table 5.6 AGILE: correlation matrix

	(1)	(2)	(3)	(4)	(5)	(6)	(7)$_D$	(8)	(9)$_D$	(10)
(1) PP1										
(2) PP2	0.94									
(3) PP3	0.81	0.80								
(4) CR1	0.46	0.41	0.44							
(5) CR2	0.44	0.41	0.47	0.91						
(6) CR3	0.44	0.45	0.64	0.77	0.78					
(7) TEST1$_D$	0.48	0.49	0.49	0.28	0.30	0.43				
(8) TEST2	0.53	0.52	0.58	0.42	0.42	0.52	0.70			
(9) TEST3$_D$	0.38	0.34	0.42	0.23	0.15	0.30	0.55	0.73		
(10) TEST4	0.48	0.48	0.46	0.46	0.48	0.48	0.60	0.84	0.54	
AGILE	0.79	0.77	0.80	0.78	0.79	0.79	0.61	0.79	0.50	0.77

D - item deleted as a result of an exploratory factor analysis
All correlation coefficients are significant ($p < 0.01$)

Table 5.7 POTENCY: descriptive statistics and correlation matrix

	Mean	S.D.	Min	Max	(1)$_D$	(2)	(3)	(4)	(5)	(6)$_D$	(7)
(1) Pot1$_D$	5.90	1.05	2	7							
(2) Pot2	5.69	1.14	2	7	0.50						
(3) Pot3	5.60	1.18	2	7	0.61	0.75					
(4) Pot4	5.28	1.36	2	7	0.53	0.58	0.62				
(5) Pot5	5.78	0.83	3	7	0.51	0.63	0.59	0.58			
(6) Pot6$_D$	6.14	0.84	3	7	0.18	0.26	0.33	0.30	0.52		
(7) Pot7	4.95	1.52	1	7	0.53	0.36	0.49	0.65	0.50	0.54	
POTENCY	5.45	0.98	3	7	0.66	0.79	0.84	0.86	0.78	0.48	0.78

D - item deleted as a result of an exploratory factor analysis
All correlation coefficients are significant ($p < 0.01$)

Team Potency Team potency was conceptualized as a configural team property. Scrum Masters were asked to rate the team's level of confidence by stating their agreement to seven questionnaire items. Scrum Masters were expected to have a good overview of the team, by virtue of their role and to reliably estimate the shared confidence level of the team. The construct was directly measured at the team level, i.e. the referent of each questionnaire item was the team. Thus, aggregation of the data was not required. The results of an exploratory factor analysis of the retrieved answers led to the removal of two measurement items to ensure measurement validity. The rating of the five remaining items were averaged to a single team level score, called *POTENCY*. The descriptive statistics as well as the correlation matrix of the measurement items are shown in Table 5.7.

Shared Mental Models and Backup Behavior As described in Sect. 4.3.2, shared mental models and backup behavior were measured on a dyadic level. Both constructs were conceptualized as a configural property of the team. All developers

Table 5.8 BACKUP and SHARED: descriptive statistics and correlation matrix

	Mean	S.D.	Min	Max	(1)	(2)	(3)	(4)	
(1) BB1	5.43	0.63	4.07	6.75					
(2) BB2	5.64	0.50	4.24	6.58	0.75				
(3) BB3	5.62	0.63	4.18	6.64	0.86	0.83			
(4) BB4	5.77	0.59	4.33	6.75	0.85	0.84	0.89		
BACKUP	5.61	0.55	4.26	6.56	0.93	0.90	0.96	0.95	
	Mean	S.D.	Min	Max	(5)	(6)	(7)	(8)	(9)
(5) SMM1	5.40	0.50	4.20	6.54					
(6) SMM2	5.40	0.51	3.91	6.33	0.68				
(7) SMM3	5.66	0.49	4.40	6.46	0.55	0.50			
(8) SMM4	5.50	0.42	4.51	6.4	0.50	0.59	0.58		
(9) SMM5	5.17	0.57	3.84	6.64	0.49	0.59	0.48	0.63	
SHARED	5.43	0.40	4.48	6.39	0.80	0.84	0.76	0.80	0.81

were asked to rate their personal work relationship with three randomly selected colleagues in the team. In addition, all developers rated the perceived similarity of their personal knowledge relative to three randomly selected members in respect to three essential areas of expertise in software development teams (see He et al. 2007).

Both constructs were calculated as additive models (Chan 1998), i.e. the team level score is a summation of the dyadic level answers regardless of the natural variance among these units. To standardize, the arithmetic mean was used with all data points of each team. The respective items loaded in an exploratory factor analysis on a single factor. Hence, no item had to be removed. The resulting scores were labeled BACKUP and SHARED. Table 5.8 show the descriptive statistics and the correlation matrix of these items.

Team Performance and Technological Uncertainty Technological uncertainty and team performance were conceptualized as global properties. Product owners and Scrum Masters were the single informants to evaluate these team variables. Technological uncertainty was calculated as an additive model. The three items covered different independent categories of technological uncertainty that software development teams may face. Already at the team level, the provided answers of the Scrum Master were added to a final score labeled UNCERTAIN.

The Area Product Owners assessed the performance of the participating teams based on four measurement items (see Sect. 5.2). Due to high correlation among them, the four team performance items were averaged with equal weights to a single team level index labeled PERF. Descriptive statistics and the correlation matrices are provided in Table 5.9.

Discriminant Validity and Measurement Reliability

Except for task uncertainty, all variables in the research model were measured reflectively. As required, the measurement indicators show high levels of correlation (see Tables 5.6, 5.7, 5.8, 5.9, and 5.10) and form a single factor in an exploratory factor analysis. Table 5.11 shows the results of an exploratory factor analysis with varimax rotation including all measurement indicators in the model. The final list of measurements is uni-dimensional and loads onto the respective latent variables. All cross-loadings are at least 0.2 smaller than the smallest loading on the respective constructs and thus meet the proposed thresholds (Homburg and Giering 1996). Finally, measurement reliability for all variables can be concluded as each variable's Cronbach's Alpha value is larger than the expected minimum of 0.7 (Homburg and Giering 1996).

5.3.2 Effects on Team Potency and Team Performance

In a first step, the hypothesized positive relationship between the extent of using agile software development practices (AGILE) and team confidence (POTENCY)

Table 5.9 UNCERTAIN and PERF: descriptive statistics and correlation matrix

	Mean	S.D.	Min	Max	(1)	(2)	(3)	
(1) TUN1^R	3.89	1.68	1	7				
(2) TUN2^R	2.84	1.60	1	7	0.62			
(3) TUN3^R	2.74	1.43	1	7	0.40	0.67		
UNCERTAIN	9.47	3.98	3	21	0.82	0.91	0.80	
	Mean	S.D.	Min	Max	(4)	(5)	(6)	(7)
(4) Perf1	4.98	1.42	2	7				
(5) Perf2	5.11	1.59	2	7	0.91			
(6) Perf3	5.08	1.27	2	7	0.82	0.86		
(7) Perf4	5.05	1.21	2	7	0.84	0.78	0.77	
PERF	5.07	1.28	2.25	7	0.96	0.96	0.92	0.90

^{R}reversed coding

Table 5.10 Research variables: descriptive statistics and correlation matrix

	Mean	S.D.	Min	Max	α	(I)	(II)	(III)	(IV)	(V)
AGILE	0.35	0.16	0.04	0.75	0.87					
POTENCY	5.45	0.98	3.00	7.00	0.86	0.24*				
SHARED	5.43	0.40	4.48	6.39	0.86	0.26**	0.21*			
BACKUP	5.61	0.55	4.26	6.56	0.95	0.3***	0.08	0.46***		
UNCERTAIN	9.47	3.98	3.00	21.00	–	−0.03	−0.26*	−0.17	0.10	
PERF	5.07	1.28	2.25	7.00	0.95	0.02	0.35***	0.11	−0.07	−0.17

$^*p < 0.1$; $^{**}p < 0.05$; $^{***}p < 0.01$

Table 5.11 Measurement model: factor loadings and reliabilities

Construct	Item	AGILE	POTENCY	SHARED	BACKUP	PERF	α
AGILE	PP1	**0.89**	0.04	−0.04	0.21	0.05	
	PP2	**0.88**	−0.07	−0.03	0.18	0.03	
	PP3	**0.83**	0.12	0.07	0.24	0.04	
	CR1	**0.60**	0.40	0.26	0.07	−0.40	0.90
	CR2	**0.58**	0.35	0.33	0.05	−0.44	
	CR3	**0.52**	0.38	0.29	0.23	−0.33	
	Test2	**0.68**	0.39	0.13	−0.16	0.11	
	Test4	**0.59**	0.37	0.35	−0.16	0.11	
POTENCY	Pot2	0.09	**0.81**	0.11	−0.04	0.21	
	Pot3	0.15	**0.74**	0.00	−0.13	0.29	
	Pot4	0.21	**0.64**	0.00	0.35	0.30	0.86
	Pot5	0.13	**0.76**	−0.02	0.14	0.03	
	Pot7	0.02	**0.61**	−0.11	0.18	0.36	
SHARED	SMM1	0.13	0.12	**0.66**	0.33	−0.09	
	SMM2	0.01	0.07	**0.75**	0.32	0.02	
	SMM3	0.22	0.14	**0.60**	0.38	0.31	0.86
	SMM4	0.14	0.06	**0.62**	0.32	0.12	
	SMM5	0.03	−0.08	**0.80**	0.26	0.09	
BACKUP	BB1	0.16	0.08	0.19	**0.86**	−0.10	
	BB2	0.11	−0.04	0.33	**0.77**	−0.17	
	BB3	0.11	0.05	0.16	**0.93**	−0.06	0.95
	BB4	0.11	−0.01	0.16	**0.92**	0.03	
PERF	Perf1	0.02	0.11	0.06	−0.08	**0.93**	
	Perf2	−0.03	0.13	0.05	−0.05	**0.92**	
	Perf3	−0.01	0.05	0.14	−0.05	**0.86**	0.95
	Perf4	0.03	0.24	−0.08	−0.01	**0.81**	

Exploratory factor analysis with varimax rotation method
Technological uncertainty was conceptualized as a formative construct

was tested. Then, the positive relationship between higher team confidence (POTENCY) and team performance (PERF) was analyzed. Both models control for the size of the team, a common control variable in team effectiveness research. The following models were specified:

$$POTENCY = \alpha_0 + \alpha_1 AGILE + \alpha_2 TeamSize + \epsilon_1 \tag{5.1}$$

$$PERF = \beta_0 + \beta_1 POTENCY + \beta_2 TeamSize + \epsilon_2 \tag{5.2}$$

The descriptive statistics and regression coefficients of these variables are shown in Table 5.10. The results (see Table 5.12) indicate that the use of agile development practices positively influences team potency (beta = 1.65, $p < 0.05$). The model predicts 7 % of the variance of team potency. Team potency, in turn, predicts 12 %

Table 5.12 Estimated parameters for models 5.1 and 5.2

	(5.1) POTENCY	(5.2) PERF	(5.2) PERF
AGILE	1.65**	0.35	
	(0.70)	(1.10)	
TeamSize	0.05	0.06	0.01
	(0.05)	(0.07)	(0.07)
POTENCY			0.46***
			(0.16)
Constant	4.43***	4.45***	2.50**
	(0.54)	(0.85)	(1.10)
Observations	79	65	63
R-squared	0.07	0.01	0.12
F test	2.94	0.29	4.12

Standard errors in parentheses
$*p < 0.1; **p < 0.05; ***p < 0.01$

of team performance (beta = 0.46, $p < 0.01$). There is no significant direct effect of using agile development practices on team performance. However, there is a weakly significant, full mediation effect ($p < 0.1$, Sobel-Test (Baron and Kenny 1986)) of using agile development practices through a higher team potency on team performance. In summary, the data supports the theorized propositions.

Regression diagnostics. In addition to this test, the standard regression diagnostics were followed. In particular, answers of five teams were identified as potentially influential data points in the models. Therefore, the effect of removing the answers of these teams on the overall results was analyzed. This sensitivity analysis, however, showed no substantial impact on the significance level, the strength of the estimated coefficients, nor an effect on the explained variance of the dependent variable. Therefore, results from the full data set are presented as no theoretical or structural reasons could be found to justify a removal of the answers of those teams. Furthermore, linearity of the tested relations, homoscedasticity of the residuals, and multicollinearity of the independent variables were not found to be an issue in the data.

5.3.3   Effects on Shared Mental Models, Backup Behavior, and Team Performance

The remaining hypotheses were tested using the same regression analysis approach. First, the impact of agile software development practices (AGILE) on the sharedness of team members mental model (SHARED) and the intensity of providing backup within the team (BACKUP) was tested. Second, the moderated effect of team backup behavior in case of high technological uncertainty was modeled and tested. For that purpose, the following equations were specified. In addition to these variables, the model again controls for the size of the studied teams.

$$SHARED = \delta_0 + \delta_1 TeamSize + \delta_2 AGILE + \epsilon_3 \qquad (5.3)$$

$$BACKUP = \rho_0 + \rho_1 TeamSize + \rho_2 AGILE + \rho_3 SHARED + \epsilon_4 \qquad (5.4)$$

$$PERF = \eta_0 + \eta_1 TeamSize + \eta_2 AGILE$$
$$+ \eta_3 (AGILE * UNCERTAIN) + \epsilon_5 \qquad (5.5)$$

The results for the parameters are displayed in Table 5.13. They support for the proposed hypotheses, i.e. the use of agile development practices on the sharedness

Table 5.13 Estimated parameters for models 5.3–5.5

	(5.3) SHARED	(5.4) BACKUP	(5.4) BACKUP
AGILE	0.68**	0.93**	0.64*
	(0.30)	(0.37)	(0.36)
SHARED			0.43***
			(0.13)
TeamSize	−0.00	−0.03	−0.03
	(0.02)	(0.02)	(0.02)
Constant	5.21***	5.63***	3.37***
	(0.22)	(0.27)	(0.74)
Observations	81	81	81
R-squared	0.06	0.11	0.22
F test	2.69	4.82	7.18

Standard errors in parentheses
*$p < 0.1$; **$p < 0.05$; ***$p < 0.01$

	(5.5) PERF
BACKUP[a]	−0.16
	(0.27)
UNCERTAIN[a]	−0.06*
	(0.03)
BACKUP[a] × UNCERTAIN[a]	0.18***
	(0.06)
TeamSize	0.02
	(0.07)
Constant	4.95***
	(0.65)
Observations	62
R-squared	0.09
F test	3.57

Robust standard errors in parentheses
*$p < 0.1$; **$p < 0.05$; ***$p < 0.01$
[a]Values mean centered

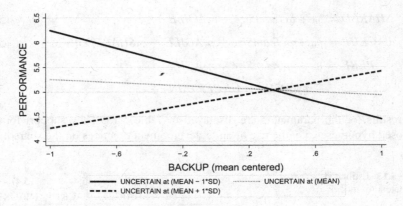

Fig. 5.9 Technological uncertainty moderation effect

of team members' mental models (beta = 0.68, p < 0.05). Moreover, it reveals the effect of team backup behavior (beta = 0.93, p < 0.05).

The second column of Table 5.13 shows that higher levels of team backup behavior are associated with a higher sharedness of team members' mental models (beta = 0.43, p < 0.01) and use of agile practices (beta = 0.64, p < 0.1). In total, 22 % of the variance of team backup behavior can be explained with the model. In a second step, the indirect effect of using agile practices on backup behavior through shared mental models was tested. The Sobel test revealed a significant indirect effect (p < 0.1).

Next, the relationship between team backup behavior and team performance under varying levels of technological uncertainty was estimated. The analysis does not indicate any direct effect of backup behavior on team performance at the mean value of task uncertainty. However, the moderating effect of technological uncertainty significantly improves the effect of using agile practices. Specifically, in case of high technological uncertainty the impact of backup behavior on team performance is positive and significant (beta = 0.19, p < 0.01). In case of low task uncertainty, backup behavior exerts even a negative effect on team performance (see Fig. 5.9).

Figure 5.9 displays this interaction effect at the mean and plus/minus one standard deviation level of technological uncertainty with mean centered values of technological uncertainty and backup behavior (Aiken and West 1992). The prediction line is only positive at high levels of technological uncertainty, whereas a negative effect can be observed in case of average or low technological uncertainty.

Regression diagnostics. The standard regression diagnostics measures did not reveal any statistical issues. A sensitivity analysis of potentially influential data points showed no substantial impact on the significance level, the strength of the estimated coefficients, nor an effect on the explained variance of the dependent variable. Therefore, results from the full data set are presented here. Linearity of the tested relations, homoscedasticity of the residuals, and multicollinearity of the independent variables were not found to be of any concern.

5.4 Integrated Prediction Model

Section 4.4.2 introduced component-based structural equation model (SEM-PLS) as an appropriate statistical technique to estimate theoretical research models using empirical survey data (Chin 1998b). While the previous chapter estimated the postulated hypotheses (see Sect. 3.3) independent from each other, PLS allows a simultaneous estimation. The SmartPLS software package (Version 2.0.M3) was used for the estimations (Ringle et al. 2005).

The results of the PLS analysis are presented as recommended according to previous literature on how to report PLS results (Chin 2010; Gefen et al. 2011). Initially, reliability and validity of the measurement model are discussed. Then, results of the structural model test are presented. As this model focuses on prediction of the dependent variable team performance, missing values in the empirical data set have been replaced with the mean values of the given responses for the particular measurement item. This procedure increased the sample size from 67 to 81 without distorting the data set and thus improved the overall quality of the prediction model.

5.4.1 Measurement Model

The previous section reported the descriptive statistics of the model variables including means and standard deviations (see Tables 5.6, 5.7, 5.8, 5.9, and 5.10). This section discusses the quality of the measurement model.

The quality of the measurement model can be assessed in terms of *measurement reliability* and *measurement validity*. These measurement attributes examine the accuracy of the measurement scale compared to the theoretical construct. Churchill (1979) formalizes this idea for an arbitrary measurement value X_0 as follows: $X_0 = X_T + X_S + X_R$ with X_T as the true value, X_S the systematic and X_R the random error. A measure X_0 is considered *valid* when differences in the observed scores reflect true differences in the measurement value ($X_0 = X_T$). A measure is *reliable* when there is no random measurement error ($X_R = 0$). Hence, reliability is necessary for validity, but not sufficient. Chin (2010) recommends to assess both reliability at the indicator and the construct level as well as convergent and discriminant validity of the measures when reporting PLS results.

- *Indicator reliability*. Table 5.14 shows the contribution of each measurement item to the respective latent variables. Literature recommends a threshold bigger than 50 % of their variance with the latent variable, i.e. factor loadings higher than 0.707 (Chin 1998b; Homburg and Giering 1996). Table 5.14 presents the loadings and the weights of all measures on their variables. With the exception of one

Table 5.14 Integrated
model: indicator reliability of
the reflective variables

Variable	Item	Loadings	Weights
AGILE	PP1	0.84	0.17
	PP2	0.81	0.15
	PP3	0.85	0.21
	CR1	0.77	0.12
	CR2	0.77	0.15
	CR3	0.81	0.20
	Test2	0.75	0.12
	Test4	0.72	0.15
POTENCY	Pot2	0.82	0.27
	Pot3	0.86	0.32
	Pot4	0.83	0.26
	Pot5	0.78	0.19
	Pot7	0.69	0.20
SHARED	SMM1	0.82	0.25
	SMM2	0.89	0.25
	SMM3	0.82	0.25
	SMM4	0.81	0.23
	SMM5	0.81	0.22
BACKUP	BB1	0.92	0.31
	BB2	0.89	0.25
	BB3	0.96	0.27
	BB4	0.93	0.25
PERF	Perf1	0.96	0.29
	Perf2	0.94	0.26
	Perf3	0.90	0.24
	Perf4	0.91	0.28

All loadings were significant (p < 0.001)

item, all loadings were larger than the recommended value of 0.707 indicating more than half of the variance to be shared with the latent variable. The loadings were tested for significance using the bootstrap routine with 1000 samples. All loadings came out to be significant (p < 0.01). Moreover, the weights of these reflective measures are equally distributed implying an equal contribution of variance of indicators to the latent variable. In summary, measurement reliability at the indicator level can be assumed.

- *Construct reliability and construct convergence* ensure appropriate representation of the combined indicators for a latent construct. Three common indicators were hereby checked (Chin 2010): (1) The average variance extracted (AVE),[6] expected to be higher than 0.5, is satisfied by all variables (see Table 5.15). (2)

---

[6] $AVE = \sum \lambda_i^2 / \left(\sum \lambda_i^2 + \sum_i var(\varepsilon_i) \right)$.

Table 5.15 Integrated model: composite reliability, ave, and correlations

	α	CR	AVE	AGILE	BACKUP	PERF	POT	SMM
AGILE	0.91	0.93	0.63	**0.79**				
BACKUP	0.95	0.96	0.86	0.33	**0.93**			
PERF	0.94	0.96	0.86	−0.05	−0.03	**0.93**		
POTENCY	0.86	0.90	0.64	0.32	0.13	0.33	**0.80**	
SHARED	0.89	0.92	0.69	0.38	0.42	0.11	0.28	**0.83**

Diagonal elements display the square root of AVE = Average Variance Extracted
α = Cronbach's alpha, CR = composite reliability

Composite reliability (CR)[7] is another indicator for construct reliability. The CR values satisfy the recommended values (Homburg and Giering 1996). All CR values are larger than 0.6. Some items had to be deleted after this analysis. The recalculated values are presented in Table 5.15. (3) The Cronbach's alpha[8] values are higher than the expected 0.7 indicating *convergent validity*.

- *Discriminant validity* assesses the correlation of the respective item to the construct of interest as opposed to any other construct in the model. For PLS models, the square root of the AVE is expected to be bigger than the corresponding correlation values (Fornell and Larcker 1981). Table 5.15 presents the square root of the AVE values in the matrix diagonal and the respective correlation values below. The data meets the Fornell-Larcker criterion for all pairs of variables, suggesting discriminant validity.

Common method bias. The dependent variable was measured from a different source than the independent variables as the product owners assessed the teams whereas the team members indicated their intensity of using agile practices and the mediating variables in the model. This setup was expected to mitigate common method bias (Podsakoff et al. 2003; Sharma et al. 2009).

Above results prove the collected data to satisfy the common requirements for measuring latent variables. Therefore, the constructs are assumed to be measured correctly. Hence, the structural model results are discussed in the following sections.

5.4.2   Structural Model

The next step is the test of the structural model. First, the strength of the model is described and the validity of the research hypotheses is reported. In particular, the share of variance explained in the dependent variables (R^2), the validity of the proposed postulated hypotheses (standardized path coefficients, and p-values), the

---

[7]$CR = \left(\sum \lambda_i\right)^2 / \left((\sum \lambda_i)^2 + \sum_i var(\varepsilon_i)\right)$.

[8]Cronbach's $\alpha = N/(N-1) * \left(1 - \sum_i \sigma_i^2 / \sigma_t^2\right)$ where N is the number of items, σ_i is the variance of item i, and σ_t is the variance of the variable score.

effect sizes (f^2), and the predictive power Q^2 are discussed. The PLS algorithm and the bootstrapping re-sampling method with 81 cases and 1000 re-samples were used to estimate the structural model.

Model evaluation. The predictive power of the model can be determined using the ratio of variance explained in the dependent variable compared to its overall variance. R^2, also referred to as coefficient of determination, is a standardized measure ranging from 0 to 1 indicating the explanatory accuracy of the independent variables in regard to the dependent variable (Wooldridge 2013). An R^2 value of 1 is hereby defined as explaining 100 % of the variance can be explained. Homburg and Giering (1996) suggest that the value should be higher than 0.4 while others claim that no universal threshold can be determined. In this study, 43 % of the variance in team performance was explained with the proposed model, while team potency and the moderated effect of backup behavior account for 36 % of the variance and the control variables add additional 7 % (see Fig. 5.10).

Hypotheses testing. First, the strength of the hypothesized relationships between the model variables are examined. The path coefficients indicate the extent to which a marginal increase in the independent variable is reflected in the dependent variable. The significance level provides confidence about the robustness of these findings. PLS uses a bootstrapping approach to calculate these significance level based on 1000 sub-samples of the sample. Most of the proposed hypotheses can be explained by the model (see Fig. 5.10). Table 5.16 summarizes the results providing the t-values and path coefficients.

The model provides support for the adoption intensity of software development practices to increases the sharedness of the mental models of team members (H1). Moreover, shared mental models (H2b) and agile software development (H2a) enhance the backup within the teams. The path coefficients are significant at a 2.5 % and 1 % level. Backup behavior does not directly impact team performance (H3a). Only in case of high technological uncertainty, backup improves team performance (H3b). This relationship can be reported at a 5 % confidence level.

The adoption of agile development practices exerts a second effect via higher team confidence. Team potency is positively influenced by the usage of agile software development practices (H4). The relationship is significant at a 1 % confidence level. Furthermore, higher team potency increases the externally assessed team performance (H5), also at a 1 % significance level.

The strength of each endogenous variable explaining team performance was further evaluated. $f^{2;9}$ is the effective size, a common statistic measure to estimate the change in R^2 upon addition of an endogenous variable to the model (Chin 1998b). The effect size of a latent variable indicates how much R^2 changes if the respective variable is removed from the model. Chin (1998b) recommends the following thresholds: 0.02 (small), 0.15 (medium), 0.35 (large) effects. Table 5.17 presents the effect sizes for the team performance. The three significant predictor variables have a small or medium effect on team performance.

---

[9]$f^2 = \left(R^2_{incl} - R^2_{excl}\right)/\left(1 - R^2_{incl}\right).$

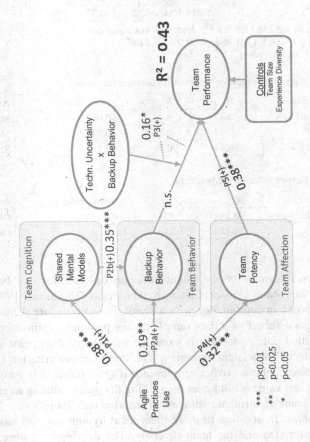

Fig. 5.10 Estimation of the integrated prediction model

Table 5.16 Effects of using agile practices on team performance

Hyp.	Independent var.	Dependent var.	Path	Sig.	t-val.	Support
H1	AGILE	SHARED	0.38	***	3.94	YES
H2a	AGILE	BACKUP	0.33	**	2.09	YES
H2b	SMM	BACKUP	0.35	***	3.37	YES
H3a	BACKUP	PERFORMANCE	−0.05	n.s.	0.60	NO
H3b	BACKUP×UNCERTAIN	PERFORMANCE	0.16	*	1.66	YES
H4	AGILE	POTENCY	0.32	***	3.79	YES
H5	POTENCY	PERFORMANCE	0.37	***	4.15	YES

***/**/* significant at the 1 % / 2.5 % / 5 % level, *n.s.* not significant
$p < 0.01$: t = 2.334; $p < 0.025$: t = 1.965; $p < 0.05$: t = 1.648
df = 999 (1000 bootstrap samples)

Table 5.17 Effect sizes of all predictor variables on team performance

Endogeneous variable	R^2_{incl}	R^2_{excl}	Effect size f^2	Assessment
BACKUP×UNCERTAIN	0.43	0.40	0.05	Small
POTENCY	0.43	0.30	0.23	Medium
ExperienceDiversity	0.43	0.36	0.13	Small

Table 5.18 Stone-Geisser criterion the predictor

Endogeneous variable	Q^2_{incl}	Q^2_{excl}	Stone-Geisser Q^2	Assessment
BACKUP×UNCERTAIN	0.35	0.35	0.01	Ok
POTENCY	0.35	0.25	0.16	Ok

The predictive relevance of the latent endogenous variables can be further assessed using the Stone-Geisser Criterion (Geisser 1975; Stone 1974). PLS deploys this approach in combination with a blindfolding procedure (Chin 1998b). Blindfolding omits a subset of a data sample during parameter estimation to then estimate the omitted data sets. This is executed until every data point has been omitted at least once. For a latent variable η, the Stone-Geisser criterion $Q^{2,10}$ can be calculated. The model has predictive relevance if Q^2 is larger than zero. In case of zero, the predicted value is not better than taking the mean value as an estimator. All predictors of team performance suffice this criterion (see Table 5.18).

Control variables. In addition to these theoretical hypotheses, the model controlled for the team size and the team diversity. The developers' rating of their experience in professional software development was utilized to calculate each team's experience diversity in the sample as the standard deviation of the team members' years of experience as professional software developers. The team size

---

[10]$Q^2 = 1 - \left(\sum E_\omega / \sum O_\omega \right)$ where E_ω are the squared errors of the predicted values and O_ω the squared error using the mean as prediction value.

did not have a significant effect on team performance ($\beta = 0.01$, t-value: 0.13). Experience diversity, however, had a significant effect ($\beta = 0.28$, t-value: 3.08).

5.5 Summary

This study examines the effect of the adoption of agile software development practices on team performance. The research model hypothesizes a direct effect on team potency, team shared mental models, and team backup behavior. Subsequently, team potency and backup behavior are theorized to directly impact the performance of the team. Hence, an indirect effect of using agile software development practices on team performance through various teamwork aspects was studied.

Data from 81 software development teams containing 491 developers, 79 Scrum Masters, and 67 product owners was collected to empirically test this model. This chapter provided an overview of the study sample (Sect. 5.1). Then, insights in the performance ratings of the teams were discussed. Second, the research hypotheses were tested (see Sect. 5.3) using regression analysis techniques. The last section of this chapter integrated all research hypotheses into a combined model. The SEM-PLS approach was used to estimate the parameters of this team performance prediction model.

In conclusion, the proposed hypotheses are supported by the empirical data. The strength of the relationship between the model variables is low to medium, the statistical analyses provide medium to high confidence level for these statements. The following chapter will discuss and interpret the findings in the context of previous studies.

Chapter 6
Discussion

In this chapter, the results of this study are discussed and its contributions are highlighted. Section 6.1 briefly summarizes the study findings followed by the discussion of the theoretical and practical contributions in Sects. 6.2 and 6.3. The limitations of this study as well as opportunities for future research are finally outlined in Sect. 6.4.

6.1 Summary of the Research Findings

This study confirms previous findings that agile software development positively influences the performance of software development teams (i.a. Lee and Xia 2010; Maruping et al. 2009a; Ramesh et al. 2012; Sarker et al. 2009). The study further advances the understanding of agile software development and helps better explain the performance implications. In the following paragraphs, the three research questions are recapitulated and their results are summarized (Fig. 6.1).

RQ1: What Is the Performance of a Software Development Team?

The interview and survey results confirm the prevailing opinion of team performance as a multidimensional concept. The study distinguishes between four performance dimensions, categorized as *outcome-oriented* and *process-oriented*. These are (1) software quality as an outcome-oriented performance dimension as well as (2) delivery progress, (3) delivery transparency, and (4) delivery predictability as process-oriented performance dimensions. In the collected survey data, these four performance dimensions explain 76 % of the variance in product owners' overall team performance perceptions. The delivery velocity ratings are the best predictor for team performance ($\beta = 0.55$, $p < 0.001$), while delivery transparency

© Springer International Publishing Switzerland 2016
C. Schmidt, *Agile Software Development Teams*, Progress in IS,
DOI 10.1007/978-3-319-26057-0_6

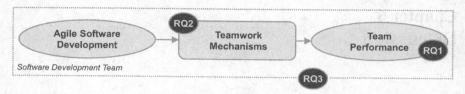

Fig. 6.1 Research objectives

($\beta = 0.27$, p < 0.01), and software quality ratings ($\beta = 0.19$, p < 0.05) are also significant, but less relevant (see Fig. 5.7 on page 95).

RQ2: What Are the Latent Teamwork Mechanisms Affected by Agile Software Development in Software Development Teams?

This study postulates a mediated performance effect of agile software development through affective, behavioral, and cognitive teamwork mechanisms (see Sect. 3.3). These propositions were derived from team effectiveness theories and tested with data collected through a survey with professional software development teams at SAP SE. Overall, the test results confirm the effects on shared mental models (team cognition, $\beta = 0.38$, p < 0.01), backup behavior (team behavior, $\beta = 0.19$, p < 0.025), and team confidence (team affection, $\beta = 0.32$, p < 0.01). These results are illustrated in Fig. 5.10 on page 111.

RQ3: How Does Agile Software Development Influence the Performance of Software Development Teams?

The empirical data confirm the study's basic assumption that software development teams work in highly dynamic environments. Team adaptation was found as an important mechanism determining the performance of software development teams as the two related markers of team adaptation were more pronounced in high performance teams. In case of high *technological uncertainty*, team *backup behavior* was positively related with team performance ($\beta = 0.16$, p < 0.05). *Shared mental models* were found as important antecedents of team backup behavior ($\beta = 0.35$, p < 0.01). The findings further demonstrate *team confidence* ($\beta = 0.38$, p < 0.01) as an important antecedent of team performance.

Overall, the survey results support the theorized mediation effect of agile software development on team performance through these teamwork mechanisms. The integrated performance prediction model explains 43 % of the variance in the team performance ratings (see Fig. 5.10 on page 111).

6.2 Theoretical Contributions

The study results outlined above offer a number of theoretical contributions, both relevant for IS development and team effectiveness research.

Better Understanding of the Impact of Agile Software Development on Teamwork Mechanisms

Agile software engineering evolved from the knowledge of experienced consultants and industry best practices (see Sect. 2.2). While the number of scientific publications demonstrates a clear interest of academic scholars (see Sect. 2.3), theory-based research on agile software development remains limited (Dingsøyr et al. 2012; Dybå and Dingsøyr 2008). This study addresses this research gap by grounding the research in established theories from team effectiveness research (see Chap. 3). Previous scholars have taken a similar approach and analyzed various teamwork factors and their performance implications in agile software development teams. Exemplary studies discussed coordination mechanisms (Li and Maedche 2012; Strode et al. 2011, 2012; Xu and Cao 2006), control mechanisms (Maruping et al. 2009a), or team autonomy (Lee and Xia 2010), communication (Hummel et al. 2013a; Rosenkranz et al. 2013), social loafing (McAvoy and Butler 2006), control (Maruping et al. 2009a), or collective mindfulness (McAvoy et al. 2013; Nagle et al. 2011) (see overview in Table A.1). This study advances the knowledge about agile development teams with two additional perspectives. The study integrates theoretical arguments from (a) *team adaptation theory* and (b) *team confidence theory*.

Add (a) The study builds on previous studies which have emphasized the importance of adaptation in software development teams (Lee and Xia 2010; MacCormack et al. 2001). For instance, Lee et al. (2010) examined software development teams and their ability to react to changing software requirements. The author agrees on change being an inherent characteristic of software development projects, while broadening the perspective. The study assumes software development teams to not only face volatile requirements, but to be exposed to frequent technological, task-specific, and/or organizational change throughout the development process. Consequently, team adaptation is considered an essential teamwork factor determining the performance of software development teams. Team adaption theory explains the team mechanisms enabling team adaption. Based on this theory, the study investigates two decisive mechanisms of team adaptation in software development teams, namely shared mental models and backup behavior, and links them to the use of agile development practices. Surprisingly, no previous study has extended the explanations provided by team adaptation theory to study agile software development teams before.

In addition to these contributions, the study findings have wider implications. Solving tasks together with a colleague (pair programming) or reviewing fellow colleagues' work (code review) are work practices seamlessly transferable to work contexts beyond the software development domain. The study results therefore also contribute to a better understanding of team adaptation in other knowledge-intensive contexts, such as new product development (Bhattacharya et al. 1998). Furthermore, the discussed mechanisms of team adaptation help better understand the development of teams' dynamic capabilities (Eisenhardt and Martin 2000) necessary to succeed in dynamic work environments.

Add (b) The study offers a second explanatory perspective on the team performance effect of agile software development practices. A team's level of confidence was suggested as another influential factor of team performance (Bandura 1986). Confident teams are expected to set higher goals, to be more determined to achieve their goals, and show greater persistence in the face of obstacles, challenges, or setbacks (see Sect. 3.1). The positive impact of agile software development practices on team confidence provides a novel explanation why agile software development positively affects the performance of software development teams. While the literature on team confidence has mostly focused on performance implications, less attention has been paid to the antecedents of team confidence. Studies on the emergence of collective confidence beliefs have mostly focused on past performance or leadership and only rarely examined the behaviors of team members (see the review article by Gully et al. 2002). Thus, this study also contributes to team confidence literature showing a positive relationship between the use of agile development practices and team confidence. The results demonstrate an influence of individual level behavior on team confidence. No previous study has revealed such a relationship before.

Better Explanation of Teamwork and the Impact on Team Performance

On the one hand, the positive relationship between team confidence and backup behavior on team performance is an empirical confirmation of previous studies in the software development domain. On the other hand, it is a previously unrecognized explanation why the adoption of agile development practices leads to higher team performance.

The study further confirms previous findings of uncertainty being an inherent characteristic of software development projects (Nidumolu 1995). While the use of agile practices was unconditionally positively related with team backup behavior, backup was only found to be beneficial in case of high uncertainty. When facing predictable tasks, the empirical findings even revealed a negative impact of backup behavior on team performance (see Fig. 5.9 on page 106). With this result, the study is among the first to provide a reason for the effectiveness of agile software development in uncertain work contexts. No previous study has demonstrated this effect so far.

Over the last decades, team effectiveness research has elucidated a wide spectrum of influencing factors of team performance (i.a. Cohen and Bailey 1997; Mathieu et al. 2008). Moreover, there is anecdotal evidence that developers' expertise with a technology, developers' programming skills, and team leadership are the essential predictors of team performance. Nevertheless, the integrated research model is able to explain 43 % of the variance of the team performance ratings. Given the multitude of factors influencing team performance, this outcome is encouraging and sets the scene for more team-based research projects to advance the knowledge about agile software development.

Finally, the study underlines the importance of teamwork in software development projects. The study provides proof for the benefits of teamwork mechanisms leading to successful software development. Obviously, developers working alone neither develop these collective mechanisms nor do they benefit from them. For instance, developers working outside a team setting can never ask for support or assistance when needed. Therefore, the study findings corroborate previous work claiming a superiority of team-based work structures over a group of individual workers. Thus, the study contributes to the discussion why teams outperform the same group of software developers working alone.

Development of an Instrument for Measuring Team Performance

Cumulative research on the performance of software development teams requires clear assessment criteria. A review of previous studies on software development teams, however, has revealed weaknesses in the current approaches. Apart from conceptual diversity, reliable measurement instruments to empirically assess the performance of agile software development teams are needed. Unfortunately, many of the existing approaches are—for various reasons (see discussion in Sect. 3.2)—not applicable to evaluate development teams in agile software development projects. This study addresses this gap by providing an overview of existing performance concepts and, subsequently, develop a new measurement instrument to assess the performance of agile software development teams.

Research has shown a tenfold difference in quality and productivity between programmers with the same level of experience. Similar differences are assumed at the team level (McConnell 2010). The collected data of this study confirm these findings with significant differences in the performance assessment of the studied software development teams. Some teams delivered satisfying software only every other sprint, while the high performance teams almost always delivered to promise. To better understand reasons for these team performance differences, new team-based performance measures were required and therefore developed for this study.

Better Understanding of the Team Performance Construct

The studied agile development practices were originally introduced as quality assurance techniques (Schwaber and Beedle 2002). Consequently, many studies examined the effect of agile software development on the quality of the delivered software (see Fig. 3.6). This study, however, has taken a broader perspective and analyzed the effect on team performance. For that purpose, the teams' key stakeholders provided their subjective performance ratings for all participating teams. For agile software development teams, Product Owners (POs) are the key team stakeholder. Hence, the study first analyzed how POs assess the performance of their teams and derived a new measurement instrument to assess the performance of agile software development teams.

POs frequently promise new features to their customers and expect their teams to implement new software functionality. Only if a team delivers to promise, POs can keep their word to their customers. Hence, delivery reliability and delivery progress are highly relevant performance dimensions, aside the software quality dimensions. This study follows this multidimensional perspective of the team performance construct. Evaluating agile software development in terms of its impact on software quality only may unnecessarily restrict the evaluation perspective.

The survey results confirm this approach. The analysis of the performance ratings indicate that the process-oriented performance dimensions (transparency and delivery progress) are decisive determinants of POs' team performance perception. These findings help not only to better understand the performance construct for agile development teams, but allow a more comprehensive evaluation approach for agile software development compared to previous studies.

Development of an Instrument for Measuring Shared Mental Models and Backup Behavior

Team effectiveness research has developed numerous procedures to measure shared mental models of work teams, while no measurement instrument to quantify team backup behavior was found at all. The existing measures are very time-consuming and can—for economical reasons—not be used in large-scale field studies with professional software developers[1] (see Sect. 4.3). Therefore, a new procedures to quantify backup behavior and shared mental models in software development teams were developed and successfully deployed.

The new questionnaire-based approach offers an efficient and promising way to operationalize these latent constructs (see Sect. 4.3). Moreover, the proposed measurement procedures allow much more detailed insights into teams' inner structures compared to previous measurement approaches. For instance, researchers could analyze configural or shared multi-level constructs and their emergence in work teams (Klein et al. 1994). This level of detail is particularly interesting to study in agile software development teams. The agile Scrum methodology, for

---

[1]Even with the newly developed measurement instrument, this study went to the limits of what was economically acceptable by the researched company. The overall work time spent by all study participation added up to about €36,000 (600 respondents 45 min; conservative estimation of €80/h per respondent).

example, suggests to develop software in cross-functional teams, i.e. teams with no role specialization such as testers or user interface specialists. Such fundamental decisions may significantly influence the communication or cognitive structure of teams and thus, their performance. The proposed measurement procedures provide researchers with the necessary data to analyze the resulting change in inner team structures to understand the effects on the teams. No previous measurement approach provided such detailed insights before.

Embedded Research as a Valuable Research Approach for ISD Researchers

The embedded research approach was a central element of this study. The research setting offered valuable insights into various software development teams and offered the necessary access to conduct a survey with a large number of comparable software development teams. Future IS researchers may replicate a similar research setup in other companies. The gained insights will help the IS research community close the gap between academia and industry, a necessary step as IS research still lags behind the advancements in industrial software engineering.

Furthermore, the combined perspective may help researchers to detect emerging development methods early without neglecting the required rigor for conducting academic studies. Embedded research not only allows scholars to work on theoretical explanations of existing development methods, but increase their awareness of emerging trends. Ideally, researchers will position themselves to guide and consult software development companies with context-specific software development methods derived from their theoretical understanding. Overall, this study is considered as an interesting case study for embedded research in the IS domain.

6.3 Practical Implications

The studied agile software development practices were originally introduced as quality assurance techniques for individual developers (Beck 2000; Schwaber and Beedle 2002). Consequently, decision makers may assess their usefulness in respect to the impact on software quality and delivered feature scope of individual developers. This study, however, adopts a team perspective emphasizing the social aspects of software development and the importance of teamwork factors. The results clearly demonstrate the effect of using agile software development practices on various teamwork mechanisms. Hence, agile development practices should not be seen as a trade-off between immediate quality benefits and the required effort for applying the practices. Instead, project leaders and developers are advised to include long-term effects on emergent teamwork mechanisms into their evaluation.

In contrast to other areas of engineering, software engineers are exposed to frequent changes in their working environment (Boehm 2006). Therefore, new development methods, technologies, and management approaches frequently emerge. This trend is likely to continue in the coming years as the global economy becomes more information-intensive. Not every new direction is likely to become mainstream and many of these new developments might just be recycled concepts. This poses a challenge for managers to understand if and when they should deploy new software development methods. Many organizations either adopt a trial-and-error approach or simply follow the herd. This study provides a third approach: understanding the underlying concepts and mechanisms which drive the newly proposed software development methods. This approach allows decision makers to predict the impact and effectiveness of new methods in relevant project contexts. Applied to the impact of agile software development on shared mental models and backup behavior, this study presents decision makers with important teamwork aspects to consider when evaluating the merits of new software development practices.

The study confirms previous findings of uncertainty as a significant influencing factor for the performance of software development teams. Even though many sources of uncertainty are beyond the control of project leaders, they should be aware of its negative influences on team performance. As a consequence, projects leaders are advised to maximize their efforts to avoid uncertainty for their development teams wherever possible. For projects facing project endogenous technological uncertainty, agile software development practices are now demonstrated as a helpful mean to mitigate the negative impact on team performance due to an increased provision of backup among team members.

SAP SE is one of the largest software development organizations. While agile software development was originally introduced as an approach for small teams, the study results confirm the trend of agile software engineering becoming a mainstream development approach adopted by large-scale global players (West et al. 2010). The introduction of agile software development means a cultural change to a development organization. Despite the extensive investment into the training program—overall more than 5000 SAP developers participated—many developers still do not use the studied agile practices (see Sect. 5.1). The descriptive data of this study clearly indicate a significant variation of the adoption intensity by the studied developers and teams. This underpins the notion of necessary long-term efforts to transform a traditional development organization into an agile one.

6.4   Limitations of the Study and Future Research

The embedded research approach has both advantages and disadvantages. On the one hand, it provides unique access to software development teams to conduct such large-scale surveys, to interview numerous people on the same topic, and observe several teams during their daily work. On the other hand, embedded researchers may develop a biased perspective on the researched phenomenon as context-specific characteristics influencing the research phenomena may not be considered. Furthermore, all study participants are part of the same organization.

In this study, all teams were even located in Germany and primarily developed application software. While the resulting study sample controls for contextual factors arising from inter-firm differences, the study results may be limited in their generalizability.

Future researchers are therefore encouraged to replicate this study in other contexts. In particular, researchers may survey teams developing various types of software, working in different cultural backgrounds, or in smaller companies. An extended survey sample would further improve the control over yet unconsidered contingency factors to capture confounding factors in the model. Especially, the newly developed measurement approach for shared mental models, backup behavior, and team performance would benefit from additional validations in other research contexts. Researcher may test the effect of shared mental models, backup behavior, and team confidence also in non-agile software development teams. Comparing results between teams of both development paradigms may provide valuable insights for the IS field and the evaluation of the agile software development.

Another limitation of the study is its static perspective for studying team adaptation, an inherently dynamic phenomenon. The study used static markers of team adaptation as proxy variables assuming that adaptive teams develop these markers over time (Rosen et al. 2011). While this approach is an accepted way to circumvent this challenge in cross-sectional studies, a dynamic perspective may have provided more detailed insights into team adaption. Future studies are therefore advised to measure teamwork in agile development teams at different points in time. The resulting longitudinal data could be used to analyze causal relationships over time and additionally analyze cyclic or reinforcing effects of agile software development. Alternatively, the performance of the participating teams could be measured after an extended waiting period post surveying the team members.

There are certain limitations inherent to the used measurement methods. The study results are based on subjective ratings. In particular, developers estimated their level of automated tests on a 10-point Likert scale in retrospective or the software quality was subjectively rated by the Area Product Owners. Future studies may complement these subjective measures with objective metrics. Possible objective metrics may include automatically calculated code coverage of teams' software code base. Furthermore, some teams have distinct quality indicators, such as customer satisfaction ratings of the delivered software, software adoption rates, generated revenue with the developed software, or returning customer error messages, potentially suited as objective metric. Extraction of such data for all participating teams was beyond the scope of this study. Future studies may also include objective performance indicators for the evaluation of the agile development approach.

On a different note, the study collected data from at least five respondents per team. This data, however, were aggregated to team scores by calculating the arithmetic mean for each team, compressing the gathered information. Future work may apply multilevel analysis techniques to discover intra-team variances for more accurate research models. Moreover, scholars may analyze the data for nonlinear relationships and investigate hierarchical effects.

Future research may elaborate on the conceptual and empirical elaboration of the team performance construct. Aside the conceptual discussion, new measurement instruments need to be developed and tested. This study provided a new approach which needs to be discussed and further validated. In addition, researchers should delineate the differences between the team performance, team effectiveness, and software development project success concepts. Other researchers may examine effects of agile software development on individual performance metrics, such as developers' level of satisfaction, motivation, or perceived stress at work.

Finally, team effectiveness research provided a broad spectrum of explanations improving the understanding of the agile development paradigm. So far, there are only a few studies leveraging this body of knowledge. Future studies may analyze other teamwork mechanisms and their effect on the performance in agile software development teams. Combining these findings with the results of this study may advance the understanding of agile software development even further.

Chapter 7
Conclusion

Many software companies follow an agile development approach today (VersionOne 2012). Originally introduced as a counter-movement from the plan-driven approach, agile software development is mainstream today (West et al. 2010). The approach gained its popularity through the postulation of the Agile Manifesto and the persuasiveness of its four core values in 2001 (Fowler 2002). These agile values are reflected in numerous development methods and practices which were introduced by experienced consultants in the end of the 1990s and beginning 2000s and later labeled as "agile methods". Scrum (Schwaber and Beedle 2002) and Extreme Programming (Beck 2000) are the most popular today. Scrum is a team-based development framework, often combined with Extreme Programming development practices shaping the daily implementation work of individual developers, such as pair programming, automated testing, or code review. Despite its popularity, a theoretical understanding of agile software development is still in its infancy (Dingsøyr et al. 2012; Dybå and Dingsøyr 2008).

This study addressed this research gap. It examined the impact of agile software development practices on the performance of development teams. First, the study examined the team performance concept. Existing performance concepts and measurement approaches found in previous studies were compared with insights from 15 project leaders at SAP SE. The findings led to the development of a new measurement instrument to assess the performance of agile software development teams. Then, consulting and scholarly literature on agile software development were analyzed. The gained insights were combined with existing theories, concepts, and measurement methods provided in team effectiveness research (i.e. Cohen and Bailey 1997; Kozlowski and Bell 2003; Mathieu et al. 2008). Drawing on team adaptation theory (Burke et al. 2006b; Rosen et al. 2011) and knowledge on team confidence (Bandura 1986; Gully et al. 2002), a theoretical research model was derived. Agile software development was proposed to not only directly influence the performance of software development teams, but simultaneously improve team confidence, shared mental models, and backup behavior of software development

© Springer International Publishing Switzerland 2016
C. Schmidt, *Agile Software Development Teams*, Progress in IS,
DOI 10.1007/978-3-319-26057-0_7

teams. The positive impact of backup behavior on team performance was suggested to be more pronounced in teams facing high technological uncertainty.

The research model was tested with data from 81 software development teams at SAP SE. From all teams, developers, Scrum Masters, and Product Owner were invited to answer role-specific questionnaires. While developers and Scrum Masters rated the adoption intensity of agile software development and the studied teamwork mechanisms, the Product Owners assessed the team performance. The collected data was analyzed with regression and structural equation modeling techniques. First, the inner structure of the performance construct was examined. Then, the explanatory power of shared mental model, backup behavior, and team confidence for team performance were tested.

The study provides support for the theorized mediation effect on team performance through these teamwork mechanisms. First, the use of agile development practices leads to higher team confidence. This finding is relevant as more confident teams were shown to be more determined to achieve their goals, set higher goals, and exert more effort when facing difficulties (Gully et al. 2002). Hence, this study finds team confidence as a determining factor of team performance in agile software development teams. Second, the study results show that agile software development leads to better common understanding in the teams (shared mental models) and more intense backup behavior among team members. Finally, team backup behavior was found to be more relevant for team performance in case of high technological uncertainty.

This study is a response to the frequent calls for more theory-based, industrial case studies on agile software development (Dingsøyr et al. 2012; Dybå and Dingsøyr 2008). First, it advances the understanding of the performance concept of software development teams. Second, it contributes to the still limited theoretical understanding of agile software development and its impact on team performance. The demonstrated hidden teamwork mechanisms provide prior unrecognized theoretical explanations for the alleged performance effect. These insights are expected to help decision makers in industry to make more rational decisions about the use of agile software development practices. In addition, the study introduced new measurement instruments to assess the performance of software development teams as well as shared mental models and backup behavior. Future studies should build on the provided insights and examine further teamwork aspects to advance the understanding of agile software development.

Appendix A
Appendix

A.1 Agile Information Systems Development: Literature Review

Section 2.3 provides an overview of existing studies on agile software development in the *software engineering literature (SE)* as well as the *information systems research (IS)* literature streams. While there are various review articles providing a comprehensive overview of the SE field (see Table 2.5 on page 31), no review article exists summarizing the IS research literature. Hence, this study reviewed the central IS outlets for studies on agile software development published between 2000 and 2014.

Table A.1 provides an overview of 72 articles found as a result of the structured literature analysis. The table includes the *research focus*, the *research context*, the used *research methods*, as well as the *theoretical foundations* of each article. The list of the reviewed IS outlets are listed at the bottom of the table.

© Springer International Publishing Switzerland 2016
C. Schmidt, *Agile Software Development Teams*, Progress in IS,
DOI 10.1007/978-3-319-26057-0

Table A.1 Publications on agile software development in IS research

Publication		Research focus					Context			Research method						Foundation
Author(s)	Outlet	Agility	Adoption	Adaptation	Project mgmt.	Teamwork	Distributed	Large-scale	Maintenance	Case study	Survey	Experiment	Simulation	Lit. review	Conceptual	Theory or model
Batra et al. (2006)	AMCIS			x			x								x	
Bonner et al. (2010)	AMCIS	x									x					Theory of innovation diffusion
Brown et al. (2004)	AMCIS	x													x	
Cho et al. (2006)	AMCIS					x	x	x		x						
Dabrowski et al. (2011)	AMCIS		x				x	x				x				
Elbanna and Murray (2009)	AMCIS					x				x						Theory of collective mindfulness
Gregory et al. (2013)	AMCIS				x					x						Theory of organizational controls
Hummel and Rosenkranz (2013)	AMCIS					x					x					Team input-process-output model
Jain and Meso (2004)	AMCIS					x									x	Theory of complex adaptive systems
Karekar et al. (2011)	AMCIS		x							x						
Russo et al. (2013)	AMCIS		x							x						Theory of innovation diffusion
Sun and Schmidt (2013)	AMCIS				x										x	
Xu and Cao (2006)	AMCIS				x										x	Theory of coordination
Yang et al. (2009)	AMCIS				x					x	x					Leadership theory
Bajec et al. (2004)	ECIS	x								x				x	x	
Hummel and Rosenkranz (2013)	ECIS					x					x				x	Organizational communication theory; media naturalness theory
Keaveney and Conboy (2006)	ECIS				x					x						

Study	Venue	Theory
Kude et al. (2014)	ECIS	Team adaptation theory
Lawrence and Rodriguez (2012)	ECIS	Lasswell value framework
McAvoy et al. (2006)	ECIS	Agency theory
McAvoy and Butler (2006)	ECIS	Theory of collective mindfulness
Nagle et al. (2011)	ECIS	Theory of innovation diffusion
Overhage and Schlauderer (2012)	ECIS	
Spohrer et al. (2013)	ECIS	
Tanner and Wallace (2012)	ECIS	Theory of practice
Vidgen and Wang (2006)	ECIS	Theory of complex adaptive systems
Wang and Conboy (2009)	ECIS	Theory of complex adaptive systems
Wang et al. (2008)	ECIS	
Wang and Vidgen (2007)	ECIS	Theory of complex adaptive systems
Wang et al. (2011)	ECIS	
Cao et al. (2013)	EJIS	Adaptive structuration theory
Cao et al. (2009)	EJIS	Adaptive structuration theory
Fitzgerald et al. (2006)	EJIS	
Karlsson and Ågerfalk (2009)	EJIS	Activity theory
Lyytinen and Rose (2006)	EJIS	IT innovation and org. learning model
Mangalaraj et al. (2009)	EJIS	Theory of innovation diffusion
Maruping et al. (2009b)	EJIS	Transactive memory systems theory
McAvoy and Butler (2009)	EJIS	Group think theory
Port and Bui (2009)	EJIS	Home ground theory
Sarker et al. (2009)	EJIS	
Berger and Beynon-Davies (2008)	ICIS	Theory of innovation diffusion

(continued)

A.1 (continued)

Publication		Research focus				Context				Research method						Foundation
Author(s)	Outlet	Agility	Adoption	Adaptation	Project mgmt.	Teamwork	Distributed	Large-scale	Maintenance	Case study	Survey	Experiment	Simulation	Lit. review	Conceptual	Theory or model
Lee et al. (2010)	ICIS				x		x				x					Organizational ambidexterity theory
Li and Maedche (2012)	ICIS					x	x			x						Theory of coordination
Lohan et al. (2010)	ICIS				x					x					x	Beyond budgeting model
Schlauderer and Overhage (2013)	ICIS		x								x					Theory of innovation diffusion
Schmidt et al. (2013)	ICIS					x									x	Team adaptation theory
Zheng et al. (2007)	ICIS	x													x	Organizational improvisation theory
Baskerville and Pries-Heje (2004)	ISJ	x								x						
Berger and Beynon-Davies (2009)	ISJ							x		x						
Charaf et al. (2013)	ISJ				x	x				x						Theory of language
Cram and Brohman (2013)	ISJ				x					x					x	Control theory
McAvoy et al. (2013)	ISJ					x				x						Theory of collective mindfulness
Persson et al. (2012)	ISJ				x		x			x						Control theory
Wang et al. (2012)	ISJ		x							x						Innovation assimilation theory
Zheng et al. (2011)	ISJ	x					x	x		x						Organizational improvisation theory
Austin and Devin (2009)	ISR		x					x						x	x	
Conboy (2009)	ISR	x												x	x	
Harris et al. (2009)	ISR				x					x						Control theory

Study	Journal														Theory
Maruping et al. (2009a)	ISR								x						Control theory
Ramesh et al. (2012)	ISR	x				x			x					x	Theory of ambidexterity
Sarker and Sarker (2009)	ISR	x				x			x					x	
Vidgen and Wang (2009)	ISR	x				x			x					x	Theory of complex adaptive systems
Goh et al. (2013)	JAIS			x			x		x						Control theory
Rosenkranz et al. (2013)	JIT			x					x						Speech act theory
Edberg et al. (2012)	JMIS	x					x	x	x						
Fruhling and Vreede (2006)	JMIS	x							x						
Keith et al. (2013)	JMIS	x							x						Theory on interdependence and coord.
Baiijepally et al. (2009)	MISQ	x		x							x				
Lee and Xia (2010)	MISQ			x					x	x					Social identity and self-categor. theory
Strode et al. (2011)	PACIS			x					x					x	Theory of coordination
van der Vyver et al. (2003)	PACIS	x							x						Theory of complex adaptive systems
Ralph and Narros (2013)	PACIS	x							x						Theory of complex adaptive systems
Total 2000–2014	72	18	6	12	18	11	5	1	50	11	2	1	2	28	
		18%	6%	12%	18%	11%	5%	1%	50%	11%	2%	1%	2%	28%	

AMCIS - American Conference on Information Systems, *ECIS* - European Conference on Information Systems, *EJIS* - European Journal of Information Systems, *ICIS* - International Conference on Information Systems, *ISJ* - Information Systems Journal, *ISR* - Information Systems Research, *JAIS* - Journal of the Association for Information Systems, *JIT* - Journal of Information Technology, *JMIS* - Journal of Management Information Systems, *MISQ* - Management Information Systems Quarterly, *PACIS* - Pacific Asia Conference on Information Systems

A.2 Team Performance Interviews: Interview Guideline

Einführung
(5 min)

– Ziel der Studie

– Garantie von Anonymität und Vertraulichkeit

– Zustimmung zur Aufzeichnung des Interviews

Hintergrund
(5 min)

– Position bei SAP

– Anzahl Teams im Verantwortungsbereich

– Produkt und Technologie

Explorativ
(25 min)

Allgemein

– Sind Unterschiede in der Leistung der Teams feststellbar?

– Woran werden diese festgemacht? (nicht: was beeinflusst diese!)

Teamspezifisch

Beim Vergleich des besten Teams und dem Team mit dem größten Verbesserungspotential:

– Woran kann man die unterschiedliche Leistung feststellen?

– Was sind die zentralen Leistungsindikatoren?

Gibt es eine Situation, in der ein Team als besonders leistungsstark/-schwach aufgefallen ist:

– Woran war dies erkennbar?

Über das letzte Jahr hinweg gesehen ...

– Gab es Leistungsunterschiede der Teams?

– Woran konnte man diese festmachen?

Scrum-Einführung

Wenn man die Teams vor/nach der Scrum-Einführung vergleicht:

– Hat sich die Leistungsdefinition verändert? Worin?

– Gab es unterschiedliche Leistungsdimensionen?

– Waren unterschiedliche Aspekte gewichtiger/weniger wichtig?

Methoden zur Leistungsbewertung

– Wird die Leistung der Teams offiziell bewertet?

– Wie läuft dies ab? / Werden Tools eingesetzt?

Konfirma-torisch
(10 min)

Es wurden Erfolgsindikatoren aus der Literatur abgeleitet:

– Softwarequalität; Dienstleistungsqualität des Team

– Zuverlässigkeit; Innovationsfähigkeit; Mehrwert des Team

– Verhalten; Einstellung; Zufriedenheit des Teams

Wie relevant sind diese bei der Leistungsbestimmung?

A.3 Survey: Data Collection Process

1. **Vorbereitung der Erhebung**

   a. Erstkontakt
   Telefon/Mail: Anfrage zur Teilnahme
   b. Absage oder Zusage
   Ansprechpartner und Termin festhalten

2. **Datenerhebung: 30 min Meeting mit Team**

   a. Checkliste

      i. Süßigkeiten in Korb; Gewinnspiel-Box; Lose; Ampeln
      ii. Schilder (zufällig vorsortiert); Fragebögen; Stifte

   b. Team Meeting

      1. Ansprache
      *"Herzlich willkommen, wir freuen uns, dass ihr an der Studie teilnehmt.
      Wir führen eine Studie zu agiler Softwareentwicklung mit 80 Teams bei SAP durch. Hierzu
      haben wir unterschiedliche Fragebögen für Scrum Master und Entwickler."*
      2. Scrum Master
      "Wer ist der Scrum Master?"
      Scrum Master erhält Schild, Fragebogen und Stift
      3. Entwickler
      Alle anderen Teammitglieder erhalten einen Entwickler-Fragebogen und Stifte.
      *"Auf der zweiten Seite gibt es eine Besonderheit zu beachten. Hierzu erhält jeder ein
      Schild.*
      (Schild hochheben, siehe Abb. 4.1 auf Seite 72). *Auf diesem findet ihr eure persönliche
      Nummer.*
      Auch auf der Rückseite ist diese nochmals zu sehen. (zeigen)
      Außerdem findet ihr für 3 Kollegen A, B und C im Raum jeweils eine Nummer.
      Bitte tragt auf der zweiten Seite des Fragebogens (Fragebogen hochhalten) *eure Nummer
      und die Nummern dieser drei Kollegen ein. Ihr findet einige Fragen zu euch und diesen
      Kollegen.*
      Es wäre super, wenn ihr bitte die Nummern jetzt eintragt, die auf den Schildern stehen."
      Anzahl Entwickler ermitteln; entsprechenden Schildersatz zufällig verteilen
      Fragebögen austeilen mit Stiften
      4. Süßigkeiten verteilen
      5. Beginn Umfrage *"Dies ist kein Schultest, es gibt keine richtigen oder falschen Antworten.
      Wir freuen uns über ehrlichen Antworten.*
      Rückfragen bitte direkt stellen."
      6. Team füllt Frabebögen aus
      7. Fragebögen einsammeln

         a. Check, ob alle Bögen eingesammelt wurden
         b. Check, ob alle Nummern eingetragen wurden

      8. Scrum Master erhält USB-Ampel mit Installationsanweisung
      9. Scrum Master füllt Gewinnspiellos aus und wirft es in die Gewinnspielbox
      10. Danksagung an Team für Teilnahme an der Studie

3. **Nachbereitung**

  i.. Stifte einsammeln
  ii. Fragebögen eineindeutig stempeln zur Zuordnung bei Transkription
  iii. Teambogen ausfüllen
  iv. Fragebögen abheften in Ordner
  v. Doppelte Transkription

A.4   Survey: Overview

AgileSE Research Study – Study Overview

In a joint research project between the University of Mannheim and SAP, we conduct a study on the impact of agile software engineering *(Scrum, pair programming, code reviews, automated testing, iterative development, continuous quality assurance, etc.)*. The study is carried out by Christoph Schmidt. He is a PhD student at the Chair of General Management and Information Systems ('Wirtschaftsinformatik') of Prof. Dr. Heinzl. Further, he works half time for SAP in the "AgileSE Research Project" led by Dr. Juergen Heymann (PI COO Development Methods).

During the last years, many software development teams at SAP have started using Scrum and have participated in the agile software engineering training program. In general, SAP has chosen a clear direction towards agile software engineering with a strong focus on team work. Our research seeks to better understand the underlying drivers of team-centric agile software development.

Study concept

We conduct a team-based study for which we invite (area) product owners, scrum masters and developers of about 60-70 SAP development teams. The scrum master and the developers allow an intra-team perspective, while the area product owner provides an external perspective on a team. During a 30 minute meeting, we would like to ask developers and the scrum master to fill out a paper-based questionnaire which covers aspects from agile software engineering (see below). Our pretests show that it takes about 20 min to complete the questionnaire.

Team meeting (30 min)	**Developers** answer the questionnaire „*AgileSE Research Study – questions for developers*".	
	• Part 1	Adoption intensity of agile development practices *(Pair programming[1]/Code review[2], automated testing[3], …)*
	• Part 2	Mutual assistance[4] and common understanding in the team[5]
	• Part 3	Team leadership[6], Knowledge distribution in the team
	• Part 4	Perceived impact of agile software engineering Areas of improvement in the team
	Scrum Master answers the questionnaire "*AgileSE Research Study – questions for scrum masters*".	
	• Part 1	Adoption intensity of various Scrum aspects[7]
	• Part 2	Iterative and collaborative work mode (central for agile SE)
	• Part 3	Task-specific knowledge in the team
	• Part 4	Team context[8]
Area Product Owner Meeting	**Area Product Owner** answers "*AgileSE Research Study – questions for (area) product owners*".	
	• Part 1	Software quality
	• Part 2	Software delivery process
	• Part 3	Team task characteristics
	• Part 4	Overall effectiveness of the team

Exemplary questions

[1] How much of your code do you develop with a programming partner?
[2] How much of your new code is reviewed by at least one colleague?
[3] For how much of your new code do you write automated tests?
[4] We regularly provide feedback to each other on work results. *(agreement scale)*
[5] We agree what needs to be done before a task is considered 'done'. *(agreement scale)*
[6] *The product owner is clear and explicit about what he/she wants our team to do. (agreement scale)*
[7] The team rather reduces the scope than delaying deadlines. *(agreement scale)*
[8] What is the sprint length?

Results and outcomes

Team Report

All participating teams receive a **team report** with the aggregated answers of all developers in the team after we will have finished the study. In the team report, the team members' answers are aggregated and reported in comparison to the answers of all peer teams participating in the study. The team might jointly discuss this report in a retrospective.

Second, all teams participating in the study will receive a **"USB traffic light"** which can be used to display the status of the team's automated tests on the continuous integration server.

Lottery

Third, all teams will participate in a **lottery**. Two winner teams can choose to be either invited for a **wine tasting** or a **go-cart team event**.

Studienreport

Finally, we will summarize our research findings in **study report** which will contain insights from all participating teams. We seek to better understand the impact of agile software engineering in various work context of software development teams.

Data privacy

Participation in the study is obviously voluntary and anonymous. All answers will be made anonymous. The area product owner or the team's managers will not see the answers of the team. The team will not see the answers of the area product owner. In summary, our study report will not allow insights into the answers of single teams.

The study has been approved by the **data protection officer** of SAP and the **German workers' council**. Complying with their requirements, we are only allowed to conduct the study with **at least four developers plus a scrum master** of each participating team.

> **It would be great if your team would participate in our study and thus support our research. Thank you in advance.**

Christoph Schmidt   christoph.schmidt01@sap.com
(d056196)   christoph.schmidt@uni-mannheim.de

A.5   Survey: Developer Questionnaire

AgileSE Research Study – questions for Developers

In a joined research project with the University of Mannheim, we are conducting a study on the impact of **agile software engineering** at SAP. The study is conducted by Christoph Schmidt, who is a half-time employee at SAP and a PhD student at the University of Mannheim at the Institute for Enterprise Systems (Prof. Dr. Heinzl).

We invite your team to participate in the study and kindly ask you to fill out this questionnaire, which will take about 20 minutes. For the purpose of this study, we define the development team as 'developers & scrum master'.

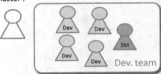

We would highly appreciate to get your honest opinion on our questions. There are no right or wrong answers. Your thoughtful answers will not only help the success of the study, but will also improve the **AgileSE trainings** at SAP. For methodological reasons, some questions seem to cover similar aspects from different perspectives.

 We offer a **team report** for your team with the team's aggregated answers compared to all participating teams after the study is completed.

and   *Lottery*

 Every team will receive a **team traffic light**. Further, <u>two of the participating teams</u> will win a **cart race** or a **wine tasting** team event as a thank you.

*Study disclaimer: The survey has been approved by the <u>German SAP workers' council</u> and <u>SAP's data protection officer</u>. We will not pass any data to management that would allow insights into the answers of a single team. **The data is ONLY used for research purposes** and we guarantee to work confidentially with the data.*

Christoph Schmidt   christoph.schmidt01@sap.com & christoph.schmidt@uni-mannheim.de
Prof. Dr. Armin Heinzl   heinzl@uni-mannheim.de

How many years of experience do you have in professional software development in total? *(please do NOT answer if you do not feel ok to do so)*	☐ <1 year ☐ 1-3 years	☐ 4-6 years ☐ 7-10 years	☐ 11-15 years ☐ > 15 years
How long have you been working in this team? *(please do NOT answer if you do not feel ok to do so)*	☐ <3 months ☐ 3-6 months	☐ 6-9 months ☐ 9-12 months	☐ 1-3 years ☐ > 3 years
How much of your work time is development time? *(understanding requirements, coding, testing, integrating, bug fixing, … activities directly related to software dev.)*		%	
I agree that my answers are included in a team report.		☐ yes	☐ no

In case of less than 6 respondents we are not allowed to provide a team report without your explicit permission. *(SAP data privacy policy)*

AgileSE Research Study

SAP · UNIVERSITY OF MANNHEIM · InES

Part 1/4: *Please rate how much you use the following agile development practices.*

	0%-9%	10%-19%	20%-29%	30%-39%	40%-49%	50%-59%	60%-69%	70%-79%	80%-89%	90%-100%

Pair programming *"programming with a partner, while one is the coding driver and the other is the observer"*

How much of your **code** do you develop with a programming partner?										
How much of your **coding time** do you work with a programming partner?										
With how many of your **team members** do you pair program regularly?										

Refactoring *"process of changing a software system in such a way that it does not alter the external behavior of the code yet improves its internal structure"*

How much of your **development time** do you roughly spend ...

... **simplifying existing code** without changing its functionality?										
... **identifying and eliminating redundancies** in the software code?										
... **improving the code quality?**										

Automated and manual testing

For how much of *your* new code do *you* write **automated tests** *before* writing the productive code *(test-driven development)* ?										
For how much of *your* **new code** do *you* write **automated tests** at all *(before or after writing the productive code)* ?										
For how many of *your* **new tests** do *you* use **test isolation** *(test double, mocking, ...)* ?										
How much of *your* **new functionality** is regularly tested with **automated integration tests?**										
How much of *your* **new functionality** is regularly tested with **automated UI tests** *(e.g. selenium tests)* ?										
How much of *your* **new functionality** is regularly tested with **manual exploratory tests?**										
For how much of *your* **new functionality** do you run **acceptance tests** *(e.g. defined by the product owner)* ?										

Code review

How much of your **new code** is **reviewed** by at least one colleague?										
How much of your **modified code** is **reviewed** by at least one colleague?										
How many of your **team members** regularly review code you have developed?										

AgileSE Research Study

Part 2/4

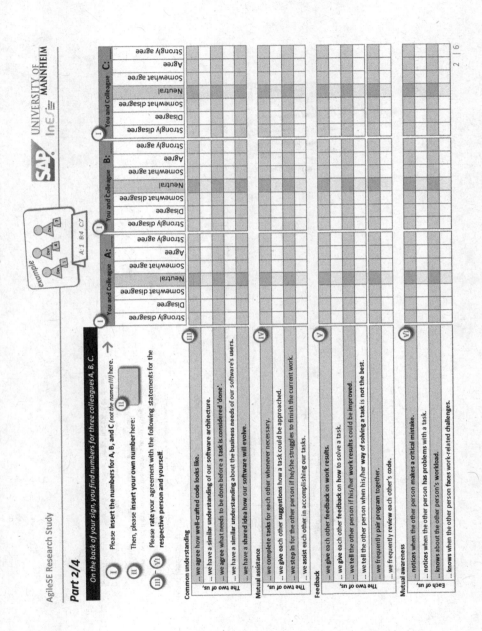

SAP | UNIVERSITY OF MANNHEIM | InES

On the back of your sign, you find numbers for three colleagues A, B, C.

(I) Please insert the numbers for A, B, and C *(not the names(II))* here.

(II) Then, please insert your own number here:

(III) – (VI) Please rate your agreement with the following statements for the respective person and yourself.

example

A: 1 B: 4 C: 7

Common understanding

(III) The two of us,
... we agree how well-crafted code looks like.
... we have a similar understanding of our software architecture.
... we agree what needs to be done before a task is considered 'done'.
... we have a similar understanding about the business needs of our software's users.
... we have a shared idea how our software will evolve.

Mutual assistance

(IV) The two of us,
... we complete tasks for each other whenever necessary.
... we give each other suggestions how a task could be approached.
... we step in for the other person if he/she struggles to finish the current work.
... we assist each other in accomplishing our tasks.

Feedback

(V) The two of us,
... we give each other feedback on work results.
... we give each other feedback on how to solve a task.
... we tell the other person if his/her work results could be improved.
... we tell the other person when his/her way of solving a task is not the best.
... we frequently pair program together.
... we frequently review each other's code.

Mutual awareness

(VI) Each of us,
... notices when the other person makes a critical mistake.
... notices when the other person has problems with a task.
... knows about the other person's workload.
... knows when the other person faces work-related challenges.

You and Colleague A: / B: / C:

Columns (for each colleague A, B, C):
Strongly disagree | Disagree | Somewhat disagree | Neutral | Somewhat agree | Agree | Strongly agree

AgileSE Research Study

UNIVERSITY OF MANNHEIM
SAP. InES

Part 3/4: *Please rate the following team work aspects.*

please consider the
whole team *now!*
(Developers & Scrum master)

Team performance

	Strongly disagree	Disagree	Somewhat disagree	Neither agree or disagree	Somewhat agree	Agree	Strongly agree
Recently, our team seems to be having **problems** in its level of performance and accomplishments.							
Those who receive or use our software often have **complaints about our work.**							
The software quality provided by our team is **improving over time.**							
Critical quality errors occur **frequently** in our team.							
Others in the company who interact with us often **complain** about **how our team functions.**							

Team leadership

The team's key stakeholder *(in a Scrum context: the **product owner**)* ...

	Strongly disagree	Disagree	Somewhat disagree	Neither agree or disagree	Somewhat agree	Agree	Strongly agree
... is **clear and explicit about what** he/she wants our team to do *(product vision, backlog specification).*							
... keeps a **watchful eye** on how the team is **progressing.**							
... shows that he/she cares a great deal **about us** being a good team.							
... goes new ways by **asking** team members for **ideas** and **advice.**							
... **alerts** the team when he/she notices **things that could be done** better.							

AgileSE Research Study

Continued

**please consider the
whole team!**
(Developers & Scrum master)

Knowledge in the team

	Strongly disagree	Disagree	Somewhat disagree	Neither agree or disagree	Somewhat agree	Agree	Strongly agree
Each member of my team **has special expertise**.							
I **know which** team members have **expertise** in specific areas.							
Different team members are **responsible for expertise** in different areas.							
The **expertise** of several different team members **is needed** to complete our deliverables.							
I am **comfortable** accepting work suggestions from other team members.							
I am **confident relying** on the information that other **team members** bring into discussions.							
I **do not** have much **faith** in other members' **"expertise"**.							
I **trust** that other members' **task-related knowledge** is credible.							
Our team works together in a **well-coordinated** fashion.							
We **accomplish** our tasks **smoothly** and **efficiently.**							
Our team has very **few misunderstandings** about what to do.							
There is **often confusion** in our team about how we will accomplish our tasks.							

Team cohesion

Please indicate how you would describe your team.

Please tick one box per line.

close							distant
cooperative							conflictual
integrating							fragmenting
team-oriented							self-oriented

AgileSE Research Study

SAP. InEɼ UNIVERSITY OF MANNHEIM

Continued

**please consider the
whole team!**
(Developers & Scrum master)

Scale: Strongly disagree | Disagree | Somewhat disagree | Neither agree or disagree | Somewhat agree | Agree | Strongly agree

Team internal support

The team members **help and support** each other as best they can.

If **conflicts** come up, they are easily and quickly **resolved.**

Discussions and controversies are **conducted constructively.**

Suggestions and contributions of team members are **respected.**

Our team is able to **reach consensus** regarding important issues.

Suggestions and contributions of team members are **discussed and further developed.**

Team relationship

The people on this team **get on my nerves.**

There is a lot of **unpleasantness** among people on our team.

Dealing with the members of this team often leaves me **feeling irritated and frustrated.**

Often, I am **disappointed** with the other **members** of this team.

Time pressure

I have **too much work and too little time** to do it.

I find this organization **a relaxed place to work.**

I often have to deal with **work-related problems in my off hours.**

I feel like **I never have a day off.**

Many employees at my level get **"burned out"** by the demands of their jobs in this organization.

AgileSE Research Study

SAP | InES | UNIVERSITY OF MANNHEIM

Part 4/4: *Please rate which benefits you see in the context of AgileSE.*

Impact of AgileSE

Only if you have participated in the AgileSE training

To what extent (%) have the following aspects changed since the last release that was **developed without AgileSE?** *(before the AgileSE training)*

	%
Number of reported defects	
Rework efforts	%

e.g. +20% or -50% (rough estimates)

To what extent have the following aspects changed since the last release that was **not developed with AgileSE?** (before the AgileSE training)

	Got worse drastically	Got worse	Did not change	Got better	Improved significantly
Delivered feature scope per development cycle *(in a Scrum context: in a sprint)*					
Internal software quality *(code readability, understandability, testability, maintainability)*					
External software quality *(functionality, usability, reliability, accuracy, performance)*					
Customer satisfaction with the software quality we deliver					
My work stress at the end of the development cycle *(in a Scrum context: end of a sprint)*					
My work stress at the end of the release *(before RTC)*					

Which of the following improvement areas would help your team the most to perform better?

*Please indicate the **three top aspects.** Either choose from the options or add new ones.*

☐ Better programming skills in the team   ☐ Better communication within the team   ☐ Better work equipment
☐ Better testing skills in the team   ☐ Better communication with our POs   ☐ Better development tools
☐ Better software architecture   ☐ Better communication with our customers/users   ☐ Better work environment
☐ Better atmosphere among team members   ☐ Better communication with other teams   ☐ More motivated team members

☐ _____   ☐ _____

Thank you very much for your contribution!

6 | 6

A.6   Survey: Scrum Master Questionnaire

AgileSE Research Study – questions for Scrum Masters

In a joined research project with the University of Mannheim, we are conducting a study on the impact of **agile software engineering** at SAP. The study is conducted by Christoph Schmidt, who is a half-time employee at SAP and a PhD student at the University of Mannheim at the Institute for Enterprise Systems (Prof. Dr. Heinzl).

We invite your team to participate in the study and kindly ask you to fill out this questionnaire, which will take about 20 minutes. For the purpose of this study, we define the development team as 'developers & scrum master'.

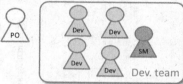

As part of the study, we invite **you as the Scrum Master** to answer central questions for your team which do not need to be answered by all members.

We would highly appreciate to get your honest opinion on our questions. There are no right or wrong answers. Your thoughtful answers will not only help the success of the study, but will also improve the **AgileSE trainings** at SAP. For methodological reasons, some questions seem to cover similar aspects from different perspectives.

   We offer a **team report** for your team with the aggregated answers of all developers compared to all participating teams after the study is completed. As you are the only person of your team answering this Scrum master questionnaire, your answers will not be included in to the team report for data privacy.

and

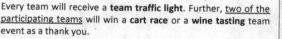   Every team will receive a **team traffic light**. Further, <u>two of the participating teams</u> will win a **cart race** or a **wine tasting** team event as a thank you.

Lottery

*Study disclaimer: The survey has been approved by the <u>German SAP workers' council</u> and <u>SAP's data protection officer</u>. We will not pass any data to management that would allow insights into the answers of a single team. **The data is ONLY used for research purposes** and we guarantee to work confidentially with the data.*

Christoph Schmidt   christoph.schmidt01@sap.com & christoph.schmidt@uni-mannheim.de
Prof. Dr. Armin Heinzl   heinzl@uni-mannheim.de

Team background

Team name		
How many people work on the team? *(Developers & Scrum master)*	_____ members	
How many people have joined or left the team during the last 12 months?	_____ members have joined the team.	
	_____ members have left the team.	
More than 80% of the team is located in ...	□ Same room	□ Same location
	□ Same floor	□ Same time zone
	□ Same building	□ Different time zones
For how long has the team been working in Scrum mode?	_____ years	□ We do not use Scrum at all.
What is the sprint length?	_____ weeks	
How much time has passed since the team has participated in the AgileSE training?	_____ months	□ We have not participated in the training at all.
How often is the team's software released (RTC)?	_____ months	
Which programming language(s) does the team mainly use?	□ ABAP	□ Java Script / HTML5
	□ Java	□ _____
	□ C / C++ / C#	□
What type of software does the team develop?	□ Platform	□ Mobile Apps
	□ Applications	□ _____
How much time did the team roughly spend on the following activities during the last three months?	____ % Development of completely new functionality	
	____ % Extension of existing functionality	
	____ % Major redesign of existing functionalities	
	____ % Small enhancements & mainly bug fixes	
Does the team use a peer code review system?	□ No, we do not use one.	
If so, which one?	□ Yes, we use 'Review board'.	
	□ Yes, we use 'Git Gerrit'. □ Yes, we use _____	
If the team also does offline code reviews, how many reviews are not documented in the system at all?	_____ % of our code reviews are offline.	
What are the main CSS application components the team works on? e.g. BC-XI-CON-ABA-HTTP or CA-GTF-PCF-SRV-SAM	_____	
	_____	
	_____	
How much new code did the team roughly add during the last three months *(rough estimate, e.g. 1:5 or 1:1000)*	_____ : _____	
	new code *existing code*	
With how many teams does the team currently work together on its product(s)?	□ Our team works alone on its product(s).	
	_____ other teams work with us on our product(s).	
What is the rough number of customers of the team's software?	_____ internal customers (other SAP teams)	
	_____ external customers (SAP external organizations)	

AgileSE Research Study

SAP UNIVERSITY OF MANNHEIM InES

Part 1/4: *Scrum* in *agile software development teams*

Iterative Meetings

At the beginning of a development cycle *(e.g. Sprint)* ...

... our **key stakeholder** *(in a Scrum context: our product owner)* always **explains new user stories.**

... we always create a **list of prioritized tasks** to work on.

... we always **estimate** our tasks and make commitments.

At the end of a development cycle *(e.g. Sprint)* ...

... we always have a **review meeting** with our key stakeholder *(in Scrum: our product owner)* to demonstrate new features.

... we always present our progress in a **live demo** *(e.g. to the product owner)*.

Iterative Development

We implement our software in **short iterations.**

The team rather **reduces the scope** than delaying deadlines.

We always **start** development tasks according to the key stakeholder's **priority** *(in a Scrum context: our product owner)*.

At the end of every development cycle, our code **meets product quality requirements.**

We have time-boxed **daily standup** meetings in which all team members participate.

Retrospectives

After every development cycle, we have **retrospective meetings.**

We regularly **reflect** on how we perform our tasks.

We regularly **consider** potential **domains of improvements.**

We regularly develop **action plans** to improve our work.

	Strongly disagree	Disagree	Somewhat disagree	Neither agree or disagree	Somewhat agree	Agree	Strongly agree

AgileSE Research Study

UNIVERSITY OF MANNHEIM
InES

SAP.

Continued: **Scrum** *in agile software development teams*

	Strongly disagree	Disagree	Somewhat disagree	Neither agree or disagree	Somewhat agree	Agree	Strongly agree

Continuous Integration

Developers **integrate** new or modified code into our existing code base on a **daily basis.**

We **combine** new code with existing code on a **daily basis.**

Our team has **dedicated "integration phases"** during which we integrate new or modified **code of different developers.**

Coding Standards

We have a set of agreed upon **coding standards** in this team.

Members of this team have a **shared understanding** of how code is to be written.

Everyone on this team **uses** his/her **own standards** for coding.

Code Ownership

Anyone on this team **is allowed to change** any part of existing code at any time.

Members of this team **feel comfortable changing any part** of the existing code at any time.

If anyone wants to change a piece of code, they **need the permission** of the individual(s) that coded it.

AgileSE Research Study

Part 2/4: *Iterative team work* of agile teams

The model on the right shows six activities (a–f) that every software development team pursues independent of the used development methodology.

Please answer the following questions regarding these activities.

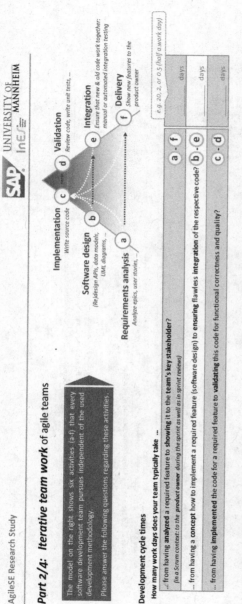

Implementation
Write source code

Software design
(Re)design APIs, data models, UML diagrams, …

Requirements analysis
Analyze epics, user stories, …

Validation
Review code, write unit tests, …

Integration
Ensure that new & old code work together; manual or automated integration testing

Delivery
Show new features to the product owner

Development cycle times

How many work days does your team typically take …

… from having **analyzed** a required feature to **showing** it to the team's key stakeholder?
(in a Scrum context: to the product owner during the sprint as well as in sprint reviews) **a – f**

… from having a **concept** how to implement a required feature (software design) to **ensuring flawless integration** of the respective code? **b – e**

… from having **implemented** the code for a required feature to **validating** this code for functional correctness and quality? **c – d**

For which time horizon does your team typically …

… **analyze** requirements **upfront**, *so that developers know exactly what functionality needs to be developed during this time period?* **a – c**

… **specify** the software design upfront, *so that developers have a concept how to implement the software during this time period ?* **b – c**

After how many development days does the team typically …

… **validate** new or modified code for **functional correctness and quality?** **d – c**

… **integrate** new or modified code into the **existing code base?** **e – c**

… **show** new or modified code to the **team's key stakeholder?**
(in a Scrum context: to the product owner during the sprint as well as in sprint reviews) **f – c**

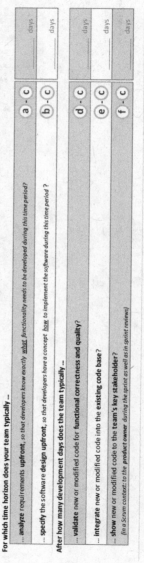

e.g. 20, 2, or 0.5 (half a work day)

days

days

days

days

days

days

days

days

AgileSE Research Study

Continued: *Collaborative team work* of agile teams

SAP
InEr≡ UNIVERSITY OF MANNHEIM

Requirements analysis
Analyze epics, user stories, ...

(a) — (b) — (c) — (d) — (e) — (f)

Software design
(Re)design APIs, data models, UML diagrams, ...

Implementation
Write source code

Validation
Review code, write unit tests, ...

Integration
Ensure that new & old code work together: manual or automated integration testing

Delivery
Show new features to the product owner

Stakeholder interaction

How many team members have **analyzed requirements** during the last six months?
(e.g., analyzing epics/user stories with the product owner to understand requirements)

⌐→ When analyzing **one typical requirement**, how many team members usually work together to make contributions?

(a) _____ persons	
(a) _____ persons	

How many team members have **shown features** to the team's key stakeholder during the last six months?
(In a Scrum context: to the product owner during the sprint as well as in sprint reviews)

⌐→ When showing **one typical feature** to the team's key stakeholder, how many team members usually work together to make contributions?

(f) _____ persons	
(f) _____ persons	

Collaboration

How many **work of team members** have done the following **activities** during the last six months?

Software (re)design	*(Re)design APIs, data models, UML diagrams, ...*	(b) _____ persons
Source code implementation	*Write source code*	(c) _____ persons
Source code validation	*Review code, write unit tests, ...*	(d) _____ persons
Source code integration	*Ensure that new & old code work together: manual or automated integration testing*	(e) _____ persons

How much **work** of these activities is regularly done through **intensive collaboration** by **at least two** team members *(rather than done by individuals working alone?)*

Software (re)design	*(Re)design APIs, data models, UML diagrams, ...*	(b) _____ %
Source code implementation	*Write source code*	(c) _____ %
Source code validation	*Review code, write unit tests, ...*	(d) _____ %
Source code integration	*Ensure that new & old code work together: manual or automated integration testing*	(e) _____ %

AgileSE Research Study

SAP | UNIVERSITY OF MANNHEIM | InE ⫶

Part 3/4: *Expertise in the team*

Current level of expertise in the team

that is necessary to accomplish the team tasks

	How much of the **expertise** that is necessary to accomplish the team tasks is currently located inside the team?									
	0% - 9%	10% - 19%	20% - 29%	30% - 39%	40% - 49%	50% - 59%	60% - 69%	70% - 79%	80% - 89%	90% - 100%
Engineering skills & technical knowledge *(coding and testing expertise, design patterns, programming language, development tools, etc.)*	☐	☐	☐	☐	☐	☐	☐	☐	☐	☐
Software architecture knowledge *of the product(s) that the team develops*	☐	☐	☐	☐	☐	☐	☐	☐	☐	☐
Application domain knowledge *(knowledge about customer processes that the software supports, supported user activities, embodied business rules, etc.)*	☐	☐	☐	☐	☐	☐	☐	☐	☐	☐

Part 4/4: Team context

Dynamism of the Environment

The following aspects changed a lot during the last six months:

... **underlying software components** we build our software on *(APIs, libraries, platforms, etc.)*

... **technology** we use *(Programming language, persistence technology, servers, etc.)*

... software **development tools** that the team depends on *(IDEs, integration tools, testing landscape, build tools, etc.)*

... **team membership** *(joining or leaving team members)*

... team manager(s) or key stakeholder *(in a Scrum context: to the product owner)*

	Strongly disagree	Disagree	Somewhat disagree	Neither agree or disagree	Somewhat agree	Agree	Strongly agree

Common Understanding in the Team

Team members have a common understanding of the **technologies** used in the development process.

Team members have a common understanding of the **development procedures.**

Team members have a common understanding of the **application domain** that the software is to support.

Team members share **one vision of the product** that the team develops.

Team Task Complexity

Concerning the last six months, the team faced tasks ...

... for which there was a **clearly known way how** to solve them.

... for which the team's **preexisting knowledge** was of great help to solve them.

... for which the team's preexisting **work procedures and practices** could be relied upon to solve them.

AgileSE Research Study

SAP. | UNIVERSITY OF MANNHEIM InES

Continued: Team work

Team Culture

	Strongly disagree	Disagree	Somewhat disagree	Neither agree or disagree	Somewhat agree	Agree	Strongly agree
If you make a mistake on this team, it is **never held against you**.							
Members of this team are able to **bring up problems** and tough issues.							
People on this team sometimes **reject others** for being different.							
It is **safe to take a risk** on this team.							
It is **difficult to ask** other members of this team for **help**.							

Team Confidence

	Strongly disagree	Disagree	Somewhat disagree	Neither agree or disagree	Somewhat agree	Agree	Strongly agree
Our team has **confidence** in itself.							
Our team believes it can become unusually good by producing **high-quality work**.							
Our team expects to be known as a **high-performing team**.							
Our team feels it **can solve any problem** it encounters.							
Our team believes **it can be very productive**.							
Our team can **get a lot done** when it works hard.							
No task is too tough for our team.							

AgileSE Research Study

Continued: Team work

For methodological reasons, some questions cover similar aspects from different perspectives.

Peer Awareness

How often do members of your team ...

	Almost never	Rarely	Sometimes	Often	Almost always
... see what other team members do on the job?					
... notice how other team members behave at work?					
... notice what other team members do at work?					
... take action if another team member does his/her job incorrectly?					
... correct other team members when they make mistakes?					
... let other team members know if they do something wrong?					
... tell a manager if another team member misbehaves?					
... tell a manager if a team member disregards team rules?					
... let someone know if another team member is dishonest?					
... talk about how other team members do their job?					
... discuss how everyone performs at work?					
... let others know that another team member does good work?					
... congratulate other team members if they are recognized for doing good work?					
... tell other team members that they did a good job?					

Thank you very much for your contribution!

A.7 Survey: Area Product Owner Questionnaire

AgileSE Research Study – questions for (Area) Product Owners

In a joined research project with the University of Mannheim, we are conducting a study on the impact of **agile software engineering** at SAP. The study is conducted by Christoph Schmidt, who is a half-time employee at SAP and a PhD student at the University of Mannheim at the Institute for Enterprise Systems (Prof. Dr. Heinzl).

We have invited your teams to participate in the study. Now, we kindly ask you to fill out this questionnaire, which will take about 20 minutes. For the purpose of this study, we define the development team as 'developers & scrum master'.

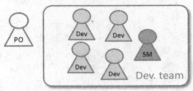

Complementary to the teams' answers, we invite you to rate your satisfaction with your development teams. In particular, we ask about the **software quality** the teams deliver, your satisfaction with the **software delivery process**, i.e., *how* the teams deliver software, and about the **overall effectiveness** of the teams. Additionally, there are questions about the **teams' tasks**.

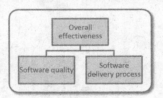

We would highly appreciate to get your honest opinion on our questions. There are no right or wrong answers. Your thoughtful answers will not only help the success of the study, but will also improve the **AgileSE trainings** at SAP. For methodological reasons, some questions seem to cover similar aspects from different perspectives.

> *Study disclaimer: The survey has been approved by the <u>German SAP workers' council</u> and <u>SAP's data protection officer</u>. We will not pass any data to management that would allow insights into the answers of a single team or your answers. **The data is ONLY used for research purposes** and we guarantee to work confidentially with the data. **The teams will not see your answers.***

Christoph Schmidt   christoph.schmidt01@sap.com & christoph.schmidt@uni-mannheim.de
Prof. Dr. Armin Heinzl   heinzl@uni-mannheim.de

AgileSE Research Study

SAP / UNIVERSITY OF MANNHEIM / InES

Part 1/4: Software quality

(1) Please insert the names of the participating teams in the boxes here.

(2) Then, please rate the following statements.

APO = Area product owner
PO = Product owner

Overall team effectiveness
Software quality
Software delivery process

	Team A											Team B										
	Never ~ 10% of the occasions	Rarely ~ 20% of the occasions	Here and then ~ 30% of the occasions	Occasionally ~ 40% of the occasions	Sometimes ~ 50% of the occasions	Frequently ~ 60% of the occasions	Very often ~ 70% of the occasions	Usually ~ 80% of the occasions	Almost always ~ 90% of the occasions	Always ~ 100% of the occasions		Never ~ 10% of the occasions	Rarely ~ 20% of the occasions	Here and then ~ 30% of the occasions	Occasionally ~ 40% of the occasions	Sometimes ~ 50% of the occasions	Frequently ~ 60% of the occasions	Very often ~ 70% of the occasions	Usually ~ 80% of the occasions	Almost always ~ 90% of the occasions	Always ~ 100% of the occasions

External software quality

When the team presents new features, the team's software does what it is supposed to do.

The team's key stakeholder *(in a Scrum context: product owner)* is **satisfied** with the **software quality** the team delivers.

When the team presents new features, they could fearlessly be shipped to the customer.

The capabilities of the software **meet** the needs of the team's customers *(SAP internal or external)*.

Overall, the team's software **contributes** to SAP's reputation as a high quality software company.

The team delivers software that fully covers the requested functionality.

The software the team delivers meets technical requirements.

Internal software quality

The team complies with done criteria.

The software code is **reusable.**

The software code is **maintainable.**

The software code is easily **testable.**

The software code is **clean** *(e.g., naming, structure, readability, formatting)*.

Project perspective

The APO/PO **rejects** presented development tasks *(in a Scrum context: backlog items)* of the team due to quality issues.

The team has to **rework** presented features to **fix issues** from previous development cycles *(in a Scrum context: sprints)*.

AgileSE Research Study

SAP.   UNIVERSITY OF MANNHEIM   InES

Part 2/4: Software delivery process

Overall team effectiveness — Software delivery process — Software quality

For methodological reasons, some questions cover similar aspects from different perspectives.

	Team A							Team B						
	Strongly disagree	Disagree	Somewhat disagree	Neither agree or disagree	Somewhat agree	Agree	Strongly agree	Strongly disagree	Disagree	Somewhat disagree	Neither agree or disagree	Somewhat agree	Agree	Strongly agree

Team progress

This team has a **high velocity** of delivering new features.

The **progress** of the team is always **satisfying.**

The team continously makes **excellent progress** with new features.

This team is a high performance team regarding the **speed** of **delivering features.**

Predictability

I trust the team to **deliver** at the end of a development cycle **what it forecasts** before the cycle.

The team always meets the **objectives** that are **set at the beginning** of a development cycle.

When the team **promises** to do something, **I am sure it does so.**

I am confident that the team **delivers forecasted features.**

Transparency

The team **communicates issues** to affected stakeholders whenever necessary.

Product stakeholders *(PO & APO)* are **always well-informed** about problems.

Whenever problems occur, the team **informs** affected **stakeholders outside the team.**

AgileSE Research Study

SAP | UNIVERSITY OF MANNHEIM | InES

Part 3/4: Team tasks

For methodological reasons, some questions cover similar aspects from different perspectives.

	Team A							Team B						
	Strongly disagree	Disagree	Somewhat disagree	Neither agree or disagree	Somewhat agree	Agree	Strongly agree	Strongly disagree	Disagree	Somewhat disagree	Neither agree or disagree	Somewhat agree	Agree	Strongly agree

Requirements volatility

The software requirements the team works on ...

... **were changing quite a bit** during the last three months.

... **will change quite a bit** in the future.

... are **quite different** from those originally identified.

Team task diversity

The team works on a **broad spectrum of different tasks** *(new dev., maintenance, documentations, consulting others)*.

The team faces **very heterogeneous requirements**.

The team has to be familiar with details from **many different software components** *(e.g., libraries, APIs)*.

The team works on **various software layers** in the technology stack *(e.g., persistence, application logic, UI)*.

Architectural modularity

How would you describe the **software the team develops**?

The team's software has a **highly modular** architecture.

The team's software can be **decomposed** into separate, independent functional sub-units.

The team can **change key component(s)** of its software **without redesigning** others.

From a technical point of view, **large parts** of the team's software **could be reused** in other products.

AgileSE Research Study

SAP | UNIVERSITY OF MANNHEIM · InES

Continued: *Reaction to change*

For methodological reasons, some questions cover similar aspects from different perspectives.

Reaction to change

When **changes** occur in the following categories, the team is able to **effectively incorporate** these **changes:**

	Team A							Team B						
	Strongly disagree	Disagree	Somewhat disagree	Neither agree or disagree	Somewhat agree	Agree	Strongly agree	Strongly disagree	Disagree	Somewhat disagree	Neither agree or disagree	Somewhat agree	Agree	Strongly agree
Changing **requirements** *(e.g. reprioritizations, new requirements)*														
Changing **technological resources** *(e.g. programming languages, APIs, platforms, servers)*														
Changing **people** *(e.g. changing team members, product owners, managers)*														

Considering the last six months,
how much **additional effort** was required by the team to **incorporate changes** in the following categories?

	Team A							Team B						
	Very little effort	Little effort	Minor effort	Moderate effort	Some effort	Much effort	Very much effort	Very little effort	Little effort	Minor effort	Moderate effort	Some effort	Much effort	Very much effort
Changing **requirements** *(e.g. reprioritizations, new requirements)*														
Changing **technological resources** *(e.g. programming languages, APIs, platforms, servers)*														
Changing **people** *(e.g. changing team members, product owners, managers)*														

AgileSE Research Study

Part 4/4: Overall team effectiveness

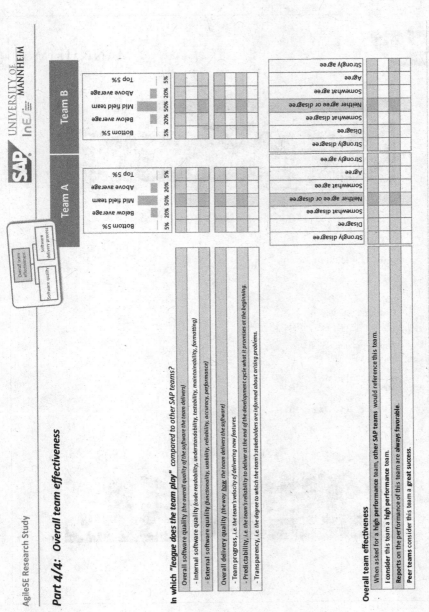

In which "league does the team play" compared to other SAP teams?

Overall software quality *(the overall quality of the software the team delivers)*

- Internal software quality *(code readability, understandability, testability, maintainability, formatting)*
- External software quality *(functionality, usability, reliability, accuracy, performance)*

Overall delivery quality *(the way how the team delivers the software)*

- Team progress, i.e. the team's velocity of delivering new features.
- Predictability, i.e. the team's reliability to deliver at the end of the development cycle what it promises at the beginning.
- Transparency, i.e. the degree to which the team's stakeholders are informed about arising problems.

Overall team effectiveness

When asked for a high performance team, other SAP teams would reference this team.

I consider this team a high performance team.

Reports on the performance of this team are always favorable.

Peer teams consider this team a great success.

Thank you very much for your contribution!

A.8   Survey: Team Report

UNIVERSITY OF MANNHEIM

Institute for Enterprise Systems (InES)
University of Mannheim

AgileSE Research Study

Christoph Schmidt
SAP AG / University of Mannheim

Prof. Dr. Armin Heinzl
University of Mannheim

Dr. Juergen Heymann
SAP AG

December 2013 - March 2014

AgileSE Research Study

SAP AG has trained more than 4000 developers in agile software engineering methodology with the Agile Software Engineering Program (P&I COO Development Methods) during the last years. In a joint research project with the Institute of Enterprise Systems at the University of Mannheim, we conducted the AgileSE Research Study to better understand the impact on SAP's software development teams. The study took place between December 2013 and March 2014. First study results show a high variance among the participating teams regarding their intensity of using the taught methods. In general, the adoption rate is quite high.

>> Respondents

Overall, **76 teams** have participated with more than **500 individual respondents**. The **average team size** was **9 team members** with an **average response rate** of **71% per team**. Figure 1 shows the teams' programming languages, their software product type, and their location.

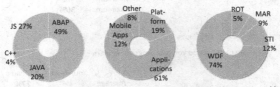

Figure 1: Participating teams' programming language, software product type, and location

>> This Team Report

This team report provides your team's aggregated answers and compares them with all participating teams. We only consider answers of those respondents who specifially indicated on the first page of the questionnaire to be included in the team report and who said to develop software at least 20% of their time. We send this report to the participating team only and will not distribute any team-specific data to the line or the product management.

Here is a short example how to read the following charts.

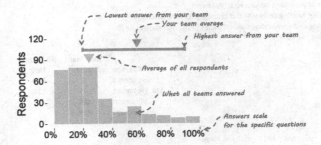

Study disclaimer: The survey has been approved by the German SAP workers' council and SAP's data protection officer. The data is only used for research purposes and we guarantee to work confidentially with the data.

Agile Software Development Practices

The questionnaire covered various agile software engineering practices such as pair programming, automated testing, refactoring, and code review. Your team's answers are shown in comparison to the answers of all respondents. To give you an overview, we averaged your answers for some questions that are rather similar. The respective charts are marked with an asterisk and show the distribution of the average response values.

>> Pair Programming

How much of your code do you develop with a programming partner?*
How much of your coding time do you work with a programming partner?*

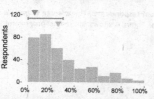

	Your Team	All Teams
Average	6%	26%
Responents	9	363
Std. Deviation	10%	23%
Minimum	0%	
Maximum	30%	

With how many of your team members do you pair program regularly?

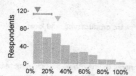

	Your Team	All Teams
Average	4%	27%
Responents	9	359
Std. Deviation	7%	24%
Minimum	0%	
Maximum	20%	

>> Refactoring

How much of your time do you roughly spend ...
... simplifying existing code without changing its functionality?*
... identifying and eliminating redundancies in the software code?*
... improving the code quality?*

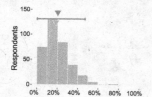

	Your Team	All Teams
Average	20%	18%
Responents	9	359
Std. Deviation	14%	13%
Minimum	0%	
Maximum	47%	

>> Automated Testing

For how much of your new code do you write automated tests before writing the productive code, i.e. test-driven development?

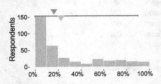

	Your Team	All Teams
Average	**17%**	**23%**
Responents	9	360
Std. Deviation	30%	29%
Minimum	0%	
Maximum	90%	

For how much of your new code do you write automated tests at all, i.e. before or after writing the productive code?

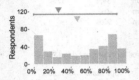

	Your Team	All Teams
Average	**27%**	**47%**
Responents	9	361
Std. Deviation	38%	32%
Minimum	0%	
Maximum	90%	

For how many of your new tests do you use test isolation, i.e. test double, mocking?

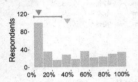

	Your Team	All Teams
Average	**6%**	**36%**
Responents	9	349
Std. Deviation	11%	32%
Minimum	0%	
Maximum	30%	

How much of your new functionality is regularly tested with automated integration tests?

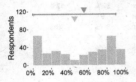

	Your Team	All Teams
Average	**56%**	**45%**
Responents	9	351
Std. Deviation	36%	33%
Minimum	0%	
Maximum	90%	

How much of your new functionality is regularly tested with automated UI tests?

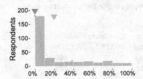

	Your Team	All Teams
Average	**0%**	**20%**
Respondents	7	326
Std. Deviation	0%	28%
Minimum	0%	
Maximum	0%	

How much of your new functionality is regularly tested with manual exploratory tests?

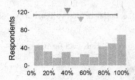

	Your Team	All Teams
Average	**37%**	**51%**
Respondents	9	353
Std. Deviation	34%	32%
Minimum	0%	
Maximum	90%	

For how much of your new functionality do you run acceptance tests, e.g. defined by the PO?

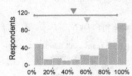

	Your Team	All Teams
Average	**43%**	**57%**
Respondents	7	337
Std. Deviation	42%	33%
Minimum	0%	
Maximum	90%	

>> Code Review

How much of your new code is reviewed by at least one colleague?*
How much of your modified code is reviewed by at least one colleague?*

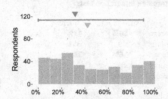

	Your Team	All Teams
Average	**32%**	**42%**
Respondents	9	361
Std. Deviation	30%	30%
Minimum	0%	
Maximum	90%	

How many of your team members regularly review code you have developed?

	Your Team	All Teams
Average	**6%**	**24%**
Respondents	9	358
Std. Deviation	7%	24%
Minimum	0%	
Maximum	20%	

Team Work Factors

We asked several questions about how your team works together. Your answers were agreggated to a single indicator. Your answers are the orange line; the green dashed line shows the average of all teams. Some questions were asked negativeley. We inverted your answers to those questions and marked them with a † sign below.

>> Team Atmosphere

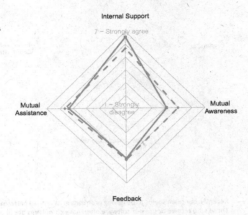

Internal Support	The team members help and support each other as best they can.
	If conflicts come up they are easily and quickly resolved.
	Discussions and controversies are conducted constructively.
	Suggestions and contributions of team members are respected.
	Our team is able to reach consensus regarding important issues.
	Suggestions and contributions of team members are discussed and further developed.
Mutual Assistance	We complete tasks for each other whenever necessary.
	We give each other suggestions how a task could be approached.
	We step in for the other person if he/she struggles to finish the current work.
	We assist each other in accomplishing our tasks.
Feedback	We give each other feedback on work results.
	We give each other feedback on how to solve a task.
	We tell the other person if his/her work results could be improved.
	We tell the other person when his/her way of solving a task is not the best.
Mutual Awareness	Each of us notices when the other person makes a critical mistake.
	Each of us notices when the other person has problems with a task.
	Each of us knows about the other person's workload.
	Each of us knows when the other person faces work-related challenges.

>> Team Spirit

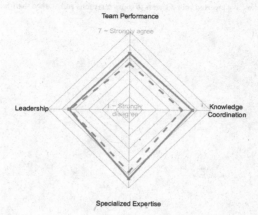

Team Performance	Recently, our team seems to be having problems in its level of performance and accomplishments.† Those who receive or use our software often have complaints about our work.† Critical quality errors occur frequently in our team.† Others in the company who interact with us often complain about how our team functions.†
Leadership	The product owner is clear and explicit about what he/she wants our team to do, product vision, backlog specification. The product owner keeps a watchful eye on how the team is progressing. The product owner shows that he/she cares a great deal about us being a good team. The product owner goes new ways by asking team members for ideas and advice. The product owner alerts the team when he/she notices things that could be done better.
Spec. Expertise	Each member of my team has special expertise. I know which team members have expertise in specific areas. Different team members are responsible for expertise in different areas. The expertise of several different team members is needed to complete our deliverables.
Knowledge Coordination	Our team works together in a well-coordinated fashion. We accomplish our tasks smoothly and efficiently. Our team has very few misunderstandings about what to do. There is often confusion in our team about how we will accomplish our tasks.†

>> Team Capabilities

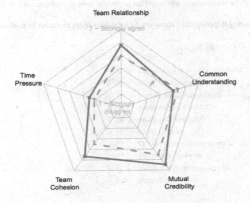

Team Relationship

The people on this team get on my nerves.†
There is a lot of unpleasantness among people on our team.†
Dealing with the members of this team often leaves me feeling irritated and frustrated.†
Often, I am disappointed with the other members of this team.†

Time Pressure

I have too much work and too little time to do it.
I find this organization a relaxed place to work.†
I often have to deal with work-related problems in my off hours.
I feel like I never have a day off.
Many employees at my level get "burned out" by the demands of their jobs in this organization.

Team Cohesion

How would you describe your team: close 7 - distant 1
How would you describe your team: cooperative 7 - conflictual 1
How would you describe your team: integrating 7 - fragmenting 1
How would you describe your team: team-oriented 7 - self-oriented 1

Mutual Credibility

I am comfortable accepting work suggestions from other team members.
I am confident relying on the information that other team members bring into discussions.
I do not have much faith in other members expertise.†
I trust that other members' task-related knowledge is credible.

Common Understanding

We agree how well-crafted code looks like.
We have a similar understanding of our software architecture.
We agree what needs to be done before a task is considered 'done'.
We have a similar understanding about the business needs of our software's users.
We have a shared idea how our software will evolve.

Improvement Areas

Finally, we asked your team about potential areas of improvement. First, we show the top ten answers of all participants of the study. Then, you find your team's top seven answers as well as additional comments. The numbers indicate the share of the respondents who saw that particular area of improvement for their team.

Which of the following improvement areas would help your team the most to perform better?

>> Top Ten Answers from All Teams

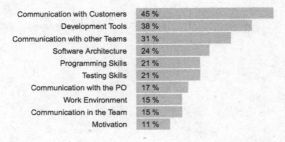

Communication with Customers	45 %
Development Tools	38 %
Communication with other Teams	31 %
Software Architecture	24 %
Programming Skills	21 %
Testing Skills	21 %
Communication with the PO	17 %
Work Environment	15 %
Communication in the Team	15 %
Motivation	11 %

>> Top Seven Answers from Your Team

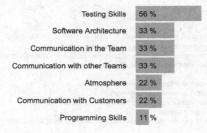

Testing Skills	56 %
Software Architecture	33 %
Communication in the Team	33 %
Communication with other Teams	33 %
Atmosphere	22 %
Communication with Customers	22 %
Programming Skills	11 %

Additional comments from your team:

- Better testing framework
- better quality of things we include (from other teams)

Institute of Enterprise Systems at the University of Mannheim

The Institute of Enterprise Systems (InES - http://ines.uni-mannheim.de) at the University of Mannheim works on an interdisciplinary basis across faculties. The institute was founded in 2011 on the initiative of the Ministry of Science, Research and Arts of the federal state of Baden-Württemberg (MWK) and the University of Mannheim.

InES pursues two main purposes:

- Achieving high-quality results in research by following an interdisciplinary research approach
- Transferring know-how into the practical world in middle-sized enterprises as well as large corporations

Participating Researchers in this Study:

Prof. Dr. Armin Heinzl
Chair of General Management and Information Systems
Institute of Enterprise Systems
University of Mannheim
heinzl@uni-mannheim.de

Christoph Schmidt
Institute of Enterprise Systems
SAP AG
christoph.schmidt@uni-mannheim.de
christoph.schmidt01@sap.com

Dr. Thomas Kude
Chair of General Management
and Information Systems
University of Mannheim
kude@uni-mannheim.de

Kai Spohrer
Chair of General Management
and Information Systems
University of Mannheim
spohrer@uni-mannheim.de

Agile Software Engineering Program at SAP

The Agile Software Engineering Program at SAP AG aims at establishing agile software development practices such as test-driven development, test isolation, refactoring, continuous integration etc. as standard practices of the SAP development culture.

Dr. Juergen Heymann
SAP AG
P&I COO Development Methods
juergen.heymann@sap.com

Bibliography

Abrahamsson, P., Conboy, K., & Wang, X. (2009). Lots done, more to do: The current state of agile systems development research. *European Journal of Information Systems, 18*(4), 281–284.

Abrahamsson, P., Salo, O., Ronkainen, J., & Warsta, J. (2002). Agile Software Development Methods: Review and Analysis. 2002 (478). Research Report. http://www.vtt.fi/inf/pdf/publications/2002/P478.pdf.

Aiken, L. S., & West, S. G. (1992). *Multiple regression: Testing and interpreting interactions.* Newbury Park, CA: Sage.

Akgün, A. E., Byrne, J., & Keskin, H. (2005). Knowledge networks in new product development projects: A transactive memory perspective. *Information and Management, 42*(8), 1105–1120.

Akgün, A. E., Keskin, H., Byrne, J., & Imamoglu, S. Z. (2007). Antecedents and consequences of team potency in software development projects. *Information and Management, 44*(7), 646–656.

Al-Fatish, F., Roemer, M., Fassunge, M., Reinstorf, T., & Staader, J. (2011). ASE: Immer besser mit starken Teams! Agile Software Engineering bei der SAP. *Object Spectrum 1*, 1–3.

Anderson, D. J. (2004). *Agile management for software engineering: Applying the theory of constraints for business results.* The coad series. Upper Saddle River, NJ: Prentice Hall.

Andreessen, M. (2011, August 20). Why software is eating the world. *Wall Street Journal.*

Argote, L. (1982). Input uncertainty and organizational coordination in hospital emergency units. *Administrative Science Quarterly, 27*(3), 420–434.

Austin, R. D., & Devin, L. (2009). Weighing the benefits and costs of flexibility in making software: Toward a contingency theory of the determinants of development process design. *Information Systems Research, 20*(3), 462–477.

Baccarini, D. (1996). The concept of project complexity: A review. *International Journal of Project Management, 14*(4), 201–204.

Bajec, M., Krisper, M., & Rupnik, R. (2004). The scenario for constructing flexible, people focused systems development methodologies. In *European Conference on Information Systems.*

Balijepally, V. G., Mahapatra, R. K., Nerur, S., & Price, K. H. (2009). Are two heads better than one for software development? The productivity paradox of pair programming. *Management Information Systems Quarterly, 33*(1), 91–118.

Bandura, A. (1977). Self-efficacy: Toward a unifying theory of behavioral change. *Psychological Review, 84*(2), 191–215.

Bandura, A. (1986). *Social foundations of thought and action: A social cognitive theory.* Englewood Cliffs, NJ: Prentice-Hall.

Banker, R. D., Davis, G. B., & Slaughter, S. A. (1998). Software development practices, software complexity, and software maintenance performance: A field study. *Management Science, 44*(4), 433–450.

© Springer International Publishing Switzerland 2016
C. Schmidt, *Agile Software Development Teams*, Progress in IS,
DOI 10.1007/978-3-319-26057-0

Baron, R. M., & Kenny, D. A. (1986). The moderator-mediator variable distinction in social psychological research: Conceptual, strategic, and statistical considerations. *Journal of Personality and Social Psychology, 51*(6), 1173–1182.

Baskerville, R., Levine, L., Pries-Heje, J., Ramesh, B., & Slaughter, S. (2001). How internet software companies negotiate quality. *Computer, 34*(5), 51–57.

Baskerville, R., & Pries-Heje, J. (2004). Short cycle time systems development. *Information Systems Journal, 14*(3), 237–264.

Baskerville, R., Ramesh, B., Levine, L., Pries-Heje, J., & Slaughter, S. (2003). Is internet-speed software development different? *IEEE Software, 20*(6), 70–77.

Batra, D., Sin, T., & Ying, S. (2006). Modified agile practices for outsourced software projects. In *Americas Conference on Information Systems*.

Beck, K. (2000). *Extreme programming explained: Embrace change*. Reading, MA: Addison-Wesley.

Begel, A., & Nagappan, N. (2007). Usage and perceptions of agile software development in an industrial context: An exploratory study. In *International Symposium on Empirical Software Engineering and Measurement* (pp. 255–264). Washington, DC: IEEE.

Begel, A., & Simon, B. (Eds.). (2010). *Novice professionals: Recent graduates in a first software engineering job* (Chapter 6, pp. 495–516). Sebastopol, CA: O'Reilly Media.

Berger, H., & Beynon-Davies, P. (2008). Knowledge based diffusion: A case study experience. In *International Conference on Information Systems*.

Berger, H., & Beynon-Davies, P. (2009). The utility of rapid application development in large-scale, complex projects. *Information Systems Journal, 19*(6), 549–570.

Bettenhausen, K. L. (1991). Five years of groups research: What we have learned and what needs to be addressed. *Journal of Management, 17*(2), 345–381.

Bhattacharya, S., Krishnan, V., & Mahajan, V. (1998). Managing new product definition in highly dynamic environments. *Management Science, 44*(11), 50–64.

Bhattacherjee, A. (2012). *Social science reserach: Principles, methods, and practices*. Zurich: Global Text Project.

Boehm, B. (2006). A view of 20th and 21st century software engineering. In *International Conference on Software Engineering* (pp. 12–29). New York, NY: ACM.

Bok, H. S., & Raman, K. S. (2000). Software engineering productivity measurement using function points: A case study. *Journal of Information Technology, 15*(1), 79–90.

Bollen, K., & Lennox, R. (1991). Conventional wisdom on measurement: A structural equation perspective. *Psychological Bulletin, 110*(2), 305.

Bollen, K. A. (1989). *Structural equations with latent variables*. New York, NY: Whiley.

Bommer, W. H., Johnson, J. L., Rich, G. A., Podsakoff, P. M., & MacKenzie, S. B. (1995). On the interchangeability of objective and subjective measures of employee performance: A meta-analysis. *Personnel Psychology, 48*(3), 587–605.

Bonner, N. A., Teng, J. T. C., & Nerur, S. (2010). The perceived advantage of agile development methodologies by software professionals: Testing an innovation-theoretic model. In *Americas Conference on Information Systems*.

Brill, S. (2014, March 10). Code red - inside the nightmare launch of healthcare.gov and the team that figured out how to fix it. *Times,* 26–36.

Börjesson, A., & Mathiassen, L. (2005). Improving software organizations: Agility challenges and implications. *Information Technology and People, 18*(4), 359–382.

Brooks, F. P. (1995). *The mythical man-month: Essays on software engineering*. Reading, MA: Addison-Wesley.

Brown, R., Nerur, S., & Slinkman, C. (2004). Philosophical shifts in software development. In *Americas Conference on Information Systems*.

Bryman, A., & Bell, E. (2011). *Business research methods*. New York, NY: Oxford University Press.

Burke, S., Stagl, K. C., Klein, C., Goodwin, G. F., Salas, E., & Halpin, S. M. (2006). What type of leadership behaviors are functional in teams? A meta-analysis. *The Leadership Quarterly, 17*(3), 288–307.

Burke, S., Stagl, K. C., Salas, E., Pierce, L., & Kendall, D. (2006). Understanding team adaptation: A conceptual analysis and model. *Journal of Applied Psychology, 91*(6), 1189–1207.

Campbell, D. J. (1988). Task complexity: A review and analysis. *Academy of Management Review, 13*(1), 40–52.

Cannon-Bowers, J. A., Salas, E., & Converse, S. (Eds.). (1993). *Shared mental models in expert team decision making* (Chapter 12, pp. 221–246). Castellan, NJ: Lawrence Erlbaum Associates.

Cao, L., Mohan, K., Ramesh, B., & Sarkar, S. (2013). Adapting funding processes for agile IT projects: An empirical investigation. *European Journal of Information Systems, 22*(2), 191–205.

Cao, L., Mohan, K., Xu, P., & Ramesh, B. (2009). A framework for adapting agile development methodologies. *European Journal of Information Systems, 18*(4), 332–343.

Carmeli, A., Gelbard, R., & Goldriech, R. (2011). Linking perceived external prestige and collective identification to collaborative behaviors in R&D teams. *Expert Systems with Applications, 38*(7), 8199–8207.

Chan, D. (1998). Functional relations among constructs in the same content domain at different levels of analysis: A typology of composition models. *Journal of Applied Psychology, 83*(2), 234–246.

Charaf, M. C., Rosenkranz, C., & Holten, R. (2013). The emergence of shared understanding: Applying functional pragmatics to study the requirements development process. *Information Systems Journal, 23*(2), 115–135.

Charette, R. N. (2005). Why software fails. *IEEE Spectrum, 42*(9), 42–49.

Charette, R. N. (2009). This car runs on code. *IEEE Spectrum, 46*(3), 3–11.

Chen, G., Bliese, P. D., Payne, S. C., Zaccaro, S. J., Webber, S. S., Mathieu, J. E., et al. (2002). Simultaneous examination of the antecedents and consequences of efficacy beliefs at multiple levels of analysis. *Human Performance, 15*(4), 381–409.

Chin, W. W. (1998). Issues and opinion on structural equation modeling. *Management Information Systems Quarterly, 22*(1), viii–xvi.

Chin, W. W. (1998). The partial least squares approach to structural equation modeling. *Modern Methods for Business Research, 295*(2), 295–336.

[Chin 2010] Chin, W. W. (Ed.). (2010). *How to write up and report PLS analyses* (Chapter 28, pp. 655–690). Heidelberg: Springer.

Chin, W. W., Marcolin, B. L., & Newsted, P. R. (2003). A partial least squares latent variable modeling approach for measuring interaction effects: Results from a Monte Carlo simulation study and an electronic-mail emotion/adoption study. *Information Systems Research, 14*(2), 189–217.

Cho, J., Kim, Y., & Olsen, D. (2006). A case study on the applicability and effectiveness of scrum software development in mission-critical and large-scale projects. In *Americas Conference on Information Systems*.

Chuang, S.-W., Luor, T., & Lu, H.-P. (2014). Assessment of institutions, scholars, and contributions on agile software development. *Journal of Systems and Software, 93*(7), 84–101.

Churchill, G. A. (1979). A paradigm for developing better measures of marketing constructs. *Journal of Marketing Research, 16*(1), 64–73.

Cockburn, A. (2001). *Agile software development: Software through people*. Amsterdam: Addison-Wesley.

Cockburn, A. (2005). *Crystal clear: A human-powered methodology for small teams*. The agile software development series. Boston, MA: Addison-Wesley.

Cohen, D., Lindvall, M., & Costa, P. (2004). An introduction to agile methods. *Advances in Computers, 62*, 1–66.

Cohen, S. G., & Bailey, D. E. (1997). What makes teams work: Group effectiveness research from the shop floor to the executive suite. *Journal of Management, 23*(3), 239–290.

Conboy, K. (2009). Agility from first principles: Reconstructing the concept of agility in information systems development. *Information Systems Research, 20*(3), 329–354.

Cram, W. A., & Brohman, M. K. (2013). Controlling information systems development: A new typology for an evolving field. *Information Systems Journal, 23*(2), 137–154.

Dabrowski, M., Acton, T., Drury, M., Conboy, K., & Dabrowska, A. (2011). Agile software development: A case for adequate decision support tools. In *Americas Conference on Information Systems*.

DeChurch, L. A., & Mesmer-Magnus, J. R. (2010). Measuring shared team mental models: A meta-analysis. *Group Dynamics: Theory, Research, and Practice, 14*(1), 1–14.

Dibbern, J., Goles, T., Hirschheim, R., & Jayatilaka, B. (2004). Information systems outsourcing: A survey and analysis of the literature. *ACM Sigmis Database, 35*(4), 6–102.

Dickinson, T. L., & McIntyre, R. M. (Eds.). (1997). *A conceptual framework for teamwork measurement* (Chapter 2, pp. 19–43). Mahwah, NJ: Lawrence Erlbaum Associates.

Dillman, D. A., Smyth, J. D., Christian, L. M., & Dillman, D. A. (2009). *Internet, mail, and mixed-mode surveys: The tailored design method*. Hoboken, NJ: Wiley.

Dingsøyr, T., & Dybå, T. (2012). Team effectiveness in software development: Human and cooperative aspects in team effectiveness models and priorities for future studies. In *International Workshop on Cooperative and Human Aspects of Software Engineering (CHASE)* (pp. 27–29).

Dingsøyr, T., Nerur, S., Balijepally, V., & Moe, N. B. (2012). A decade of agile methodologies: Towards explaining agile software development. *Journal of Systems and Software, 85*(6), 1213–1221.

Dönmez, D., & Grote, G. (Eds.). (2013). *The practice of not knowing for sure: How agile teams manage uncertainties*. Lecture notes in business information processing (Chapter 5, Vol. 149, pp. 61–75). Berlin/Heidelberg: Springer.

Dybå, T. (2011). Special section on best papers from Xp2010. *Information and Software Technology, 53*(5), 507–508.

Dybå, T., & Dingsøyr, T. (2008). Empirical studies of agile software development: A systematic review. *Information and Software Technology, 50*(9), 833–859.

Edberg, D., Ivanova, P., & Kuechler, W. (2012). Methodology mashups: An exploration of processes used to maintain software. *Journal of Management Information Systems, 28*(4), 271–303.

Edmondson, A. C. (1999). Psychological safety and learning behavior in work teams. *Administrative Science Quarterly, 44*(2), 350–383.

Edmondson, A. C., & McManus, S. E. (2007). Methodological fit in management field research. *Academy of Management Review, 32*(4), 1246–1264.

Eisenhardt, K. M., & Martin, J. A. (2000). Dynamic capabilities: What are they? *Strategic Management Journal, 21*(10–11), 1105–1121.

Elbanna, A., & Murray, D. (2009). Organizing projects for innovation: A collective mindfulness perspective. In *Americas Conference on Information Systems*.

Erickson, J., Lyytinen, K., & Siau, K. (2005). Agile modeling, agile software development, and extreme programming: The state of research. *Journal of Database Management, 16*(4), 88–100.

Espinosa, J A., Slaughter, S. A., Kraut, R. E., & Herbsleb, J. D. (2007). Familiarity, complexity, and team performance in geographically distributed software development. *Organization Science, 18*(4), 613–630.

Faraj, S., & Sproull, L. (2000). Coordinating expertise in software development teams. *Management Science, 46*(12), 1554–1568.

Fitzgerald, B., Hartnett, G., & Conboy, K. (2006). Customising agile methods to software practices at Intel Shannon. *European Journal of Information Systems, 15*(2), 200–213.

Fornell, C. (Ed.). (1989). *The blending of theoretical empirical knowledge in structural equations with unobservables* (Chapter 8, pp. 153–174). Paragon House, NY: Paragon House.

Fornell, C., & Larcker, D. F. (1981). Evaluating structural equation models with unobservable variables and measurement error. *Journal of Marketing Research, 18*(1), 39–50.

Fowler, F. J. (2002). *Survey research methods*. Singapore: Thousand Oaks.

Fruhling, A., & Vreede, G. D. (2006). Field experiences with extreme programming: Developing an emergency response system. *Journal of Management Information Systems, 22*(4), 39–68.

Fry, L. W. (1982). Technology-structure research: Three critical issues. *Academy of Management Journal, 25*(3), 532–552.

Gefen, D., Rigdon, E. E., & Straub, D. W. (2011). An update and extension to SEM guidelines for administrative and social science research. *Management Information Systems Quarterly, 35*(2), iii–A7.

Gefen, D., Straub, D. W., & Boudreau, M.-C. (2000). Structural equation modeling and regression: Guidelines for research practice. *Communications of the ACM, 4*(1), 1–77.

Geisser, S. (1975). A predictive approach to the random effect model. *Biometrika, 61*(1), 101–107.

Ågerfalk, P. J., Fitzgerald, B., & Slaughter, S. A. (2009). Flexible and distributed information systems development: State of the art and research challenges. *Information Systems Research, 20*(3), 317–328.

Gibson, C. B. (1999). Do they do what they believe they can? Group efficacy and group effectiveness across tasks and cultures. *Academy of Management Journal, 42*(2), 138–152.

Gladstein, D. L. (1984). Groups in context: A model of task group effectiveness. *Administrative Science Quarterly, 29*(4), 499–517.

Goh, J. C. L., Pan, S. L., & Zuo, M. (2013). Developing the agile IS development practices in large-scale IT projects: The trust-mediated organizational controls and IT project team capabilities perspectives. *Journal of the Association for Information Systems, 14*(12), 722–756.

Green, P. (2011). Measuring the impact of scrum on product development at Adobe Systems. In *Hawaii International Conference on System Sciences*.

Greer, D., & Hamon, Y. (2011). Agile software development. *Software: Practice and Experience, 41*(9), 943–944.

Gregory, T., Mathiassen, L., & Sambhara, C. (2013). Chains of control in agile software development. In *Americas Conference on Information Systems*.

Guinan, P. J., Cooprider, J. G., & Faraj, S. (1998). Enabling software development team performance during requirements definition: A behavioral versus technical approach. *Information Systems Research, 9*(2), 101–125.

Gully, S. M., Incalcaterra, K. A., Joshi, A., & Beaubien, M. (2002). A meta-analysis of team-efficacy, potency, and performance: Interdependence and level of analysis as moderators of observed relationships. *Journal of Applied Psychology, 87*(5), 819.

Guzzo, R. A., Yost, P. R., Campbell, R. J., & Shea, G. P. (1993). Potency in groups: Articulating a construct. *British Journal of Social Psychology, 32*(1), 87–106.

Hackman, R. (1987). *The design of work teams* (Vol. 129, pp. 315–342). New York, NY: Prentice Hall.

Hair, J. F., Anderson, R. E., & Black, W. C. (1995). *Multivariate data analysis: With readings*. Englewood Cliffs, NJ: Prentice Hall.

Harris, M. L., Collins, R. W., & Hevner, A. R. (2009). Control of flexible software development under uncertainty. *Information Systems Research, 20*(3), 400–419.

He, J., Butler, B. S., & King, W. R. (2007). Team cognition: Development and evolution in software project teams. *Journal of Management Information Systems, 24*(2), 261–292.

Henderson, J. C., & Lee, S. (1992). Managing I/S design teams: A control theories perspective. *Management Science, 38*(6), 757–777.

Henderson-Sellers, B., & Serour, M. K. (2005). Creating a dual-agility method: The value of method engineering. *Journal of Database Management, 16*(4), 1–24.

Henry, S. M., & Todd, S. K. (1999). Using Belbin's leadership role to improve team effectiveness: An empirical investigation. *Journal of Systems and Software, 44*(3), 241–250.

Heymann, J. (2013). Gekommen, Um Zu Bleiben. *Entwickler-Magazin, 2*(1), 2–4.

Hickey, A. M., & Davis, A. M. (2004). A unified model of requirements elicitation. *Journal of Management Information Systems, 20*(4), 65–84.

Highsmith, J. A. (2000). *Adaptive software development: A collaborative approach to managing complex systems*. New York, NY: Dorset House.

Highsmith, J., & Cockburn, A. (2001). Agile software development: The business of innovation. *Computer, 34*(9), 120–127.

Hirschheim, R., Klein, H. K., & Lyytinen, K. (1996). Exploring the intellectual structures of information systems development: A social action theoretic analysis. *Accounting, Management and Information Technologies, 6*(1), 1–64.

Hoegl, M., & Gemuenden, H. G. (2001). Teamwork quality and the success of innovative projects: A theoretical concept and empirical evidence. *Organization Science, 12*(4), 435–449.

Homburg, C., & Giering, A. (1996). Konzeptualisierung und Operationalisierung komplexer Konstrukte: Ein Leitfaden für die Marketingforschung. *Marketing: Zeitschrift für Forschung und Praxis, 18*(1), 3–24.

Huang, C. C., Chu, C. Y., & Jiang, P. C. (2008). An empirical study of psychological safety and performance in technology R&D teams. In *IEEE International Conference on Management of Innovation and Technology* (pp. 1423–1427). Bangkok: IEEE.

Huang, C. C., & Jiang, P. C. (2010). Examining transactive memory systems in R&D teams. In *International Conference on Industrial Engineering and Engineering Management* (pp. 885–890). Macao: IEEE.

Huckman, R. S., Staats, B. R., & Upton, D. M. (2009). Team familiarity, role experience, and performance: Evidence from Indian software services. *Management Science, 55*(1), 85–100.

Hummel, M. (2014). State-of-the-art: A systematic literature review on agile information systems development. In *Hawaii International Conference on System Sciences*.

Hummel, M., & Rosenkranz, C. (2013). Measuring the impact of communication in agile development: A research model and pilot test. In *Americas Conference on Information Systems*.

Hummel, M., Rosenkranz, C., & Holten, R. (2013). Explaining the changing communication paradigm of agile information systems development: A research model, measurement development and pretest. In *European Conference on Information Systems*.

Hummel, M., Rosenkranz, C., & Holten, R. (2013). The role of communication in agile systems development. *Business & Information Systems Engineering, 5*(5), 343–355.

IEEE (1990). IEEE standard glossary of software engineering terminology. In *IEEE Std 610.12-1990* (pp. 1–84).

Ilgen, D. R., Hollenbeck, J. R., Johnson, M., & Jundt, D. (2005). Teams in organizations: From input-process-output models to IMOI models. *Annual Review of Psychology, 56*(1), 517–543.

Ilieva, S., Ivanov, P., & Stefanova, E. (2004). Analyses of an agile methodology implementation. In *Euromicro Conference* (pp. 326–333). Washington: IEEE.

ISO/IEC (2001). International Standard Iso/Iec 9126 - Information Technology - Product Quality - Part1: Qualtity Model / International Standard Organization. Research Report. ISO9126.

Jain, R., & Meso, P. (2004). Theory of complex adaptive systems and agile software development. In *Americas Conference on Information Systems*.

Jalali, S., & Wohlin, C. (2012). Global software engineering and agile practices: A systematic review. *Journal of Software: Evolution and Process, 24*(6), 643–659.

Jarvis, C. B., MacKenzie, S. B., & Podsakoff, P. M. (2003). A critical review of construct indicators and measurement model misspecification in marketing and consumer research. *Journal of Consumer Research, 30*(2), 199–218.

Jugdev, K., & Müller, R. (2005). A retrospective look at our evolving understanding of project success. *Project Management Journal, 36*(4), 19–31.

Jung, D. I., & Sosik, J. J. (2003). Group potency and collective efficacy examining their predictive validity, level of analysis, and effects of performance feedback on future group performance. *Group & Organization Management, 28*(3), 366–391.

Kan, S. H. (2003). *Metrics and models in software quality engineering*. Boston, MA: Addison-Wesley.

Kang, H.-R., Yang, H.-D., & Rowley, C. (2006). Factors in team effectiveness: Cognitive and demographic similarities of software development team members. *Human Relations, 59*(12), 1681–1710.

Karekar, C., Tarrell, A., & Fruhling, A. (2011). Agile development at ABC: What went wrong? In *Americas Conference on Information Systems*.

Karlsson, F., & Ågerfalk, P. (2009). Exploring agile values in method configuration. *European Journal of Information Systems, 18*(4), 300–316.

Keaveney, S., & Conboy, K. (2006). Cost estimation in agile development projects. In *European Conference on Information Systems*.

Keith, M., Demirkan, H., & Goul, M. (2013). Service-oriented methodology for systems development. *Journal of Management Information Systems, 30*(1), 227–259.

Klein, G., & Pierce, L. (2001). Adaptive teams. In *International Command and Control Research and Technology Symposium*, DTIC Document.

Klein, K. J., Dansereau, F., & Hall, R. J. (1994). Levels issues in theory development, data collection, and analysis. *Academy of Management Review, 19*(2), 195–229.

Klein, K. J., & Kozlowski, S. W. (2000). *Multilevel theory, research, and methods in organizations: Foundations, extensions, and new directions.* Frontiers of industrial and organizational psychology. San Francisco, CA: Jossey-Bass.

Klimoski, R., & Mohammed, S. (1994). Team mental model: Construct or metaphor? *Journal of Management, 20*(2), 403–437.

Koomey, J. G., Berard, S., Sanchez, M., & Wong, H. (2011). Implications of historical trends in the electrical efficiency of computing. *IEEE Annals of the History of Computing, 33*(3), 46–54.

Kozlowski, S. W., & Bell, B. S. (Eds.). (2003). *Work groups and teams in organizations* (Chapter 17, Vol. 12, pp. 333–375). London: Wiley.

Kozlowski, S. W., & Ilgen, D. R. (2006). Enhancing the effectiveness of work groups and teams. *Psychological Science in the Public Interest, 7*(3), 77–124.

Kraut, R. E., & Streeter, L. A. (1995). Coordination in software development. *Communications of the ACM, 38*(3), 69–81.

Kude, T., Bick, S., Schmidt, C. T., & Heinzl, A. (2014). Adaptation pattern in agile information systems development teams. In *European Conference on Information Systems*.

Kude, T., Dibbern, J., & Heinzl, A. (2012). Why do complementors participate? An analysis of partnership networks in the enterprise software industry. *IEEE Transactions on Engineering Management, 59*(2), 250–265.

Larman, C., & Basili, V. R. (2003). Iterative and incremental development: A brief history. *Computer, 36*(6), 47–56.

Larman, C., & Vodde, B. (2009). *Scaling lean & agile development: Thinking and organizational tools for large-scale scrum.* Upper Saddle River, NJ: Addison-Wesley.

Lawrence, C., & Rodriguez, P. (2012). The interpretation and legitimization of values in agile's organizing vision. In *European Conference on Information Systems*.

Layman, L., Williams, L., & Cunningham, L. (2004). Exploring extreme programming in context: An industrial case study. In *Agile Development Conference* (pp. 32–41). Washington: IEEE.

Lee, A. S. (Ed.). (1999). *Researching MIS* (Chapter 1, pp. 7–27). Cambridge, MA: Oxford University Press.

Lee, C., Tinsley, C. H., & Bobko, P. (2002). An investigation of the antecedents and consequences of group level confidence. *Journal of Applied Social Psychology, 32*(8), 1628–1652.

Lee, G., DeLone, W. H., Espinosa, & J. A. (2010). The main and interaction effects of process rigor, process standardization, and process agility on system performance in distributed IS development: An ambidexterity perspective. In *International Conference on Information Systems*.

Lee, G., & Xia, W. (2005). The ability of information systems development project teams to respond to business and technology changes: A study of flexibility measures. *European Journal of Information Systems, 14*(1), 75–92.

Lee, G., & Xia, W. (2010). Toward agile: An integrated analysis of quantitative and qualitative field data on software development agility. *Management Information Systems Quarterly, 34*(1), 87–114.

Leimbach, T. (2008). The SAP story: Evolution of SAP within the German software industry. *IEEE Annals of the History of Computing, 30*(4), 60–76.

Levesque, L. L., Wilson, J. M., & Wholey, D. R. (2001). Cognitive divergence and shared mental models in software development project teams. *Journal of Organizational Behavior, 22*(2), 135–144.

Li, Y., & Maedche, A. (2012). Formulating effective coordination strategies in agile global software development teams. In *International Conference on Information Systems*.

Little, B. L., & Madigan, R. M. (1997). The relationship between collective efficacy and performance in manufacturing work teams. *Small Group Research, 28*(4), 517–534.

Lohan, G., Conboy, K., & Lang, M. (2010). Beyond budgeting and agile software development: A conceptual framework for the performance management of agile software development teams. In *International Conference on Information Systems*.

Louis, M. R., & Sutton, R. I. (1991). Switching cognitive gears: From habits of mind to active thinking. *Human Relations, 44*(1), 55–76.

Lyytinen, K., & Rose, G. M. (2006). Information system development agility as organizational learning. *European Journal of Information Systems, 15*(2), 183–199.

MacCormack, A., & Verganti, R. (2003). Managing the sources of uncertainty: Matching process and context in software development. *Journal of Product Innovation Management, 20*(3), 217–232.

MacCormack, A., Verganti, R., & Iansiti, M. (2001). Developing products on "internet time": The anatomy of a flexible development process. *Management Science, 47*(1), 133–150.

MacKenzie, S. B., Podsakoff, P. M., & Podsakoff, N. P. (2011). Construct measurement and validation procedures in MIS and behavioral research: Integrating new and existing techniques. *Management Information Systems Quarterly, 35*(2), 293–334.

Mackert, O., Hildenbrand, T., & Podbicanin, A. (2010). Vom Projekt zum Produkt - SAP's Weg zum "Lean Software Product Development". In Vom Projekt zum Produkt. Fachtagung des GI-Fachausschusses Management der Anwendungsentwicklung und -wartung im Fachbereich Wirtschaftsinformatik (WI-MAW), 01-03 Dezember 2010 in Aachen, *2010* (pp. 13–25). http://subs.emis.de/LNI/Proceedings/Proceedings178/article6206.html.

Madsen, S. (2007). Conceptualising the causes and consequences of uncertainty in IS development organisations and projects. In *European Conference on Information Systems*.

Mangalaraj, G., Mahapatra, R., & Nerur, S. (2009). Acceptance of software process innovations: The case of extreme programming. *European Journal of Information Systems, 18*(4), 344–354.

Mannaro, K., Melis, M., & Marchesi, M. (Eds.). (2004). *Empirical analysis on the satisfaction of IT employees comparing XP practices with other software development methodologies.* Lecture notes in computer science (Chapter 19, Vol. 3092, pp. 166–174). Berlin/Heidelberg: Springer.

Maraia, V. (2006). *The build master: Microsoft's software configuration management best practices.* The Addison-Wesley Microsoft technology series. Upper Saddle River, NJ: Addison-Wesley.

Marks, M. A., Mathieu, J. E., & Zaccaro, S. J. (2001). A Temporally based framework and taxonomy of team processes. *Academy of Management Review, 26*(3), 356–376.

Marks, M. A., Sabella, M. J., Burke, S., & Zaccaro, S. J. (2002). The impact of cross-training on team effectiveness. *Journal of Applied Psychology, 87*(1), 3–13.

Maruping, L. M., Venkatesh, V., & Agarwal, R. (2009). A control theory perspective on agile methodology use and changing user requirements. *Information Systems Research, 20*(3), 377–399.

Maruping, L. M., Zhang, X., & Venkatesh, V. (2009). Role of collective ownership and coding standards in coordinating expertise in software project teams. *European Journal of Information Systems, 18*(4), 355–371.

Mathieu, J. E., & Chen, G. (2011). The etiology of the multilevel paradigm in management research. *Journal of Management, 37*(2), 610–641.

Mathieu, J. E., Maynard, T., Rapp, T., & Gilson, L. (2008). Team effectiveness 1997-2007: A review of recent advancements and a glimpse into the future. *Journal of Management, 34*(3), 410–476.

McAvoy, J., & Butler, T. (2006). Looking for a place to hide: A study of social loafing in agile teams. In *European Conference on Information Systems*.

McAvoy, J., & Butler, T. (2009). The role of project management in ineffective decision making within agile software development projects. *European Journal of Information Systems, 18*(4), 372–383.

McAvoy, J., Nagle, T., & Sammon, D. (2013). Using mindfulness to examine ISD agility. *Information Systems Journal, 23*(2), 155–172.

McAvoy, J., Owens, I., & Sammon, D. (2006). Towards the development of a simple tool to assist in agile methodology adoption decisions: Agile adoption matrix. In *European Conference on Information Systems*.

McConnell, S. (Ed.). (2010). *What does 10x mean? Measuring variations in programmer productivity* (Chapter 30, pp. 567–574). Sebastopol, CA: O'Reilly Media.

McFarlan, F. W. (1981). Portfolio approach to information systems. *Harvard Business Review, 59*(4), 142–150.

McGrath, J. E. (1964). *Social psychology, a brief introduction*. New York, NY: Holt.

McIntyre, R. M., & Salas, E. (Eds.). (1995). *Measuring and managing for team performance: Emerging principles from complex environments* (Chapter 2, Vol. 22, pp. 9–45). San Francisco: Jossey-Bass.

Mellis, W., Loebbecke, C., & Baskerville, R. (2010). Moderating effects of requirements uncertainty on flexible software development techniques. In *International Research Workshop on IT Project Management*.

Meredith, S., & Francis, D. (2000). Journey towards agility: The agile wheel explored. *The TQM Magazine, 12*(2), 137–143.

Misra, S. C., Kumar, V., & Kumar, U. (2009). Identifying some important success factors in adopting agile software development practices. *Journal of Systems and Software, 82*(11), 1869–1890.

Münzing, M. (2012). *Software development team success assessment: Development of a measurement instrument*. Master Thesis, University of Mannheim.

Mohammed, S., & Dumville, B. C. (2001). Team mental models in a team knowledge framework: Expanding theory and measurement across disciplinary boundaries. *Journal of Organizational Behavior, 22*(2), 89–106.

Mohammed, S., Ferzandi, L., & Hamilton, K. (2010). Metaphor no more: A 15-year review of the team mental model construct. *Journal of Management, 36*(4), 876–910.

Moore, G. C., & Benbasat, I. (1991). Development of an instrument to measure the perceptions of adopting an information technology innovation. *Information Systems Research, 2*(3), 192–222.

Moore, G. E. (1965). *Cramming More Components onto Integrated Circuits*. Electronics, 114–117.

Morgeson, F. P., & Hofmann, D. A. (1999). The structure and function of collective constructs: Implications for multilevel research and theory development. *Academy of Management Review, 24*(2), 249–265.

Nagle, T., McAvoy, J., & Sammon, D. (2011). Utilising mindfulness to analyse agile global software development. In *European Conference on Information Systems*.

Nidumolu, S. (1995). The effect of coordination and uncertainty on software project performance: Residual performance risk as an intervening variable. In *Information Systems Research, 6*(3), 191–219.

Oosterhout, M., Waarts, E., & Hillegersberg, J. (2006). Change factors requiring agility and implications for IT. *European Journal of Information Systems, 15*(2), 132–145.

Orlikowski, W. J., & Baroudi, J. J. (1991). Studying information technology in organizations: Research approaches and assumptions. *Information Systems Research, 2*(1), 1–28.

Overby, E., Bharadwaj, A., & Sambamurthy, V. (2006). Enterprise agility and the enabling role of information technology. *European Journal of Information Systems, 15*(2), 120–131.

Overhage, S., & Schlauderer, S. (2012). How sustainable are agile methodologies? Acceptance factors and developer perceptions in scrum projects. In *European Conference on Information Systems*.

Palmer, S. R., & Felsing, J. M. (2002). *A practical guide to feature-driven development*. Upper Saddle River, NJ: Prentice Hall.

Persson, J. S., Mathiassen, L., & Aaen, I. (2012). Agile distributed software development: Enacting control through media and context. *Information Systems Journal, 22*(6), 411–433.

Petter, S., Straub, D., & Rai, A. (2007). Specifying formative constructs in information systems research. *Management Information Systems Quarterly, 31*(4), 623–656.

Podsakoff, P. M., MacKenzie, S. B., Lee, J.-Y., & Podsakoff, N. P. (2003). Common method biases in behavioral research: A critical review of the literature and recommended remedies. *Journal of Applied Psychology, 88*(5), 879–903.

Poppendieck, M., & Poppendieck, T. D. (2007). *Implementing lean software development: from concept to cash*. Upper Saddle River, NJ: Addison-Wesley.

Popper, K. R. (1935). *Logik der Forschung: Zur Erkenntnistheorie der Modernen Naturwissenschaft*. Schriften zur Wissenschaftlichen Weltauffassung. Wien: Springer.

Port, D., & Bui, T. (2009). Simulating mixed agile and plan-based requirements prioritization strategies: Proof-of-concept and practical implications. *European Journal of Information Systems, 18*(4), 317–331.

Porter, C. O., Hollenbeck, J. R., Ilgen, D. R., Ellis, A. P., West, B. J., & Moon, H. (2003). Backing up behaviors in teams: The role of personality and legitimacy of need. *Journal of Applied Psychology, 88*(3), 391–403.

Procaccino, D., Verner, J. M., Darter, M. E., & Amadio, W. J. (2005). Toward predicting software development success from the perspective of practitioners: An exploratory bayesian model. *Journal of Information Technology, 20*(3), 187–200.

Prussia, G. E., & Kinicki, A. J. (1996). A motivational investigation of group effectiveness using social-cognitive theory. *Journal of Applied Psychology, 81*(2), 187–198.

Qumer, A., & Henderson-Sellers, B. (2008). A framework to support the evaluation, adoption and improvement of agile methods in practice. *Journal of Systems and Software, 81*(11), 1899–1919.

Ralph, P., & Narros, J. E. (2013). Complexity, process and agility in small development teams: An exploratory case study. In *Pacific Asia Conference on Information Systems*.

Ramesh, B., Mohan, K., & Cao, L. (2012). Ambidexterity in agile distributed development: An empirical investigation. *Information Systems Research, 23*(2), 323–339.

Rasker, P. C., Post, W. M., & Schraagen, J. M. C. (2000). Effects of two types of intra-team feedback on developing a shared mental model in command & control teams. *Ergonomics, 43*(8), 1167–1189.

Reinartz, W., Haenlein, M., & Henseler, J. (2009). An empirical comparison of the efficacy of covariance-based and variance-based SEM. *International Journal of Research in Marketing, 26*(4), 332–344.

Rentsch, J. R., & Klimoski, R. J. (2001). Why do "great minds" think alike?: Antecedents of team member schema agreement. *Journal of Organizational Behavior, 22*(2), 107–120.

Ringle, C. M., Sarstedt, M., & Straub, D. W. (2012). Editor's comments: A critical look at the use of PLS-SEM in MIS quarterly. *Management Information Systems Quarterly, 36*(1), iii–xiv.

Ringle, C. M., Wende, S., & Will, A. (2005). *SmartPLS*. Version 2.0.M3. Hamburg: SmartPLS.

Robinson, H., & Sharp, H. (Eds.). (2005). *The social side of technical practices*. Lecture notes in computer science (Chapter 12, Vol. 3556, pp. 100–108). Berlin/Heidelberg: Springer.

Rosen, M. A., Bedwell, W. L., Wildman, J. L., Fritzsche, B. A., Salas, E., & Burke, S. (2011). Managing adaptive performance in teams: guiding principles and behavioral markers for measurement. *Human Resource Management Review, 21*(2), 107–122.

Rosenkranz, C., Charaf, M. C., & Holten, R. (2013). Language quality in requirements development: Tracing communication in the process of information systems development. *Journal of Information Technology, 28*(3), 198–223.

Rousseau, D. M. (1985). Issues of level in organizational research: Multi-level and cross-level perspectives. *Research in Organizational Behavior, 7*(1), 1–37.

Royce, W., Bittner, K., & Perrow, M. (2009). *The economics of iterative software development: Steering toward better business results*. Upper Saddle River, NJ: Addison-Wesley.

Royce, W. W. (1970). Managing the development of large software systems. In *Technical papers of Western Electronic Show and Convention* (Vol. 26, pp. 1–9). Los Angeles, CA: IEEE WESCON.

Russo, N. L., Fitzgerald, G., & Shams, S. (2013). Exploring adoption and use of agile methods: A comparative case study. In *Americas Conference on Information Systems*.

Ryan, S., & O'Connor, R. V. (2009). Development of a team measure for tacit knowledge in software development teams. *Journal of Systems and Software, 82*(2), 229–240.

Salas, E., Prince, C., Baker, D. P., & Shrestha, L. (1995). Situation awareness in team performance: Implications for measurement and training. *Human Factors: The Journal of the Human Factors and Ergonomics Society, 37*(1), 123–136.

Salas, E., Sims, D. E., & Burke, S. (2005). Is there a "big five"i in teamwork? *Small Group Research, 36*(5), 555–599.

Sambamurthy, V., & Kirsch, L. J. (2000). An integrative framework of the information systems development process. *Decision Sciences, 31*(2), 391–411.

Sarker, S., Munson, C. L., Sarker, S., & Chakraborty, S. (2009). Assessing the relative contribution of the facets of agility to distributed systems development success: An analytic hierarchy process approach. *European Journal of Information Systems, 18*(4), 285–299.

Sarker, S., & Sarker, S. (2009). Exploring agility in distributed information systems development teams: An interpretive study in an offshoring context. *Information Systems Research, 20*(3), 440–461.

Sawyer, S. (2001). Effects of intra-group conflict on packaged software development team performance. *Information Systems Journal, 11*(2), 155–178.

Sawyer, S., & Guinan, P. J. (1998). Software development: Processes and performance. *IBM Systems Journal, 37*(4), 552–569.

Scandura, T. A., & Williams, E. A. (2000). Research methodology in management: Current practices, trends, and implications for future research. *Academy of Management Journal, 43*(6), 1248–1264.

Scheerer, A., Schmidt, C. T., Heinzl, A., Hildenbrand, T., & Voelz, D. (2013). Agile software engineering techniques: The missing link in large scale lean product development. In Kowalewski, S. (Ed.), *Software engineering 2013: Fachtagung des GI-Fachbereichs Softwaretechnik* (Vol. 213, pp. 319–330). Hamburg: Gesellschaft für Informatik.

Schlauderer, S., & Overhage, S. (2013). Exploring the customer perspective of agile development: Acceptance factors and on-site customer perceptions in scrum projects. In *International Conference on Information Systems*.

Schmidt, C. T., Kude, T., Tripp, J., Heinzl, A., & Spohrer, K. (2013). Team adaptability in agile information systems development. In *International Conference on Information Systems*.

Schmidt, C. T., Spohrer, K., Kude, T., & Heinzl, A. (2012). The impact of peer-based software reviews on team performance: The role of feedback and transactive memory systems. In *International Conference on Information Systems*.

Schmidt, C. T., Srinivasa, G. V., & Heymann, J. (2014). Empirical insights into the perceived benefits of agile software engineering practices: A case study from SAP. In *International Conference on Software Engineering*.

Schmidt, R., Lyytinen, K., Keil, M., & Cule, P. (2001). Identifying software project risks: An international delphi study. *Journal of Management Information Systems, 17*(4), 5–36.

Schnitter, J., & Mackert, O. (2011). *Large-scale agile software development at SAP AG*. Evaluation of novel approaches to software engineering Heidelberg: Springer.

Schwaber, K., & Beedle, M. (2002). *Agile software development with scrum*. Series in agile software development. Upper Saddle River, NJ: Prentice Hall.

Schwaber, K., & Sutherland, J. (2011). The Scrum Guide. Research Report. https://www.scrum.org/Portals/0/Documents/Scrum.

Setia, P., Rajagopalan, B., Sambamurthy, V., & Calantone, R. (2012). How peripheral developers contribute to open-source software development. *Information Systems Research, 23*(1), 144–163.

Sfetsos, P., & Stamelos, I. (2010). Empirical studies on quality in agile practices: A systematic literature review. In *Quality of information and communications technology* (pp. 44–53). Washington, DC: IEEE.

Shah, R., & Goldstein, S. M. (2006). Use of structural equation modeling in operations management research: Looking back and forward. *Journal of Operations Management, 24*(2), 148–169.

Sharifi, H., & Zhang, Z. (1999). A methodology for achieving agility in manufacturing organisations: An introduction. *International Journal of Production Economics, 62*(1), 7–22.

Sharma, R., Yetton, P., & Crawford, J. (2009). Estimating the effect of common method variance: The method-method pair technique with an illustration from TAM research. *Management Information Systems Quarterly, 33*(3), 5.

Siau, K. (2005). A retrospective review of JDM from 2003 to 2005 and a discussion on publication emphasis of JDM for the next two to three years. *Journal of Database Management, 16*(1), 1–10.

Siau, K., Long, Y., & Ling, M. (2010). Toward a unified model of information systems development success. *Journal of Database Management, 21*(1), 80–101.

So, C. (2010). *Making software teams effective: How agile practices lead to project success through teamwork mechanisms*. Frankfurt: Peter Lang GmbH.

Sommerville, I. (2004). *Software engineering*. Harlow: Addison Wesley.

Spinellis, D., & Giannikas, V. (2012). Organizational adoption of open source software. *Journal of Systems and Software, 85*(3), 666–682.

Spohrer, K., Kude, T., Schmidt, C. T., & Heinzl, A. (2013). Knowledge creation in information systems development teams: The role of pair programming and peer code review. In *European Conference on Information Systems*.

Stajkovic, A. D., Lee, D., & Nyberg, A. J. (2009). Collective efficacy, group potency, and group performance: Meta-analyses of their relationships, and test of a mediation model. *Journal of Applied Psychology, 94*(3), 814–828.

Standish, Group I (2014). The Chaos Report / Standish Group Inc. Research Report.

Stapleton, J. (1999). DSDM: Dynamic systems development method. In *Proceedings of Technology of Object-Oriented Languages and Systems* (pp. 406–406).

Stewart, K. J., & Gosain, S. (2006). The impact of ideology on effectiveness in open source software development teams. *Management Information Systems Quarterly, 30*(2), 291–314.

Stone, M. (1974). Cross-validatory choice and assessment of statistical predictions. *Journal of the Royal Statistical Society, 36*(2), 111–147.

Strauss, A. L. (1987). *Qualitative analysis for social scientists*. Cambridge, MA: Cambridge University Press.

Strode, D. E., Hope, B. G., Huff, S. L., & Link, S. (2011). Coordination effectiveness in an agile software development context. In *Pacific Asia Conference on Information Systems*.

Strode, D. E., Huff, S. L., Hope, B., & Link, S. (2012). Coordination in co-located agile software development projects. *Journal of Systems and Software, 85*(6), 1222–1238.

Sun, W. N., & Schmidt, C. (2013). Do software professionals' job perceptions differ in organizations adopting different software process models? A survey from the industry. In *Americas Conference on Information Systems*.

Sundstrom, E., McIntyre, M., Halfhill, T., & Richards, H. (2000). Work groups: From the Hawthorne studies to work teams of the 1990s and beyond. *Group Dynamics: Theory, Research, and Practice, 4*(1), 44–67.

Sutherland, J. (1995). Business object design and implementation workshop. *ACM Sigplan OOPS Messenger, 6*, 170–175.

Takeuchi, H., & Nonaka, I. (1986). The new new product development game. *Harvard Business Review, 64*(1), 137–146.

Tanner, M., & Wallace, C. (2012). Towards an understanding of the contextual influences on distributed agile software development: A theory of practice perspective. In *European Conference on Information Systems*.

Tessem, B. (Ed.). (2003). *Experiences in learning XP practices: A qualitative study*. Lecture notes in computer science (Chapter 17, Vol. 2675, pp. 131–137). Berlin/Heidelberg: Springer.

Tripp, J. F. (2012). *The impact of agile development methodology use on project success: A contingency view*. Dissertation, Michigan State University.

Tuckman, B. W. (1965). Developmental sequence in small groups. *Psychological Bulletin, 63*(6), 384–399.

Tushman, M. L., & Nadler, D. A. (1978). Information processing as an integrating concept in organizational design. *Academy of Management Review, 3*(3), 613–624.

Uitdewilligen, S., Waller, M. J., & Zijlstra, F. R. (2010). Team cognition and adaptability in dynamic settings: A review of pertinent work. *International Review of Industrial and Organizational Psychology, 25*(2010), 293–353.

VersionOne (2012). 7th Annual State of Agile Development Survey / VersionOne Inc. Research Report. http://www.versionone.com/pdf/7th-Annual-State-of-Agile-Development-Survey.pdf.

Vidgen, R., & Wang, X. (2006). Organizing for agility: A complex adaptive systems perspective on agile software development process. In *European Conference on Information Systems*.

Vidgen, R., & Wang, X. (2009). Coevolving systems and the organization of agile software development. *Information Systems Research, 20*(3), 355–376.

Vyver, G., Koronios, A., & Lane, M. (2003). Agile methodologies and the emergence of the agile organization: A software development approach waiting for its time? In *Pacific Asia Conference on Information Systems*.

Wang, X., & Conboy, K. (2009). Understanding agility in software development through a complex adaptive systems perspective. In *European Conference on Information Systems*.

Wang, X., Conboy, K., & Pikkarainen, M. (2012). Assimilation of agile practices in use. *Information Systems Journal, 22*(6), 435–455.

Wang, X., Lane, M., & Conboy, K. (2011). From agile to lean: The perspectives of the two agile online communities of interest. In *European Conference on Information Systems*.

Wang, X., O Conchuir, E., & Vidgen, R. (2008). A paradoxical perspective on contradictions in agile software development. In *European Conference on Information Systems*.

Wang, X., & Vidgen, R. (2007). Order and chaos in software development: A comparison of two software development teams in a major IT company. In *European Conference on Information Systems*.

Weiber, R., & Mühlhaus, D. (2012). *Strukturgleichungsmodellierung: Eine Anwendungsorientierte Einführung in Die Kausalanalyse Mit Hilfe Von AMOS, SmartPLS Und SPSS*. Heidelberg: Springer.

Wellington, C. A., Briggs, T., & Girard, C D. (2005). Comparison of student experiences with plan-driven and agile methodologies. In *Annual Conference Frontiers in Education*.

West, D., Grant, T., Gerush, M., & D'Silva, D. (2010). Agile Development: Mainstream Adoption Has Changed Agility. Research Report. https://www.forrester.com/Agile+Development+Mainstream+Adoption+Has+Changed+Agility/fulltext/-/E-RES56100?objectid=RES56100.

Whetten, D. A. (1989). What constitutes a theoretical contribution? *Academy of Management Review, 14*(4), 490–495.

Whitney, K. (1994). Improving group task performance: The role of group goals and group efficacy. *Human Performance, 7*(1), 55–78.

Wildman, J. L., Salas, E., & Scott, C. P. (2013). Measuring cognition in teams a cross-domain review. *Human Factors: The Journal of the Human Factors and Ergonomics Society, 2014*(53), 911–941.

Williams, L., & Cockburn, A. (2003). Agile software development: It's about feedback and change. *Computer, 36*(6), 39–43.

Williams, L. J., Gavin, M. B., & Hartman, N. S. (2004). Structural equation modeling methods in strategy research: Applications and issues. *Research Methodology in Strategy and Management, 1*(1), 303–346.

Wold, H. (Ed.) (1982). *Soft modeling: The basic design and some extensions* (Chapter 1, pp. 1–54). Amsterdam: North-Holland.

Wood, R. E. (1986). Task complexity: Definition of the construct. *Organizational Behavior and Human Decision Processes, 37*(1), 60–82.

Wooldridge, J. M. (2013). *Introductory econometrics: A modern approach*. Mason, OH: South-Western Cengage Learning.

Xu, P., & Cao, L. (2006). Coordination in agile software projects. In *Americas Conference on Information Systems*.

Yang, H., Huff, S., & Strode, D. (2009). Leadership in software development: Comparing perceptions of agile and traditional project managers. In *Americas Conference on Information Systems*.

Yang, H.-L., & Tang, J.-H. (2004). Team structure and team performance in IS development: A social network perspective. *Information & Management, 41*(3), 335–349.

Young, M. S., Edwards, H. M., McDonald, S., & Thompson, B. (2005). Personality characteristics in an XP team: A repertory grid study. In *Proceedings of the Workshop on Human and Social Factors of Software Engineering* (pp. 1–7).

Zhang, S., Tremaine, M., Egan, R., Milewski, A., Plotnick, L., O'Sullivan, P., et al. (2008). Occurrence and effects of leader delegation in virtual teams. In *Hawaii International Conference on System Sciences*. Big Island, HI: IEEE.

Zheng, Y., Venters, W., & Cornford, T. (2007). Agility, improvisation, or enacted emergence. In *International Conference on Information Systems*.

Zheng, Y., Venters, W., & Cornford, T. (2011). Collective agility, paradox and organizational improvisation: The development of a particle physics grid. *Information Systems Journal, 21*(4), 303–333.